ROOTS SUPER JAM

COLLECTED WEST AFRICAN & DIASPORA DRUM RHYTHMS

ROOTS JAM ❖ VOLUMES 1, 2 & 3

BY

NOWICK GRAY

All three volumes of **Roots Jam** West African and Afro-Latin drumming lessons and notation in one book. Learn djembe rhythms, dunun patterns, and other hand drum and percussion parts, along with tips to improve your technique and feel. For solo practice, dance class arrangements, drum circles or ensemble performance. Download supporting audio files from DjembeRhythms.com.

Published by Cougar WebWorks
© 2016 Nowick Gray

email: now@djemberhythms.com
Web: http://djemberhythms.com

Roots Super Jam: Collected West African and Diaspora Drum Rhythms by Nowick Gray

ISBN-13: 978-1530301454
ISBN-10: 1530301459

ROOTS JAM

COLLECTED RHYTHMS
FOR
HAND DRUM AND PERCUSSION

NOWICK GRAY

Canadian Cataloguing in Publication Data

Gray, William N., 1950-
   Roots jam: collected rhythms for hand drum and
percussion

Includes bibliographical references and index.
ISBN 0-9682033-0-2

   1. Percussion instruments—Studies and exercises.
2. Drum—Studies and exercises. 3. Musical meter and
rhythm—Studies and exercises. 4. Percussion music—
Teaching pieces. 5. Percussion ensembles—Teaching
pieces. I. Title

MT655.3.G783 1997   786.8'1224'076   C97-900386-5

Roots Jam: Collected Rhythms for Hand Drum and Percussion

TABLE OF CONTENTS

Cougar Webworks
©1996 by Nowick Gray

AS A VODOUNIST ONCE EXPLAINED, "THE WHITE MAN GOES INTO CHURCH AND SPEAKS ABOUT GOD; THE INDIANS EAT MAGIC PLANTS AND SPEAK TO GOD; WE DANCE IN THE TEMPLE AND BECOME GOD."

--Wade Davis, "The Art of Shamanic Healing"

Introduction

The Rhythm Notation

The notation in this collection can be easier for drummers and percussionists to use, compared to conventional notes and lines. Because percussion notes aren't sustained but struck once, it makes sense to show the timing for these beats as single and equal. Rests are measured by the same, single-beat units. I thank Moon Bear for introducing me to the written system, based on the terminology taught by Babatunde Olatunji.

The glossary below describes the notes, primarily those played on the West African djembe.

Glossary:

       D: Dun ("Doon") = bass beat with left hand

       G: Gun ("Goon") = bass beat with right hand

       d: do ("doe") = rim beat with left hand (tip half of fingers)

       g: go = rim beat with right hand

       T: Ta = slap beat with left hand: sharp glancing stroke

       P: Pa = slap beat with right hand

       - or **space** = one-beat rest

Important note on handing:

If you prefer, switch the notation for left-right handing, above. Thus, you may read **D**, **d**, and **T** as the **strong** hand, or right hand, and **G**, **g**, **P** as the other, or left.

But don't take your "strong" hand for granted. I'm a right-hander but, when learning drum rhythms, found it more natural to lead with my left. That's why the majority of the rhythms displayed in this book will show leading with **D**, **d**, **T**. In fact it makes sense to play both ways equally well, or to alternate for balance. So you'll also find a fair number of patterns beginning with **G**, **g**, **P**. The choice is more or less arbitrary. Play with it!

Additional notes…

X = low note on bass drum or two-tone bell or percussion

x = any note on monotone percussion, or high note on two-tone percussion.

*[Another way to show hi/lo notes is hi on first line, lo on second; or by **H** and **L**]*

k = bell note when played with bass drum (jun-jun)

<u>**x**</u> = underlined (or bold) note means stressed or accented.

(d) = parenthesis means optional note(s) or way to play a given note(s)

d__g__d: = triplet, with three notes played within 2, 4 or 8 beat measure.

d_g: = two notes played as if two ends of a triplet (d_-_g) [See "*Latin feel*," below].

Example:

```
            D - D - d g d g
        Dun (rest) Dun (rest) do go do go
```

Each word in the above phrase has equal time. To get the feel of this or any rhythm, say the notes together, leaving pauses for the rests (each rest can be almost spoken, as if with a silent grunt). Try speaking it and playing it at the same time, and try it at different speeds to feel the effects of different tempos. This particular rhythm is a common phrase in a number of sixteen-beat rhythms; for example…

```
        D - d g - g d g D - D - d g d g
```

Anchors and variations...

The anchoring beats of most rhythms tend to come on the first beat of each measure. So in an eight-beat phrase like the example above, the anchoring beat is the **D** at the beginning. But there are also two four-beat measures within the eight, so a second anchor comes on the **d** of beat number five. With the anchored beats underlined and perhaps played with a slight emphasis, the phrase looks like this:

```
          ‾‾‾‾‾‾‾   ‾‾‾‾‾‾‾
        |  |  |  |  |  |  |  |
        D  -  D  -  d  g  d  g
```

In conventional music terminology, the anchors mark the beginning of each quarter note, with each quarter note comprising four sixteenth notes.

Each four-beat phrase could also be divided in half, so that an anchor can be found on every other beat (all the left-hand beats). These anchors become especially important when playing with a *Latin feel*, which adds a subtle, virtual rest after each anchor beat (playing [d g] as if were a triplet, [d - g], in the same time-space). The consistent left-right alternation of hands is important to help regulate the timing especially when playing fast.

It's helpful, however, not to overuse the lead hand, especially in a straight-ahead rhythm like the example. So to balance the body's energy (and the feel of the phrase in a subtle way, since we're talking about human music here, not digital)--and since the spaces here allow time for it--you can substitute the other hand for that second bass beat:

```
D - G - d g d g
```

Note that the anchors are gone now: not necessarily so, but only to illustrate another subtlety of phrasing. With the hands more balanced it makes sense to de-emphasize the anchors, spread the weight around.

[For more discussion about understanding rhythms, refer to the Lesson Notes.]

Note the grouping of rhythms within each of the following "Scores." I've made some attempt to align rhythms with similar beginnings or basic structure. In the first section, "Scores by Timing," I've used Bob Moses's terminology (Anchor, Contract, Swing, Expand) to group rhythms by location of the key beat of a phrase--whether on beat number 1, 2, 3, or 4, respectively. (*Please note: the use of the word "bar" in this book refers to the visual grouping of four or three single beats, as distinguished from the conventional term "bar" referring to a full measure or line*). Otherwise in organizing rhythms here I've been only partly systematic, as the task quickly leads in circles. The legendary champion Calypso band leader, "The Mighty Sparrow," was heard to say that Calypso is the mother of all rhythms. Whether this is true or not for Calypso, such an insight does lead the student down a road of ever-increasing connections between all rhythms. They all stem, after all, from the heartbeat, the walk, the day and night. The first assigment in my first Musical Improvisation and Appreciation course was to "listen to nature."

Acknowledgements

Thanks to Babatunde Olatunji, Fatala, Alpha Yaya Diallo, Joseph (Pepe) Danza, Bo Conlan, Daystar, Greg Kozak, Zave, Moon Bear, Dido Morris, Duncan Johnston, Michel Coté, and Robert (Ah) Northern: all live and wonderful teachers; to Paulo Mattioli and Doudou Rose on video and to Bob Moses, Sule Greg Wilson, Mickey Hart and Airto Moreira in written form. Not to mention all the great drumming and percussion and bass work I've loved all these years, beginning undoubtedly (and continuing to the present day) with Santana. Special thanks to Duncan for my beautiful djembe.

I've tried to note a reference for every rhythm, in order to acknowledge the music and teachings others have offered. My apologies to any such artist or teacher whose offering I have mislearned or misrepresented by my method of transcription. Many of these rhythms have been handed down in unrecorded tradition over centuries or even millenia. Each time they are recorded on tape or paper, they represent an interpretation or regional style. Rhythm is fluid and live and will not be fixed forever. In some cases I have tried to capture the feel of a rhythm from a taped recording, using my own judgement for translating the timing and the types of beat. Where I have drawn from written sources, I have translated directly from conventional music terminology. In this process I have often substituted hand strokes appropriate for my instrument of choice, the African djembe, for ones designated for other instruments, such as the conga.

Untitled rhythms: these are best considered gifts from the great infinite rhythm storehouse of the cosmos. There are three main reasons why a particular rhythm would appear without other title or reference:

 a) I've forgotten or been unable to locate the original source reference
 b) It's a rhythm I heard once and forgot about until it surfaced while improvising
 c) It's a rhythm I never consciously learned but discovered one day while improvising

Some rhythms which might have come to me in this way will appear with my own serendipitous titles. Again, apologies to any unacknowledged teachers; I trust I am repaying your generosity in the reoffering of the rhythm to others. The more I play the drum, the more the variations recollect and swirl around a central source. It's like the earth's hydrological cycle: with water evaporating and spreading all over the earth to take the flavor of the various soils, but then returning in ever-more familiar, broadening streams to the sea again. This metaphor, like the rhythms I present here, is not original with me. When I talked with Olatunji about my own uncertain path as a drummer, his advice rang clear as rain beating on the roof: "Just follow your destiny, like a river to the sea."

Here's to the river...

Nowick Gray
Argenta, B.C.
Summer 1996

Scores by Timing

Twos

2/4 time

ANCHOR: (| | | |)

```
 |   |   |   |   |   |   |   |
 T   g   -   G   D   G   -   g      Samba basic (Ted Reed)

 T   -   -   G   D   -   -   g      Samba simplified (Reed)

 d   g   -   g   d   g   -   g      Baiao

 D   -   d   g   D   -   -   G      Olatunji: Esumbuku Waya
```

1st bar:

```
 |   |   |   |   |   |   |   |
 G   -   g   d   g   d   -   -      untitled

 T   -   d   g   d   g   -   g      Baiao varation

 P   -   -   d   g   d   g   -      slow Afro-Cuban

 D   -   -   g   D   g   d   g      Gabrielle Roth: flowing

 T   g   -   g   d   g   d   g      Amazonian

 D   G   -   g   d   -   d   -      untitled

 X   -   -   -   X   -   X   -      Amazonian bass drum
```

2nd bar:

```
 |   |   |   |   |   |   |   |
 g   -   P   T   G   -   P   T      untitled

 d   -   D   g   T   -   D   g      Santana: Latin feel

 T   -   -   d   P   -   g   -      Calypso

 D   -   G   -   d   g   d   g      Olatunji: Ife. fast mode

 g   d   g   d   P   -   G   -      Earth Tribe

 T   g   T   G   T   g   d   g      Rock cha-cha
```

CONTRACT/JERK/PROPEL: (| <u>l</u> | |)

2nd bar:

```
 |  |  |  |  |  l̲  |  |
 D  P  -  P  -  g  d  -      Bomba
 D  g  d  g  d  G  d  g      Golden Mean
```

SWING: (| | <u>l</u> |)

1st bar:

```
 |  |  l̲  |  |  |  |  |
 d  -  T  g  d  -  d  -      Airto: Baiao drums
 D  g  T  -  -  G  d  g      Afro-Latin fast rock
 D  g  T  g  D  g  D  g      Bolero Rumba; slow-med. rock
 D  g  T  -  D  g  d  g      Cha-cha
 -  g  T  g  -  g  D  -      untitled
```

2nd bar:

```
 |  |  |  |  |  |  l̲  |
 D  -  P  -  d  -  g  g      rumba basic
 G  -  P  T  G  -  P  -      untitled
 d  g  T  g  D  G  T  G      Airto: Batucada
 D  -  -  G  D  -  g  -      Calypso (alt.)
 D  -  d  G  D  -  d  -      Bossa Nova
```

EXPAND: (| | | <u>l</u>)

```
 |  |  |  |  |  |  |  |
 -  g  d  g̲  -  g  d  g̲      Miles Davis "Four"
 D̲  G  d̲  P  -  G  d̲  P      Just Jam
```

1st bar:

```
 |  |  |  |  |  |  |  |
 D  g  T  P  D  g  d  g     Guaracha

 G  -  g  d  -  d  g  d     Olatunji: KiyaKiya
```

```
 |  |  |  |  |  |  |  |
 D  G  D  g  -  g  d  g     Amazonian
```

2nd bar:

```
 |  |  |  |  |  |  |  |
 -  g  d  -  d  g  -  g     Bob Moses

 D  g  T  g  D  g  T  P     Montuno
```

HYBRID:

```
 |  |  |  |  |  |  |  |
 D  -  g  g  D  -  g  g     rumba basic

 d  -  -  P  D  -  -  P     surdo

 D  -  x  G  D  -  x  G     x = shaker sound

 G  -  g  d(G)-  -(D)       Olatunji: Jingoloba
          (g)
```

```
 |  |  |  |  |  |  |  |
 d  g  d  P  d  g  T  g     Baiao variation

 T  -  d  g  d  -  D  -     Baiao (Afro-Latin version)

 x  -  x  x  x  -  x  -     boogie-woogie (triplet feel)

 d  g  d  g  D  -  D  -     Airto: Maxixe

 d  -  g  -  d  g  -  g     Earth Tribe

 D  g  d  P  D  g  T  g     Middle Eastern
```

| | | | | | | | |
P D - D P - d -   Beguine

- g d g D - d g   Samba part

P T g - P T G -   Duncan Johnston

G - g d g d G -   Olatunji: Zungo

| | | | | | | | |
D G d P - g T -   untitled

D G(D)G T - T -   untitled

D G d g T g T g   untitled

| | | | | | | | |
- g T g T P T P   untitled

- G D G d g d g   untitled

D - d g D G d g   Moving the Rock

| | | | | | | | |
D G d g D g - g   King Sunny live

D g d G - G d g   King Sunny live
  (gg)

T g d g T G - G   untitled

Fours

4/4

<u>**ANCHOR**</u> **BEAT:** (| | | |)

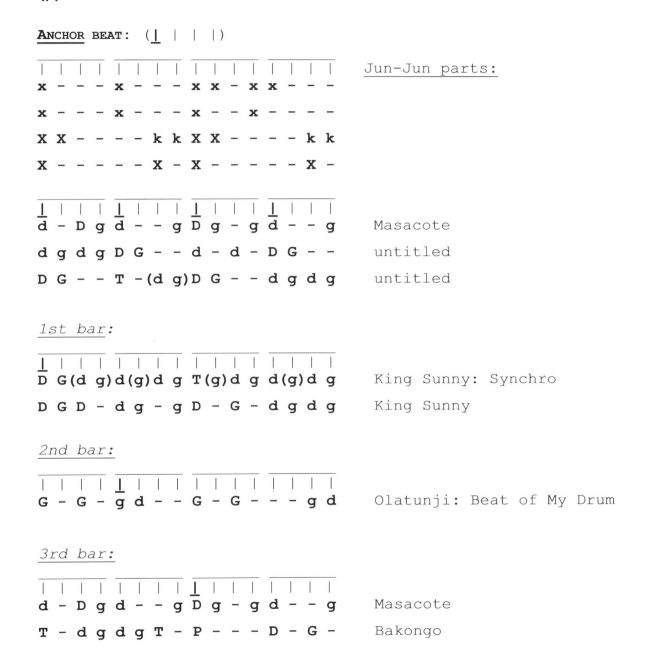

```
 | | | | | | | | | | | | | | | |     Jun-Jun parts:
 x - - - x - - - x x - x x - - -
 x - - - x - - - x - - x - - - -
 X X - - - k k X X - - - - k k
 X - - - - X - X - - - - - X -


 | | | | | | | | | | | | | | | |
 d - D g d - - g D g - g d - - g     Masacote
 d g d g D G - - d - d - D G - -     untitled
 D G - - T -(d g)D G - - d g d g     untitled
```

1st bar:

```
 | | | | | | | | | | | | | | | |
 D G(d g)d(g)d g T(g)d g d(g)d g     King Sunny: Synchro
 D G D - d g - g D - G - d g d g     King Sunny
```

2nd bar:

```
 | | | | | | | | | | | | | | | |
 G - G - g d - - G - G - - - g d     Olatunji: Beat of My Drum
```

3rd bar:

```
 | | | | | | | | | | | | | | | |
 d - D g d - - g D g - g d - - g     Masacote
 T - d g d g T - P - - - D - G -     Bakongo
```

4th bar:

```
| | | | | | | | | | | | | | | | |
D - D(G)d g d g D - D G d g - -      untitled
D - D(G)d g d g D - D G d g - -      untitled
D - G - d g d g D - G - D - d g      untitled
D - G - d g d g D - G - D - d g      untitled
   (- G -)
```

```
| | | | | | | | | | | | | | | | |
D - d g D - d g D - d g D G - -      untitled
D g - g D - G - - - D - T - d g      untitled
D - d g d G d g D - d g T - d g      Tuesday jam
D - D G d g d g D G d g T - T P      pump-down
D - - P T -(d g)D - - P T P T P      untitled
D - - g T - - - D - G d P - P -      untitled
D - - g{d -g -d}G - - d g - - -      Olatunji: Bethelehemu
d - - P D - - P d - - P D G - P      Airto: surdo
```

```
| | | | | | | | | | | | | | | | |
G - P - G - P - G - P - g d - -      Olatunji basic
G - g d - g d g D - D - d g - -      Olatunji: Ife Lo Ju Laiye
T - T g T(g)- - d g d g D G - g      untitled
T - d g T - d g T g d g D G - g      untitled
```

```
| | | | | | | | | | | | | | | | |
D - g d G - d g D - G - d g d g      Ethiopian
D - D G d - d g D - D G d g d g      King Sunny :live
```

```
| | | | | | | | | | | | | | | | |
G(d)g(d)P - d g D - d - T - - -      Alpha Yaya Diallo: 1.
d - d g d - d g d - d g d G D G      Earth Tribe
```

CONTRACT/JERK/PROPEL   (| ⌊ | |)

```
| | | | | ⌊ | | | | | | | ⌊ | |
d g d g d G - G d - g - d G - G       Dido's Jam (triplet feel)
d - r P D - r P d G - P d G - P       Airto (r = stick on rim)
```

3rd bar:

```
| | | | | | | | | | ⌊ | | | | |
D(g)d g T g D(g)d P - g T g D -        accordion in 4/4
```

4th bar:

```
| | | | | | | | | | | ⌊ | | |
TTG TTG - g d g D g d P d P - -        untitled
d g T - d g D G - g d g d G - -        shake me up
D g d g D - d g D - d g D P T P        untitled
D - d g D - d g D - d g D P d G        The Breathing Night
```

SWING: (| | ⌊ |)

```
| | | | | | | | | | | | | | | |
d G T - D g d g D g T - D g d g        slow Mambo
D g T g D g d g D g T g D g d -        Guajira
D - - G - - T - - - G D - T -          Guaguanco
```

2nd bar:

```
| | | | | | ⌊ | | | | | | | | |
d - d G - G T G d G d g d G D g        Calypso (bongo part)
```

3rd bar:

```
| | | | | | | | | | ⌊ | | | | |
D - d g D - d g - g T g D - d g        untitled
              (G D)
d g D g d g D g d g D g T P D g        Airto
```

4th bar:

```
| | | | | | | | | | | | | | _|_ |
D g T - d g D G - g d g d g D G      shake me
D - P D G - P D - D P D G - P -      Samba part
D - D G d g d g D G - G - G T g      untitled
D - d g D - d g D g d G d g T g      untitled
```

```
| | | | | | | | | | | | | | _|_ |
D - d G - - d - D G d G D G d -      Moses
D - d G - - d G - - d G D - d -      Moses
D - d - D G d G - G d - D - d -      Moses
D - d - D G d G D - d G - G d -      Moses
D - d - D - d - D G d G - G d -      Moses
```

```
| | | | | | | | | | | | | | _|_ |
D g T g D g d g D g T g D g d -      Guajira
D - - G - - T - - - - G D - T -      Guaguanco
D - d g D - d g D G d g D g T -      untitled
```

EXPAND: (| | | _|_)

1st bar:

```
| | | _|_ | | | | | | | | | | | |    Samba roll:
D g d P - P d g D - D - d g d g      w/ Latin/triplet feel
          (d g D)

D G d G - G d - D - d - D G d -      Moses
G - g D - D g d G d g d g d G d      Jesse's Calypso
```

2nd bar:

[*see Samba*]

3rd bar:

```
| | | | | | | | | | | | | | | |
D - d g T g d g D g d P - g d g    Yelle (Baaba Maal)

D - d g T - T - D g d P - g d g    Monday jam

D - d g D g - - D - d G - - - -    Savuka: Shadow Man
```

```
| | | | | | | | | | | | | | | |
D - D - D G - G d - - G - g d g    Roth: Totem

D G d G D - d - D - d G - - d -    Moses

D(g)d g D g d g D g d g - g d g    Latin/triplet feel
                (variations: alt. or selective g>G)
```

```
| | | | | | | | | | | | | | | |
D(g)d - D(G)d - D G d G - G T -    Moses

D G d g d g d g D G - P - P T P    untitled

D - d g D g d g D g T P - P T P    untitled

D - d g d g d g D G T P - P T P    untitled

D - d g d g D - P - - P - g d g    Sunjam
```

```
| | | | | | | | | | | | | | | |
G - g - g d g d g d g T - T - -    Olatunji: Primitive Fire

G - g - g d g d G - g d - d g d    untitled

P - g d g d g d g d - d g d       untitled

D - G - d g d g D G - g - g d g    Wollasidon

T - d G D - d P T - d P - - d -    conga
```

4th bar:

```
| | | | | | | | | | | | | | | |
- G d - D(G)d - D G d G - G d G    Moses
```

HYBRID ACCENT PHRASES:

```
| | | | | | | | | | | | | | | |
D - - G - - d g D - - G - - d g    Jingo

D g d G - G d g D - d g T g d g    untitled

D g d G d g d g T g d P d g T g    roll-up

D - d G - G d g D - D - d g d g    Primitive Fire variants
T)              (T) (T)

D G d G - G d G - G d - D - d -    Moses
```

```
| | | | | | | | | | | | | | | |
D - - G - - d - g d - g d - g -    Guaguanco variant

D - - G T - - P T - P - d g d g    untitled

D - - G T - - P D - - G - g d g    untitled

D - - P - g d g D - G - T - T -    Bo Conlan

D - - P T - d g D - - P T P T P    Fall Morning 1.
D g d g D - d g D - d g D P T P             2.
```

```
| | | | | | | | | | | | | | | |
d g d g d g d G - g d g d - d g    J. Brown: Make it Funky

d - d g d - d g d - d g d G D G    Earth Tribe 2

G - g d - g d g D - D - d g - -    Olatunji: Ife Lo Ju Laiye

D - d g - g d g D - d - D - - -    Hart: Island Grove

D - d - - - D - d - D - d g d g    Funk the Courthouse
        (G) (g) (G)

D - - g d - - - D - - g - g d g    Olatunji: Edunmare

D - G - D - g g D G - G D - g g    Olatunji: Ilere
```

```
| | | | | | | | | | | | | | | |
D - T P - T P - D - T - d g - -    untitled

D - d P d P T g D - d P T - T -    untitled

D - d g T g d g D G - G D - T G    untitled
```

```
| | | | | | | | | | | | | | | |
d g d d g d g g d g D g D G d g      Paradiddle Funk

d - d g d g T - d g d g d G T g      Alpha 2b.

D g D g(D)P - P(D)g D g - P T -      untitled


| | | | | | | | | | | | | | | |
- - - - - P T - - - - - P T P        untitled

D - g - T - g - T - - g - - - -      Conga

T - T - d - - P - P - g d - d -      Oyin momo ado (Olatunji)

P - P d G - P d g T P T P d G T      Edging Max

G - - - P - - - g d - g d - P -      untitled


| | | | | | | | | | | | | | | |
D G D g - g d g D G(D)G T - T -      Amazonia:

- - - " - - - - - - G D G d g d g

- - - " - - - - - - g d g T P T P

- - - " - - - - - D G - g d - d -

D G d P - g t - D G(D)G T - T -
```

8-bar Pieces

```
| | | | | | | | | | | | | | | |
D - d g D - d g t - d g t - d g      Masmoudi (Zave)
D - d g d g t - d g d g t - d g


| | | | | | | | | | | | | | | |
D - d g D g d g D g d - d - d g      untitled
 (g -)                  (g)
D - d g D g d - -(g)d - d - d g


| | | | | | | | | | | | | | | |
D - G - d g d g D - G - d g d g      untitled
D - G - d g d g D - d g d g d g
```

```
| | | | | | | | | | | | | | | |
D_____g_____g D_____g_____g      Get It
D_____g_____g D g - g D - g -

| | | | | | | | | | | | | | | |
D - G - d g d g D g d g - g d g       Boghanian (Bo Conlan)
D - G - d g d g - - - - -(g d g)

| | | | | | | | | | | | | | | |
D - d g d g d g D - d g d g - -       untitled
D - d g d g d g D G - G D - T g

| | | | | | | | | | | | | | | |
D - - g d - - - D - - g d - - -       Olatunji: Kiya Kiya, Abana
D - - g d - - G - G - g d - - -

D - - g d - - - D - - g d - - -       Olatunji: Ajaja
D - - g d g d - D - - g d - - -

| | | | | | | | | | | | | | | |      Airto:
D - G - T - - P D - G - T - - P       Xote
d g d g d g d g D - G - T - - P       (bar 5--triplet feel)

d - d - T - D G d - d - T - D G       Berimbau (D G = shaker)
d P - g T g - g d - d - T - D G
d - d - d - d )                       (alt. bar 5)

d - T - d - D G ----------------      Cavalaria 1.
d g d x d g d x d - T - d - D G       (x = buzz)

d - T - - - - - d - T - - - D G       Angola
d P - g T g - g d - T - - - D G

| | | | | | | | | | | | | | | |
D - - P D - T - D - - P D - T -       Park beat
D - - P D - T - D P - P D - T -
```

```
 | | | |  | | | |  | | | |  | | | |     funk march
 X - x x  x X - x  x x X -  X - x x
 x x X -  x x X -  x X - x  X - - -
```

```
 | | | |  | | | |  | | | |  | | | |     L. Allen: Mother Earth
 D - - -  T - - d  - - - -  - - - -
 D G - G  T - d -  d - -(g)D(g d)-
                                (d)
```

```
 | | | |  | | | |  | | | |  | | | |     Bouree dance
 x - x -  x - x -  x - x x  x - x -
 x - x -  x - x -  x x x x  x - x -
```

```
 x - x x  x - x -  x - - -  x - x -     Gavotte dance
 x - x x  x x x x  x x x x  x - x -
```

```
 | | | |  | | | |  | | | |  | | | |     Airto: surdo
 d - - P  D - - P  d - - P  D G - P     (l = left hand on rim)
 d - l P  D - l P  d G - P  d G - P
 - - - -  - - - -  - - - -  -(- l)
```

```
 | | | |  | | | |  | | | |  | | | |     Trance dance 1
 D - G -  d - d g  D - G -  d g T g
 D - G -  d - d g  D G - g  d g T g
```

Threes

3/8

```
| | | | | |
T G d P D g      Nueva onda (Afro-Lat)--anchor

d G T g D P      Afro-Cuban--expand

P   g d G D      Rainbow Train
```

```
| | | | | |
D g d G d g      Mother Rhythm

d P T g T P      Olatunji: Ajaja part

g d - g d -      Olatunji

G   g d g d      Dance of the Dogun
```

6/8

ANCHOR (| | |)

1st bar:

```
| | | | | | | | | | | |
T - d P T g T P d P T g      Counting Sheep Backwards
```

3rd bar:

```
| | | | | | | | | | | |
D - g D - g d g d G - g      Hank's tune

D - d G - g d g d G - g      (alt. hands)

D - d G d g D - - - - -      Nelson jam
```

4th bar:

```
| | | | | | | | | | | |
G - g d g d G - g d - -      Olatunji dance warmup (Zungo)

G - g d g d G - P T - -      Zungo variation

G d g D g d G d g D - T      Hank's tune (alt.)

D - g D - g D - g d g g      Xochimochi
```

PROPEL (| | |)

3rd bar:

```
 _____     _____
| | | | | | | | | | | |
G - g d g d G T g T g -     untitled
```

EXPAND (| | |)

2nd bar:

```
 _____ _____ _____
| | | | | | | | | | | |
T G d g D g - G d g D -     Alpha
```

3rd bar:

```
 _____ _____
| | | | | | | | | | | |
d - D g - G d G T g D P     Nañigo (Afro-Lat)
```

9/8

```
 ___ ___ ___ ___ ___ ___ ___
| | | | | | | | | | | | | | | | | |
D g d G d g D g d G d g D g D G D G     jam groove

D g d G d g D g d G d - d - G - G -     untitled

g d g T g d g D G - G D - - G D - -     untitled
```

12/8

```
                  Bach, A-Minor (16-bar):

 ___ ___ ___ ___ ___ ___ ___ ___
| | | | | | | | | | | | | | | | | | | | | | | |
x x x x x x x x x x x x x x x x x x x x x x x x
x - - x x x - - x x x - - x x x - - - -

                                        untitled

 ___ ___ ___ ___ ___ ___ ___ ___
| | | | | | | | | | | | | | | | | | | | | | | |
D(g)D P d g D(g)D P d g D(g)D P d g T g d P d g
```

Three-Four

3/4

```
| | | |   | | | |   | | | |
D - - - D - G - - - - -       Olatunji
      (d g)
T - G - D - G - d g d g       Bo Conlan
T - P - T - P T - P - P       Calypso (Zave)
```

```
| | | |   | | | |   | | | |
D - D g D - D - g - D -       untitled
P - P T P - P - P T P -       Olatunji: Mystery of Love (1)
- P - P - G d - T - T P       Olatunji: Mystery of Love (2)
D - d g - g d g D - d g       Future Inside Out
              (T)
D - T g - P T g - P T P       untitled
```

```
| | | |   | | | |   | | | |
D - d - - G d g D P T g       untitled
D - d - T g D P - g T g       jogging Samba
D - d - g d G - G - T g       untitled
D - d g d G d g d G d g       untitled
D - d P T g D P d g T P       monkeyshine
```

```
| | | |   | | | |   | | | |
D g d(G)d g D g d(G)d g       Alpha
d g T - d g T g d g D G       untitled
D G D - D G d G d G D -       Safari
D G D g - G D G d g d g       Amazon
D G - g d(g)D - d g d g       Olatunji: Gbogbo'ara-le nko
```

```
 |  |  |  |  |  |  |  |  |  |  |  |     Minuet phrasing
 x  -  -  x  x  -  -  x  x  -  -  x     (X1)
 x  -  -  -  -  -  -  x  -  -  x        (X3)
```

6/4

```
 |  |  |  |  |  |  |  |  |  |  |  |  |  |  |  |  |  |  |  |  |  |  |  |
 d  -  d  g  d  g  d  -  G  -  G  -  d_____g_____d  G  -  G  -     Dido's jam
```

```
 |  |  |  |  |  |  |  |  |  |  |  |  |  |  |  |  |  |  |  |  |  |  |  |
 D  -  -  G  -  d  g  d  g  d  G  -  D  -  g  -  d  -  G  -  d  -  g  -     untitled
 G  -  g  d  g  d  G  -  g  d  g  d  G  -  g  d  g  d  G  d  P  T  P  T     untitled
```

                        Moses: Yin-Yang:

```
 |  |  |  |  |  |  |  |  |  |  |  |  |  |  |  |  |  |  |  |  |  |  |  |
 d  g  D  G  d  g  D  g  D  g  D  g  D  G  d  g  D  G  d  G  d  G  d  G
```

Odd Times

5/4

```
| | | | | | | | | | | | | | | | | | | |
D g T g D G T g D P D g T g D G T g D P    untitled

D - - - d g - - D G d g d g - - D G d g    untitled

D - d g T(G)d g T g D - d g T(G)d g T g    Roth: flowing

G - d g D P - D P - D d g D P - P G - -    untitled

D - d G - g d g T g D - d G - g d g T g    untitled


| | | | | | | | | | | | | | | | | | | |
D - d P d g T(g)T(g)D - d P d g T(g)T(g)   untitled

D - d g D g d G d g D - d g D g d G d g    untitled

D__g__d G__d__g D__g__d g_____g_____g   triplets

X - k k X k k X k k X - k k X k k X k k    Clam-digging
```

15/8

```
| | | | | | | | | | | | | | |
D g D g D g g D g D g g D g g    untitled
```

7/8

4-3-4-3

```
| | | | | | | | | | | | | |    African (Zave):
x - x - x - - x x x - x x x    clave
T - T - T - - g d g - g d g    drum version

D g - G d - - g D g - G D g    Airto: Samba funk
```

4-4-3-3

| | | | | | | | | | | | | | | |
D - - d - - g - D - d - g g   Gearbox Breakdown

D - - P - g T g D - D g d g   The Jesus Stomp

G - g d - d g - G - g d g d   The In and Out of It

D - T g - P T g - P T P T g   Counting Down Dawn

| | | | | | | | | | | | | | |
G - P - - d P - G - G - P T   untitled

G - g - - d g - G - g d g d   untitled

d g T g T g d G d g d g D G   jam dance variation
        (D)

3-3-4-4

| | | | | | | | | | | | | | |
D - - d - - g - D - d - g g   untitled

D(g)d g T g D(g)d P - g T g   accordion in 7

D g d G d g - G d g D - d g   jam dance

D d g G d g D g d G d - d -   untitled
        (g - g - g)

| | | | | | | | | | | | | | |
D - d g d g D g d g d - - -   untitled

T - T g d P - g d g D g d g   untitled

G - g d g d G - g d P - P d

| | | | | | | | | | | | | | | | | | |
D - - P - g T g D - D g d g - - D G d g g   untitled

D - - P - g T g - - D G d g g D - D g d g   untitled

11/8

| | | | | | | | | | |
G d g D g d G d g g d   untitled

Arrangements

Lesson Notes and Featured Rhythms
(from Cougar WebWorks, at http://www.life-free.net/cougar/rhythm.htm)

Of Four-Four and other useful constructions

Using a typical sixteen-beat phrase (D – d g – g d g D – D – d g d g), and remembering the concept of quarter notes, we can recognize it now as that old stand-by, the four-four. With one crucial difference, which sets world-beat music apart from standard rock. Where the four-four would give us four anchors, one every four beats, the phrase above has a *rest* in the place of the second would-be anchor. This is the hitch that turns our hips, and turns us into real dancers, instead of static shakers. It's the key to the Samba (where it occurs at hitching post number three instead of two as in this example) and to the yelle (where it occurs at the fourth anchor spot instead). And here, without changing the regular order of playing hands, the emphasis shifts from the lead hand to the off-beat or upbeat hand (beat number four of the sixteen below):

D – d **g** – g d g D – D – d g d g

End of Lesson One.

Lesson Two: More variations:

Another common, basic variation is to emphasize a bit of "three" feel in the first bar, like so:

D – – g – g d g D – D – d g d g

The two rest beats after the "D" give the effect of a triplet, the basic unit of 6/8 time. Using that effect in a four-four beat gives it an extra dynamic, the second basic key to world-beat music (see above for discussion of the first).

Really, the possibilities are endless. Let's take the feel back to a "two" or low-high feel:

D – D – T – T – D – d g – g d g

Notice the similarity to the rhythm at the end of lesson one. The two halves have been switched in order, and the emphasis increased on the left-hand beats, "d" becoming "T", a clean sharp stroke without the "g." With the extra rests in the first bar, there is time enough to switch hands now for balance, if desired:

D – G – T – P – D – d g – g d g

Samba, Part One:

Now, for fun, let's slide the line left by half a bar, so that it looks like this:

```
T - T - D - d g - g d g D - D -
```

We're still in "two" feel, but now it's high-low (from T to D). This is the basis of Samba-along with the "world-beat" hitch as discussed above. There are many, many ways to carry this Samba feel; the example here is just one possibility. Focus on the high-low intro, and the "g - g" gap in the middle, and it's hard to go wrong. Reduced to the basics, it could be played simply as:

```
T - T - D - - g - g - g D - - -
```

Play around with that one for awhile and a dozen Samba beats will arrive smiling, hips rolling.

Samba, Part Two:

Here are some parts to accompany the above Samba rhythm:

First, a basic eight-beat pattern to keep it steady:

```
P - P d G - G D
```

Next, some percussion elements:

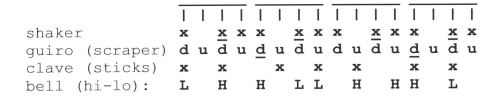

```
shaker            x   x x x   x x x   x x x   x x
guiro (scraper)   d u d u d u d u d u d u d u d u
clave (sticks)    x   x     x   x   x     x   x
bell (hi-lo):     L   H   H   L L   H   H H   L
```

d=down stroke, u=up stroke

Put it all together and have some fun!
These are only a few of the infinite variations of Samba. One of the more basic variations is to reverse the high-low swing of the drum parts, to a low-high feel:

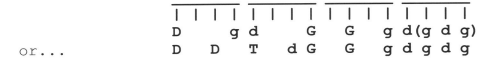

```
      D       g d     G   G   g d(g d g)
or... D   D   T   d G   G   g d g d g
```

By comparing these two you can see the common elements that gives the Samba its distinctive flavor: the low-high swing, and the hitch in the middle [G - G].

The first of these two is essentially the same as a common Nigerian rhythm taught by Olatunji:

Olatunji rhythm for Aiye Mi Re, Akiwowo, and Kiya Kiya:

Note the similarity to the low-high samba.

Triple Overtime

This is an original composition that combines the "hitch" feel of a Samba, the complexity of a round, and the steadying influence of an eight-beat repeated phrase.

Note that in the main Samba-like part (djembe 1), the low-high movement is doubled in the second two bars.

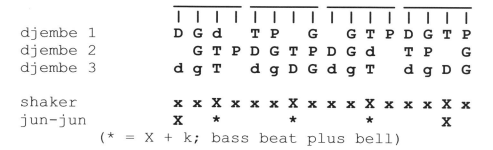

```
djembe 1   D G d   T P   G   G T P D G T P
djembe 2     G T P D G T P D G d   T P   G
djembe 3   d g T   d g D G d g T   d g D G

shaker     x x X x x x X x x x X x x x X x
jun-jun    X   *       *       *       X
           (* = X + k; bass beat plus bell)
```

Uruguayan Rhythm

This is a beat used in a local trance dance with great success. It's inspired by traditional rhythms of Uruguay taught by Pepe Danza. Very powerful, with an almost instant trance effect. The bass beats come in unusual places, and the three primary drum parts blend in a hypnotic way. Parts 2 and 3 are tricky to learn because the d G opening beats are the reverse of the usual opening. The key is to focus on that opening (d) as the one-beat. Note that it's the unplayed beat in Part 1.

```
            | | | | | | | | | | | | | | | |
Drum 1:     - g d g - g d g - g d g - g d g
Drum 2:     d G d g d G d g d G d g D - - -
Drum 3:     d G - - G - d g D - D - D - - -
Jun-Jun:    X - - X X - - X X - - X X - - X
sticks:     x - - - x - - - x - - - x - - -
```

Notes:

Part 1: To keep good time, play the silent one as a "ghost" note on the side of the drum with the left hand.

Part 3: The second G departs from strict alternation of hands by beat; but it helps give an overall balance with the final three D's, and gives a certain desired tone quality. The middle D might be varied as a G if desired; but again the repeated bass with the same hand gives a certain repetitive effect hard to achieve by using both hands.

Sticks: The stick part wasn't taught as part of the original rhythm. But we've found with the trance dance step we use (from West Africa) that it's helpful to use the regular stick beat as a constant timekeeper. It also induces its own trance effect; as the Australian aborigines do so well with sticks.

Bell and Percussion Patterns

2/4

```
| | | | | | | |
  x   x   x x x        Santana: Milagro

x   x   x x   x        Earth Tribe
```

4/4

```
| | | | | | | | | | | | | | | |
x       x       x       x       x        Af-Lat clave


      x x           x x         x        fast Af-Lat rock
x   x           x x           x
```

```
| | | | | | | | | | | | | | | |
x x x     x x   x     x   x x     x        1.
x x x     x x   x     x   x x              2.
x       x       x                          3.
```
Latin jazz: 12131--3

```
| | | | | | | | | | | | | | | |
x   x   x     x   x x   x   x x        latin percussion
```

```
| | | | | | | | | | | | | | | |
x   x   x   x   x x   x x       x        percussion: Amazonia
x   x           x   x       x x          untitled (hi-lo):
      x   x                       x
```

```
| | | | | | | | | | | | | | | |
    x x     x x       x       x x        untitled
x       x         x x   x
```

```
| | | | | | | | | | | | | | | |
x   x x x   x   x   x x x     x        swinging rock

x x   x x   x   x x x x x x x        upbeat underlay
```

```
| | | | | | | | | | | | | | | |
x   x x x   x x x   x     x   x        Funk underlay (8-bar):
x   x x x   x x x   x     x   x
```

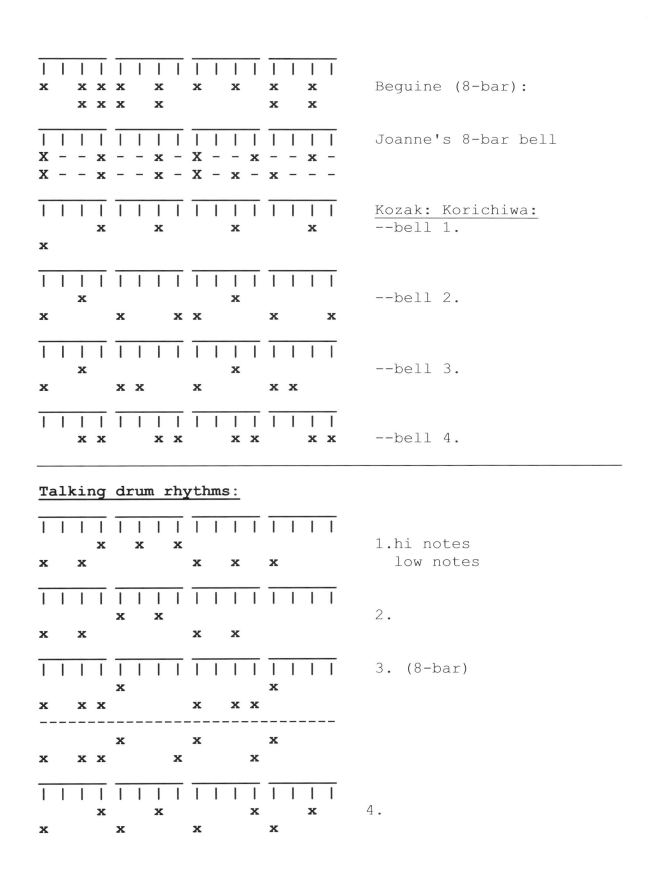

Beguine (8-bar):

Joanne's 8-bar bell

Kozak: Korichiwa:
--bell 1.

--bell 2.

--bell 3.

--bell 4.

Talking drum rhythms:

1. hi notes
   low notes

2.

3. (8-bar)

4.

Samba:

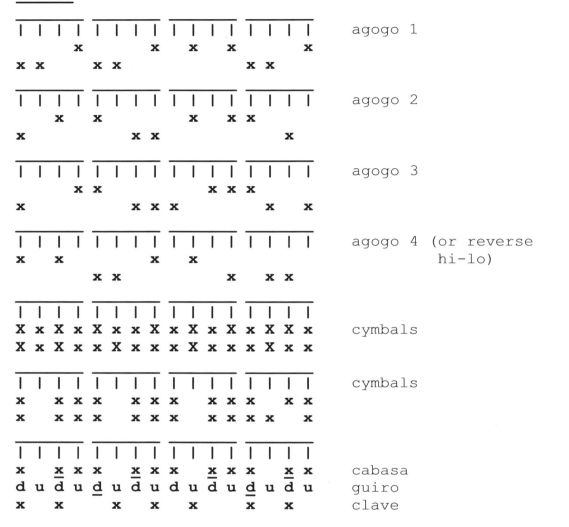

```
| | | |  | | | |  | | | |  | | | |      agogo 1
      x        x    x  x          x
x x      x x              x x

| | | |  | | | |  | | | |  | | | |      agogo 2
    x      x            x    x  x
x            x  x              x

| | | |  | | | |  | | | |  | | | |      agogo 3
    x  x            x  x  x
x            x  x  x          x      x

| | | |  | | | |  | | | |  | | | |      agogo 4 (or reverse
x      x              x      x                     hi-lo)
         x  x            x      x  x

| | | |  | | | |  | | | |  | | | |
X x X x  X x x X  x X x X  x X x X      cymbals
X x X x  x X x x  X x x X  x X x X

| | | |  | | | |  | | | |  | | | |      cymbals
x      x x x    x x x    x x x      x x
x    x  x x    x x x    x x x x      x

| | | |  | | | |  | | | |  | | | |
x    x̲ x x    x̲ x x    x x x      x̲ x    cabasa
d u d̲ u d u d̲ u d u d u d̲ u d u        guiro
x    x      x    x    x      x    x      clave
```

Reggae:

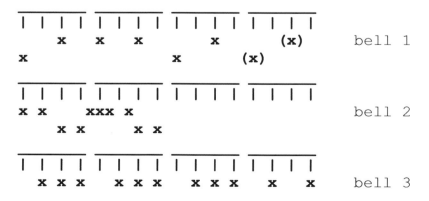

```
| | | |  | | | |  | | | |  | | | |
     x    x    x        x        (x)     bell 1
x                  x      (x)

| | | |  | | | |  | | | |  | | | |
x x    x x x x              bell 2
    x x      x x

| | | |  | | | |  | | | |  | | | |
   x x x    x x x    x x x    x      x    bell 3
```

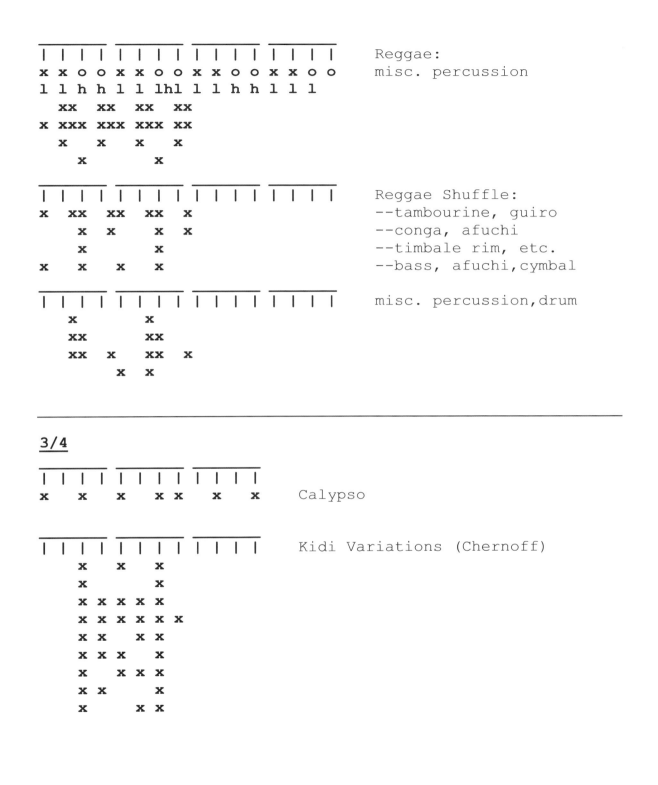

Reggae:
misc. percussion

Reggae Shuffle:
--tambourine, guiro
--conga, afuchi
--timbale rim, etc.
--bass, afuchi,cymbal

misc. percussion,drum

3/4

Calypso

Kidi Variations (Chernoff)

6/8

```
 _____ _____ _____ _____
| | | | | | | | | | | | | | | | | |
 x  x    x    x  x    x    x              Bakongo 1

 x  x    x    x  x  x       x             --part 2

 x    x    x    x  x    x    x            Earth Tribe


 _____ _____ _____ _____
| | | | | | | | | | | | | | | | | |
 x              x                         Roth: Invocation (8-bar):
 x              x    x    x               (overlay an all-24 beat)

 x    x  x  x  x       x                  Roth


 _____ _____ _____ _____
| | | | | | | | | | | | | | | | | |
      x    x  x    x    x    x            Kozak: Gadzo, Bembe:
                                         --bell, shaker
 x

 x  -  x  x  x  x  x  x  x  x  -          tin can


 _____ _____ _____ _____ _____ _____ _____ _____
| | | | | | | | | | | | | | | | | | | | | | | |   Jungle
 x        x        x        x        x        x        x        x    1.

 x  x     x     x     x  x     x     x     x  x     x     x     x    2. (hi-lo)
          x                       x                          x
```

Breaks

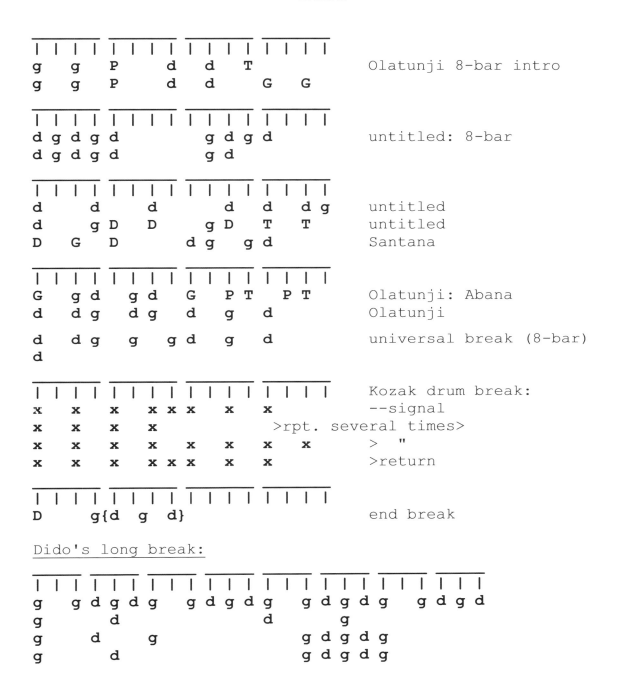

```
|  |  |  |  |  |  |  |  |  |  |  |  |  |  |  |
g     g     P        d     d     T              Olatunji 8-bar intro
g     g     P        d     d        G     G

|  |  |  |  |  |  |  |  |  |  |  |  |  |  |  |
d g d g d              g d g d                  untitled: 8-bar
d g d g d              g d

|  |  |  |  |  |  |  |  |  |  |  |  |  |  |  |
d       d       d         d     d     d g       untitled
d       g D   D       g D   T     T              untitled
D     G     D       d g     g d                 Santana

|  |  |  |  |  |  |  |  |  |  |  |  |  |  |  |
G     g d     g d     G     P T     P T          Olatunji: Abana
d     d g     d g     d     g     d              Olatunji

d     d g     g     g d     g     d              universal break (8-bar)
d

|  |  |  |  |  |  |  |  |  |  |  |  |  |  |  |  Kozak drum break:
x     x     x     x x x     x     x              --signal
x     x     x     x                  >rpt. several times>
x     x     x     x     x     x     x   x      >   "
x     x     x     x x x     x     x            >return

|  |  |  |  |  |  |  |  |  |  |  |  |  |  |  |
D       g{d  g   d}                              end break
```

<u>Dido's long break:</u>

```
 ___ ___  ___ ___  ___ ___  ___ ___  ___ ___  ___ ___  ___ ___  ___ ___
|  |  |  |  |  |  |  |  |  |  |  |  |  |  |  |  |  |  |  |  |  |  |  |  |
g     g d g d g     g d g d g     g d g d g     g d g d
g           d                 d           g
g       d       g                   g d g d g
g           d                       g d g d g
```

Duets

4/4

```
| | | | | | | | | | | | | | | |    Bo Conlan--2-part:
D   T G D   T G   G T G D   T         1.
D       g T       D   D g T   T       2.
```

```
| | | | | | | | | | | | | | | |    Olatunji: Beat of my Drum
G   G   g d       G   G       g d
G       d g       G       d g
```

```
| | | | | | | | | | | | | | | |    L. Allen: Mother Earth
    x       x       x       x       snare drum
D       T       d                   8-bar:
D G   G T   d   d   (g)D(g d)
                        (d)
```

```
| | | | | | | | | | | | | | | |
D G(d g)d(g)d g T(g)d g d(g)d g    King Sunny: Synchro
X X       k k X X       k k
D G   (T)   d g D G   (T)   d g    (sub. for jun-jun)
```

```
| | | | | | | | | | | | | | | |
D G T P   T P       T P   T P      Pan Logo (Dido)
D G   d D G   g D G   P       T
```

6/8

```
| | | | | | | | | | | |    driving blues:
  x x   x x   x x   x x    drum
X X X X X X X X            bass
```

```
| | | | | | | | | | | |    Hamish
H f g f g g H f g f g g    H=LH heel;
g   G H g       D G H g    f=heel still on, play fingertips
```

```
 |  |  |  |  |  |      Olatunji: Odun de
 g  T  P  d  P  T
 G        D  g  d
```

3/4

```
 |  |  |  |  |  |  |  |  |  |  |      Olatunji: Mystery of Love
 P     P  T  P     P     P  T  P      --high conga

       P        P        G           --lo conga (6 bars)
 d           T        T  P
```

Airto: caxixi (or shaker) duets: *top line=high pitch, bottom=low*

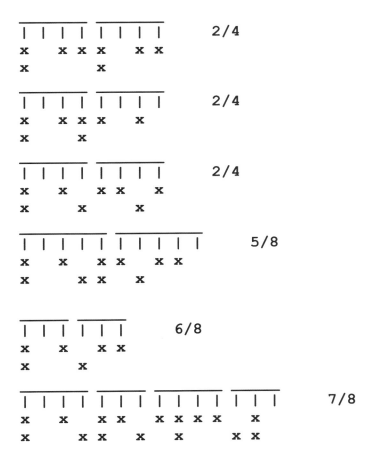

```
 |  |  |  |  |  |  |  |      2/4
 x     x  x  x     x  x
 x           x

 |  |  |  |  |  |  |  |      2/4
 x     x  x  x     x
 x        x

 |  |  |  |  |  |  |  |      2/4
 x     x     x  x     x
 x        x        x

 |  |  |  |  |  |  |  |  |      5/8
 x     x     x  x     x  x
 x        x  x     x

 |  |  |  |  |  |      6/8
 x     x     x  x
 x        x

 |  |  |  |  |  |  |  |  |  |  |  |  |  |      7/8
 x     x     x  x     x  x  x  x     x
 x        x  x     x     x        x  x
```

Bell and drum duets (adapted from Moses):

```
_____   _____   _____   _____
| | | | |   | | | | |   | | | | |   | | | |
D G d G D     d   D     d G       d
  x x x x       x x x x x     x x x x
```

```
_____   _____   _____   _____
| | | | |   | | | | |   | | | | |   | | | |
D G d G     G d     D     d     D G d
x       x x x x             x x x x
```

```
_____   _____   _____   _____
| | | |   | | | |   | | | |   | | | |
D G d G     G d G     G d     D     d
x     x x x     x x     x x       x x
    x x x       x xxx x x x     x x x x
```

```
_____   _____   _____   _____
| | | |   | | | |   | | | |   | | | |
D     d   D G d G D     d G     G d
x x     x     x       x x     x x x     x x
```

```
_____   _____   _____   _____
| | | |   | | | |   | | | |   | | | |
D     d   D G d     D G d G     G d
x x     x     x     x     x     x x x
```

```
_____   _____   _____   _____
| | | |   | | | |   | | | |   | | | |
  G d     D     d     D G d G     G d G
    x       x     x     x     x x     x     x
```

```
_____   _____   _____   _____
| | | |   | | | |   | | | |   | | | |
D     d   D G d G     G d     D     d
  x x     x     x     x x x     x x x x
```

Arranged Ensembles

Afro-Disco (8-bar)

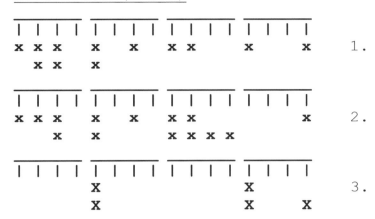

```
| | | | | | | | | | | | | | | |
x x x   x   x   x x     x     x     1.
    x x   x
```

```
| | | | | | | | | | | | | | | |
x x x   x   x   x x           x     2.
    x   x       x x x x
```

```
| | | | | | | | | | | | | | | |
        X               X           3.
        X               X   X
```

Olatunji: Fanga

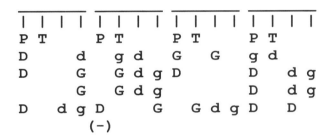

```
| | | | | | | | | | | | | | | |
P T     P T     P T     P T
D         d   g d   G   G   g d
D       G   G d g D       D     d g
        G   G d g         D     d g
D   d g D       G   G d g D   D
        (-)
```

Airto: Baiao

```
| | | | | | | |
d   T g d   d        drums: basic

T   d g d g   g      (variations)
dgdgd g d g   g
d g   g d g   g
d g d P d g T g
```

[plus:]

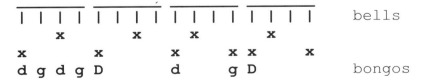

```
| | | | | | | | | | | | | | | |    bells
    x       x       x       x
x           x       x     x x     x
d g d g D           d       g D        bongos

X - k X X - X -   :  jun-jun (last X = X + k)
x - x x x - x x   :  clave
```

Airto: Cavalaria

```
| | | | | | | | | | | | | | | |
d   T   d   D G ---------------       1.
d g d x d g d x d   T   d   D G       (x = buzz)

d           d x D                     2. (bars 3-8 rest)

d           d x D                     3.
d x D   d x D   d           d x D
```

Kozak: Bamba

```
| | | | | | | | | | | | | | | |
    x       x       x       x         jun-jun
x   x   x   x   x   x   x   x         bell
x   x   x x x x   x x x       x        drum-sticks
x   X   x   X   x   X   x   X         shaker
    TP-     DG-     TP-     dg-       drum (triplets)
```

Afro-Latin Bomba:

```
| | | | | | | | | | | | | | | |
x       x       x           x   x     clave
    x x       x x       x x       x x  small bell
X X   x   x x   x x   x x x x        large bell
D   D U D   D U D   D U D   D U      guiro
      g     g d           g     g d   small conga/bongo
D P   P     g d D P   P     g d       conga/djembe
d g D P T   d       P d P T   d       low conga
```

Trance Dance

```
| | | | | | | | | | | | | | | |
x       x       x       x             clave
X   X           X   X                 bass drum
        D G             D G           djembe
  x x     x x     x x     x x         stick on drum
-       -       -   d   g   d         drum: 8-bar:
-       -       -   d g d g
```

Baka Beyond, 1

```
| | | | | | | | | | | | | | | |
D     G D g   g D   g   D   g        drum
x   x x x x x x x   x x x   x        sticks
```

Baka Beyond, 2

```
| | | | | | | | | | | | | | | |
x x           x x x           x      guiro (scraper)
D   D G d       G D G D G d   d      drum
    x           x       x            hi-lo bell: 8-bar
x               x       x
─────────────────────────────────
        x           x
    x           x
```

Conga (Afro-Latin)

```
| | | | | | | | | | | | | | | |
D   d G d G d G d       G       d     bongos or djembe
D   g   T   g   T       G             conga or djembe
D G D G D G D G D   D G D       D     tamboura or djembe
d   D G d   D G d       P       d g   drum
─────────────────────────────────
| | | | | | | | | | | | | | | |
x   x       x     x     x             clave
x   x   x x     x x     x x           timbale: sticks or bell
    O       O   O       O O           timbale: open heads
O       x x x x O       O   x   x     bell (O=hit open end)
    x       x       x       x         percussion
x       x       x       x             percussion
─────────────────────────────────
| | | | | | | | | | | | | | | |      djembe variations (Reed):
T   g   T   g   T   d P     d
T   g   D   g   T   d P     d
d   G   d   G   d   D P     D
T   D g d   D P T   D P     D
T   P   d g D P T   D P     D
T P D g d g D P T   D P     D
T   d G D   d P T   d P     d
T   d g D   d g T   d P     d
T P d g D   d g T P d P     d g
```

Kozak: Korichiwa

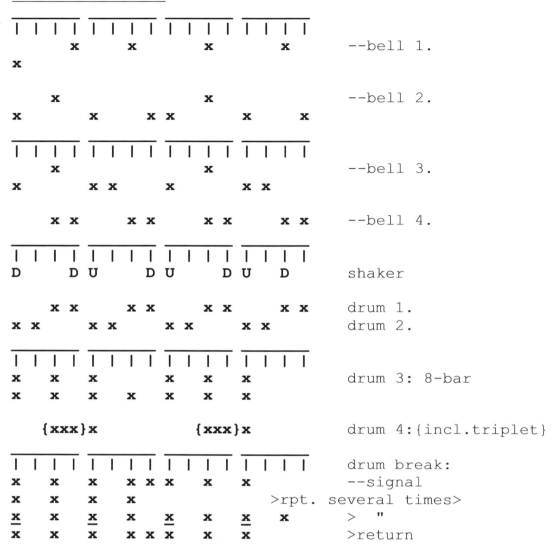

```
| | | |  | | | |  | | | |  | | | |
     x       x        x        x       --bell 1.
x

     x                x                --bell 2.
x        x        x x       x        x

| | | |  | | | |  | | | |  | | | |
     x                x                --bell 3.
x        x x      x        x x

  x x       x x      x x       x x     --bell 4.

| | | |  | | | |  | | | |  | | | |
D    D  U    D  U    D  U    D         shaker

  x x       x x      x x       x x     drum 1.
x x       x x      x x       x x       drum 2.

| | | |  | | | |  | | | |  | | | |
x    x    x      x    x    x            drum 3: 8-bar
x    x    x    x    x    x    x

    {xxx}x             {xxx}x           drum 4:{incl.triplet}

| | | |  | | | |  | | | |  | | | |     drum break:
x    x    x    x x x    x    x          --signal
x    x    x    x                        >rpt. several times>
x    x    x    x    x    x    x    x    >  "
x    x    x    x x x    x    x          >return
```

Afro-Lat. bossa nova

```
| | | |  | | | |  | | | |  | | | |
D   d G D    d    D   d G D    d
D   d G D    d G    G d g(D/g)d g
T     d G         T     d G
x x x x x x x x x x x x x x x x
```

Yesa

```
| | | |  | | | |  | | | |  | | | |
D     G     d    D        d g d g
D  g g D  g g D  g g D  g g
P T      P T      P T      P T
```

Mattioli: Lamba

```
| | | |  | | | |
G    P T g d P T      (play with triplet feel)

P      D P   g d
```

```
| | | |  | | | |  | | | |  | | | |      jun-jun: 8-bar
X    X    X       X    X    X
X  X  X       X       X  X
```

```
| | | |  | | | |
X    X x X x X x       shaker

x    x    x    x       bell/clave
```

Mattioli: Koukou

```
| | | |  | | | |
P T P T g d P      1.
P d    d g d P      1. alt.
```

```
| | | |  | | | |
     P    T    g d      2.
g d       g d      3.
```

```
| | | |  | | | |
   x x x    x x x      shaker
```

```
| | | |  | | | |  | | | |  | | | |
               X       X            jun-jun: hi
X    X    X                              lo
```

```
| | | |  | | | |  | | | |  | | | |
d    g D    D    g D    T    T      end-break
```

Alpha Yaya Diallo:

```
| | | | | | | | | | | | | | | |    variations:
G   g   P   d g D   d   T          1a.
G   g d P   d g D   d   T          1b.
G d g   P   d g D   d   T          1c.
G d g d P   d g D   d   T          1d.
```

<Break>

```
| | | | | | | | | | | | | | | |
G   d g     T   . . .              2a.
G   d P   d P   . . .              2b.
G   d g d g T   . . .              2c.
d   d g d g T   d g d g d G T g    2d.
```

```
| | | | | | | | | | | | | | | |    jun-jun
X   k k X   k k X   k k X   k k
```

```
| | | | | | | | | | | | | | | |    Break (sequence):
T       P       T       d g d(g)
T       -       -       -
T       P       T       d g d(g)
T       -       -       d g d g
T       d g d g T       d g d g
T       -       -       d g d g
T       d g d g T       d g d g
T       -       -       -
```

end: 2a (full line) +
D - d P.

Airto: bossa nova parts

```
| | | | | | | | | | | | | | | |
x     x     x     x     x          clave
D   k G D   k G D   k G D(G)k G    jun-jun
D(g)d g D g   P   P(d)g D g d(g)   drum
```

Mattioli: Kaki Lambe

```
| | | | | | | | | | | | | | | |
D     g D   P   D   g   d   P        1.
d g   g d   G   d   g   D   G        2.

| | | | | | | | | | | | | | | |
X - - X - - X - - - - - - - - -      jun-jun (8-bar):
X - - - - - - - - - - - - - - -

| | | | | | | | | | | | | | | |
X - - X - - - - X - X - - - - -      jun-jun (faster pace)

| | | | | | | | | | | | | | | |
x       x       x       x            shaker

x     x x   x   x   x   x   x        bell (8-bar):
x     x x   x   x   x   x
```

Dido Morris

```
| | | | | | | | | | | | | | | |     4/4:
G       g       G       d   d
g   d   g d     g   d   g d
x       x       x                    bell
    g d     g d     g   d   g d
X X             X X                  jun-jun

| | | | | | | | | | | |             Fume fume--12/8:
x   x   x     x   x
P     d g * P     d g *              * = dampen for P
g   g * P   g D G * P
G(d g d g)D G(d g d g)D

| | | | | | | | | | | | | | | | | | | | | | | |   break:
x   x   x     x   x     x   x   x     x   x         basic bell
G   g   G     g   g     G     g     g     g         drum

x         x   x         x     x     x              hi-lo bell:
x       x           x                              
g d g d g d g d g d g d g   P   G     P   P         3-bar drum
G                   /(end)
```

6/8

```
| | | | | | | | | | | |    Nañigo
d   D g   G d G T g D P    drum 1: combine or split
T G T G T T G T G T g g    drum 2.
x   x x x   x x   x   x    bell
x x   x   x x   x x x      clave (reverse of bell)
x x x x x x x x x x x x    maracas
x   x   x   x   x   x      shekere
D   U D   U D   U D   U    guiro
R L R L R L R L R L R L    bongos: right hand = bass
x x x x x x x x x x x x    timbales: right hand on rim
x   x   x   x   x   x              : left hand on rim
X     X     X     X        junjun and bell
```

alternate Bamba (Wollner)

```
| | | | | | | | | | | |    four drums or:...
X   x X     X   x X        1.shaker
  x X     X     X   x X    2.junjun/bell
  X x X x x X x x X        3.bell
x X x x X x x X x x X x X  4.drum
d G d g D g d G d G d G    
```

Mattioli: Linjin/Sedeba

```
| | | | | | | | | | | |    
D   D P d g D   D P d g    Linjin 1.
g   g T     g   g T        2.
X   X k     X   X k        
```

```
| | | | | | | | | | | |    
P   P   g d T   T          Sedeba 1.
g   g T     g   g T        2.
X   X   k k   k   k        
```

Baie

```
| | | | | | | | | | | | | | | | | | | | | | | |
D     G       D   d g G         G     D   d            bass drum 1
d   D         D       G   g         G   D     G   g    bass drum 2
D   d   T     D g d g T   D   d   T     D g d g T      mid drum
T   d P       T P d g D G T   d   T     T P d g D G    high drum
L   H   H H   H   H     H L   H   H H   H   H   H      bell
X     X     X     X     X     X     X     X            shaker
```

Wollner: synchopation

```
 ___  ___  ___  ___  ___  ___  ___  ___  ___  ___
 | | | | | | | | | | | | | | | | | | | | | | | |
 x x x x x x x x x x x x x x x x x x x x x x x x   1.
 X   x   x   X   x   x   -   -   X   X   -   x     2.
   x x x   x   x       x X       x   x x x   x     3.
   g d g   d   g   -   d P   -   - g   g d g   d
```
[4.improv.]

Kozak: Gadzo

```
 ___  ___  ___  ___  ___  ___
 | | | | | | | | | | | |
     x   x x   x   x   x       bell, shaker
 x

   x x x       x x x           high drum
 x       x x x       x x       low drum

 x - x x x x x x x x -         tin can
```

Kozak: Bembe (in order of appearance):

```
 ___  ___  ___  ___  ___
 | | | | | | | | | | | |
     x   x x   x   x   x       bell: 1
 x

 P T   T P   g d   d g         drum: 2
```

```
 ___  ___  ___  ___
 | | | | | | | | | | | |
 X   X   X   X X               jun-jun: 3

 g d g T G   g d g T G         drum: 4
```

```
 ___  ___  ___  ___
 | | | | | | | | | | | |
 x   x   x   x                 shaker: 5

 d   g   d   g   d g           ending
```

Sequences

Olatunji

Ashiko . . .> Samba

```
 ___  ___  ___  ___
| | | | | | | | | | | | | | | | |
D/P     D P     D P     D P     D
  P   G D P     D P   G D P     D
  P T P   G T   D P T P   G T   D
  g d g   G T   D g d g   G T   D
  P T P T       P T P T G
  g d g d G       g d g d G   P T
  g d P T G   P T g d P T G   P T
  g   P T G   G T   d P T G   G T
```

Olatunji: Rock

```
 ___  ___  ___  ___
| | | | | | | | | | | | | | | |      Olatunji: Rock
g   g d   g d   d   g   d            X4

g   g d   g d   G   G   P T
G                         P T        X1

G   G   P T   G           P T        X4
                   >>P T P T         (4th time)
G   G   P T   G         P T P T      X4
G   G   P T   G         g d g d      X4
G   G   P T   G   G   P T            X2
g   g d   g d   d   g   d            (break)
      then repeat all of above, faster
g   g d   g d   G   G   P T          ending
```

Olatunji: Jingoloba

```
| | | | | | | | | | | | | | | |
X   k k X   k k X   k k X   k k      jun-jun
P T     P T                          2 bar intro
G   g d(G)   (D)G   g d G   (D)       1. X13
      (g)
D   G     d g D   G     d g          2. X8
                                     3. part 1 X8
```

Olatunji: Ife Lo Ju

```
| | | |   | | | |   | | | |   | | | |
g   g d   g d   g   d   g           X3
g   g d   g d   G   G       P T     X1
G   G   P T     G   G       P T     X4
G   G   g d     G   G         g d   X...
g   g d   g d   g   d   g           X3
g   g d   g d   G   G     P T       end
```

Olatunji: Primitive Fire

```
| | | |   | | | |   | | | |   | | | |
G   g           G   g                 1. X1
G   g   P T P   G   g                 2. X3
                                      rpt. 1 and 2.
P T g d P T g d P T g d P T g d        3. X2
g d P T P T P T g d P T P T P T        4. X1
g d P T P T P T g d g T     T          5. X1
G   g   g d g d g d g T     T          6. X8; accel. 2nd, 6th
G   g   g d g d G   g d     d g d      7. X4
P   g d g d g d g d g d     d g d      8. X4
P T P T P T P T P T P T P T P T        9. X4
P T P T P T P T P T P T   T P T        10. X1
P T P T P T P T P T P T   T P T        11. X1
                                      rpt. 9., X3, softening
```

Olatunji: Mystery of Love

```
| | | |   | | | |   | | | |
P   P T P   P   P T P          high conga
```

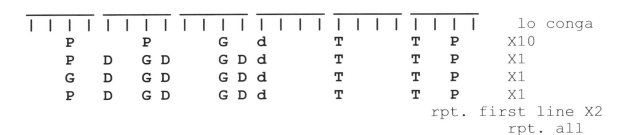

```
| | | |   | | | |   | | | |   | | | |   | | | |   | | | |   lo conga
  P         P         G   d         T       T   P           X10
  P   D   G D       G D d           T       T   P           X1
G   D   G D         G D d           T       T   P           X1
P   D   G D         G D d           T       T   P           X1
                                                   rpt. first line X2
                                                         rpt. all
```

Wilson Samba sequence/parts

| | | | | | | | | | | | | | | | | [108 bpm]
```
| | | | | | | | | | | | | | | |
    d g D G T P       d g D G T P     1. X7
T   d g T   T P   g d g D   d         2. X1
T   D G d   T P   g D G d   T         (2. variation)
T     P T   T P   g d g D   d         3. X1
d g d g D   D g   g d g D   D         4. continue
T   T g D( )D P   P d g D   D g       (4. variation)
```

Latin jazz: [*play in order: 1 2 1 3 1 - - 3*]

```
| | | | | | | | | | | | | | | |
x x x   x x   x   x   x x   x     1.
x x x   x x   x   x   x x         2.
x       x     x                   3.
```

Styles

Afro-Latin

```
| | | | | | | | | | | | | | | |    Afro-Cuban dances
d G T - D g d g D g T - D g d g    slow Mambo

D g T g D g d g D g T g D g d -    Guajira

D - - G - - T - - - G D - T -      Guaguanco

D - g - T - g - T - - g - - - -    Conga

d - D g d - - g D g - g d - - g    Masacote
```

```
| | | | | | | |    Afro-Latin: Cuban dances
D g T g D g D g    Bolero Rumba; slow-med. rock

D g T g D g T P    Montuno

D g T - D g d g    Cha-cha

D g T P D g d g    Guaracha

D g T - - G d g    Afro Latin fast rock

T g T G T g d g    Rock cha-cha

P - - d g d g -    slow Afro-Cuban

T - - d P - g -    Calypso

P G - D P - d -    Beguine

D P - P - g d -    Bomba

D - d G D - d -    Bossa Nova

T - d g d - D -    Baiao (Afro-Latin version)
```

```
| | | | | | | | | | | | | | | |    Afro-Latin style Samba:
P     d G  (P)   P      d G  (P)    conga 1
P   P d G   G D P    P d G    G D   conga 2
D   d P      D P      d G    G      conga 3
d   P D G    P d    d P G D    T    [timbale]
g   T G G    T g    g T G G    T    [" alt. handing]
```

Amazonian

```
 _____ _____   _____ _____
| | | | | | | | | | | | | | | |
 x - x - x - x - x x - x x - - x     percussion

 D G D g - g d g D G(D)G T - T -     drums:

 - - - " - - - - - G D G d g d g

 - - - " - - - - - g d g T P T P

 - - - " - - - - - D G - g d - d -

 D G d P - g T - D G(D)G T - T -
```

```
 _____ _____
| | | | | | | |      Amazonian variations:
 D G - g d - d -

 D G D g - g d g

 -G D G d g d g

 -g T g T P T P

 D G d P - g T -

 D G(D)G T - T -

 T g - g d g d g

 X - - - X - X -
```

Gabrielle Roth: The Dancing Path (Interpretations)

1. <u>Flowing</u> (add flute, violin) 120 bpm: 4 to a line:

```
 _____ _____
| | | | | | | |
 D     g D g d g
```

2. <u>Staccato</u> 184 bpm: 8 to a line:

```
 _____ _____ _____ _____
| | | | | | | | | | | | | | | |     drum variations...
 D   D G T(g D)
 D   D G d g d g D P     D P
 d g d g T   T P   P T P D   d
```

3. <u>Chaos</u> 120 bpm: 4 to a line:

```
| | | | | | | | | | | |
G d g D g d G d g D g D

d P T g T P d P T g T P

| | | | | | | | | | | |
G   g d g d G   g d        [Olatunji dance warmup]

| | | | | | | | | | | |
D(g)D P d g D(g)D P d g     8-bar patterns:
D(g)D P d g T g d P d g

d g D G d g D g D g D g     Moses: Yin-Yang (8-bar)
D G d g D G d G d G d G
```

4. <u>Lyrical</u> (guitar) (flute) 80 bpm: 4 to a line

```
| | | | | | | | | | | | | |
D   d g D g d         D   d
x   x   x x   x   x   x x x x x
D   d   d g   g   g   g d g d
```

5. <u>Stillness</u> 72 bpm: bass pulse, w/ bells, chimes, flute

High Life Rhythms

```
| | | | | | | | | | | | | | | |
d   d g d g     d g d g   g d        hi-life

| | | | | | | | | | | | | | | |
d   d g d g     d g d g   g d        Olatunji: Ki-L'abiola se?

D   d g d g d g d g   g   g d g      Olatunji: T'aiye me se

D G d g   g d   D G d g d g d        Olatunji: Bun-Bam-ba,
                                              Dominira, Mandela´

| | | | | | | | | | | |
x - x - x - - x - x - -              hi-life 3/4 percussion
D G   g d(g)D   d g d g              Olatunji: Gbogbo'ara-le nko
```

Reggae

```
| | | | | | | | | | | | | | | |
D   P           g       P           gg g    conga

D   g g       g g D   g g     T g g         rumba feel

D   g   d g d g D   g     d     P           untitled

D g d g D     P                             untitled


| | | | | | | | | | | | | | | |
D g     g d g d g D g     g d g d g         8-bar
D g     g d g


| | | | | | | | | | | | | | | |
    x   x   x           x       (x)         bell 1
x                   x       (x)


| | | | | | | | | | | | | | | |
x x     xxx x                               bell 2
    x x       x x


| | | | | | | | | | | | | | | |
x x x   x x x   x x x   x   x               bell 3


| | | | | | | | | | | | | | | |              misc. percussion
x x o o x x o o x x o o x x o o
1 1 h h 1 1 1h1 1 1 h h 1 1 1
    xx  xx  xx  xx
x xxx xxx xxx xx
    x   x   x   x
      x       x


| | | | | | | | | | | | | | | |              Reggae Shuffle:
x  xx  xx  xx  x                             --tambourine, guiro
      x x     x x                            --conga, afuchi
      x       x                              --timbale rim, etc.
x   x   x   x                                --bass, afuchi,cymbal


| | | | | | | | | | | | | | | |              misc. percussion,drum
    x       x
    xx      xx
    xx  x   xx  x
      x   x
```

Samba

```
| | | | | | | | | | | | | | | |     Basic Samba:
T   T   D       P   P   g D g D g    Hi to Lo emphasis
       (d)             (d) (d)

T   T g D(G)D P   P d g D   D g       S.G. Wilson version
       (g)
```

```
| | | | | | | | | | | | | | | |
d g d g D   D g   g d g D   D          variation
T   d g D G(d)P   P d g D G d g        variation
T   d g D G(d g)d g d g D G d g        accompaniment
```

```
| | | | | | | | | | | | | | | |
  g d g D   d g   g d g D   d g        accompaniment
g   P T G   G T   d P T G   G T        ashiko version
```

```
| | | | | | | | | | | | | | | |     Basic Samba:
D     g d     G   G   g d(g d g)     Lo to Hi emphasis
     (T)             (T)

D   d g T   d g D   d g t(g)d g        accompaniment
D g d P   P d g D   D   d g d g        Samba roll
                 (d g T P T P)
```

```
| | | | | | | | | | | | | | | |
D     g T     (G)D G   g T g d g       S.G. Wilson version
D     g T       D   D g T   T          Bo Conlan accompaniment
D   D   T   d G   G   g d g d g        Duncan version
D   d g   g d   G   G   T g d g         my version accomp.
```

```
| | | | | | | | | | | | | | | |     Airto: Batucada
x x x x x x x x x x x x x x x x     cymbal
d     P D     P d     P D     P     bass drum
X       *     X       *   *         jun-jun: * = X+k
X   k X X   k X|D   x G D   x G     jun-jun or djembe;
x=shaker
```

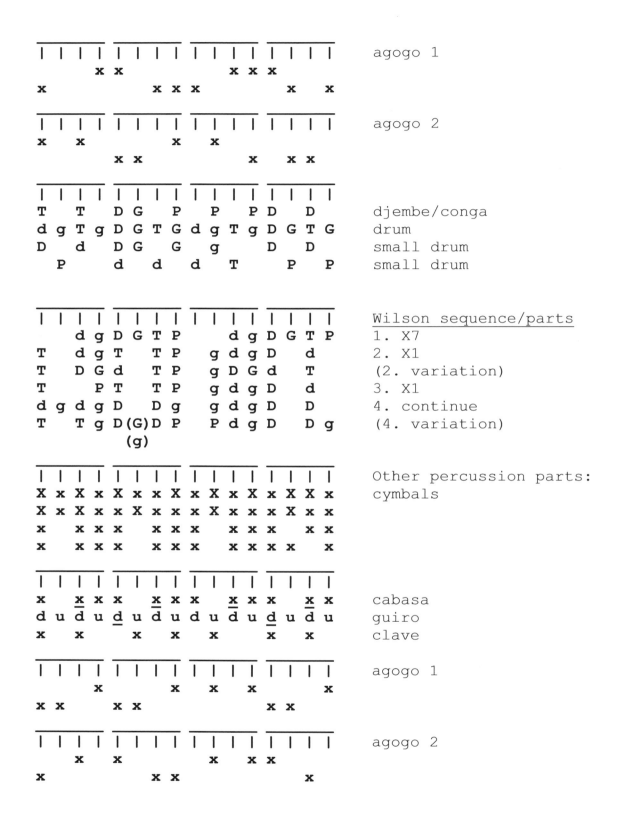

```
| | | | | | | | | | | | | | | |   agogo 1
      x x             x x x
x               x x x           x     x

| | | | | | | | | | | | | | | |   agogo 2
x     x             x     x
        x x               x     x x

| | | | | | | | | | | | | | | |   djembe/conga
T   T     D G   P   P   P D   D     drum
d g T g D G T G d g T g D G T G     small drum
D   d     D G   G     g     D   D   small drum
    P       d     d     d   T     P   P   small drum

| | | | | | | | | | | | | | | |   Wilson sequence/parts
    d g D G T P     d g D G T P   1. X7
T   d g T   T P   g d g D   d     2. X1
T   D G d   T P   g D G d   T     (2. variation)
T     P T   T P   g d g D   d     3. X1
d g d g D   D g   g d g D   D     4. continue
T   T g D(G)D P   P d g D   D g   (4. variation)
        (g)

| | | | | | | | | | | | | | | |   Other percussion parts:
X x X x X x x X x X x X x X X x   cymbals
X x X x x X x x x X x x x X x x
x     x x x     x x x     x x x     x x
x     x x x     x x x     x x x x     x

| | | | | | | | | | | | | | | |
x     x x x     x x x     x x x     x x   cabasa
d u d u d u d u d u d u d u d u   guiro
x     x       x     x   x       x   x   clave

| | | | | | | | | | | | | | | |   agogo 1
        x             x   x   x         x
x x         x x               x x

| | | | | | | | | | | | | | | |   agogo 2
    x     x             x     x x
x               x x               x
```

Samba-like variations

```
| | | |  | | | |  | | | |  | | | |
d      g T g d g   g d g D g T(P)      L.Allen: No Change

d g d g T   T P    P T P D   d         Roth--staccato

  g d g D   d g    g d g D   d g       2/4 part

| | | |  | | | |  | | | |  | | | |
D(g)d g D g    P   P(d)g D g d(g)       Bossa Nova (4/4 feel)

D   d G D   d G    G d g(D/g)d g        Bossa Nova variation

D   d g D     G    G d g D   D          Fanga (Olatunji)

d g d g D g d G    G d g D   d g        woodshed rock

| | | |  | | | |  | | | |  | | | |     Bo Conlan--2-part
D   P D G   P D    D P D G   P          1
D     g T          D   D g T   T        2.

G D G   G D G d    d G d   D G          Hart: Evening Samba

| | | |  | | | |  | | | |  | | | |     jogging Samba
d(g)Tgg d     g    g T g d G D G        (triplet feel)

| | | |  | | | |  | | | |  | | | |
d g d g D   D    Dgd Gdg Dgd Gdg        Airto

d   D G d   D G d    D G {T P T}        last bar triplet

| | | |  | | | |  | | | |  | | | |
d   d     P   P   g       D   D         Airto: drum elements
d     P   P   g   g       D   D
d   d   T P   P   g       D   D
d   d     P   G   g       D   D
```

Dance List: a personal selection

2/4

```
| | | | | | | |
D   d g D G d g        Moving the Rock

D_G d_P   G d_P        Just Jam

G   g d   d g d        Olatunji: KiyaKiya

T_P d_g T_P   g        Pele Juju: Walk & Talk

X   k k X k k          Existentialist Rumba
```

4/4

```
| | | | | | | | | | | | | | | |
G   g d   d g d G   g   P            dance warmup

D   d       D   d D   d g d g        Funk the Courthouse
          (G) (g) (G)

D       d   g   D   G   d g d g      good fast

d g d g d g d G   g d g d   d g      J. Brown: Make it Funky
```

```
| | | | | | | | | | | | | | | |
D     g   g   g D     g d   P        Friendly Funk

D     P   P   g D   D   T g d g      Vacation Samba

D G   P   P   g D G   g d g d g      Beat I Make

D   D   d     D     g   g d g        (fast)Beat I Make
        (T)       (G)
```

```
| | | | | | | | | | | | | | | |
d   l P D   l P d G   P d G   P      surdo(l=lft hand on rim)

P   P d G   G T g D P d G T g D      Roll With Me

P   P d G   P d g T P T P d G T      Edging Max
```

```
| | | | | | | | | | | | | | | |
D   D g   g d   G   G   T   g        Samba turnaround
  (d)                 (g d g)
```

```
| | | |  | | | |  | | | |  | | | |
D   G    d g d g D    g d    g d(g)    another Samba turnaround
D   G    d g d g D    G d    g d       alt. "   (Earth Tribe)
D   D    d g d g D    D g    g d(g)    alt. "
```

```
| | | |  | | | |  | | | |  | | | |
x     x     x       x   x       x      Af-Lat clave
        x x           x x         x    fast Af-Lat rock
x   x         x x         x            x
```

```
| | | |  | | | |  | | | |  | | | |
D G d P   g T   D G   G T   T          Amazonian variations in 4

D G D g   g d g   G D G d g d g

x   x   x   x   x x   x x       x      percussion: Amazonia
```

Lamba/Rock variations:

```
| | | |  | | | |  | | | |  | | | |
G   P T g d P T G   P T d g P T        djembe 1.

G   P T g d P T G   P       G          variation

G   P T g d P T *G  P  G  P*           Lamba Pop
(last 4 notes with R hand, L thumb held on drum)

P     D P   g d P     D P   g d        djembe 2.

D(g)d g T   d g D(g)d g D   D          easy drum 3.

G   P     d P   G   P T d g P T        Lambacon

G   g d   g d   G   P T g d P T        lambation
```

```
| | | |  | | | |  | | | |  | | | |
D   G   d   d g D G   g d g T g        trance-dance

D   G   d g d g D   G   T              Northern Lights dance
```

```
| | | |  | | | |  | | | |  | | | |
D_____g_____g D_____g_____g   Get It (8-bar)
D_____g_____g D g - g D - g -
```

```
| | | |   | | | |   | | | |   | | | |
D   T   D P     g D g T g D P d g       propeller

D G d g T P   G D     d g     g d g     variant prop

D g d G     g d g D     D     d g d      Magic Bus
 (-)         (G)              (d)

D   d g D   d g D   d g D P d G          The Breathing Night

D(g)d g T g D(g)d P     g T g D          accordion in 4/4
```

3/4

```
| | | |   | | | |   | | | |
D G     g d(g)D     d g d g              Gbogbo'ara-le nko (Olatunji)

D(g)d g T g D(g)d P     g                accordion

D   d   T g D P     g T g                Jogging Samba
   (G) (d)         (d)

D g d P d P d g T g T g                  Tree Samba

D   d g   g d g T   d g                  Future Inside Out

D   d   g d   G   G                      3-bar fanga
```

3/8

```
| | | | | |
d G T g D P           Afro-Cuban--expand

T G d P D P           Nueva onda

P   g d G D           Rainbow Train
```

5/4

```
| | | |   | | | |   | |
D(g)T g D G T g D P           batu-pumpa

X   k k X k k X k k           Clam-digging in Paradise
```

6/8

```
| | | | | | | | | | | |
P   P d G     P d P d G T      Process Makeup
(g) (g)       (g) (g)   (d)

P   P D   d P   P D g d        rolling rock

T   d P T g T P d P T g        Counting Sheep Backwards

G   g d g d G   g d            Olatunji dance warmup

d   D g   G d G T g D P        Nañigo

x x   x   x x   x x x          Nañigo bell


| | | | | | | | | | | |       Kozak: Gadzo/Bembe
    x   x x   x   x   x        --bell, shaker
x
```

12/8

```
| | | | | | | | | | | | | | | | | | | | | | | |
D(g)D P d g D(g)D P d g D(g)D P d g T g d P d g
```

7/8

```
| | | | | | | | | | | | | |
D g   G d     g D g   G D g      Airto: Samba funk


| | | | | | | | | | | | | |
D   T g   P T g   P T P T g      Counting Down Dawn

D     P   g T g D   D g d g      The Jesus Stomp

D     d     g   D   d   g g      Gearbox Breakdown

G   g     d g   G   g d g d      The In and Out of It
  (P)       (P)       (P T)


| | | | | | | | | | | | | |
D g d G d g   G d g D   d g      jam dance

D(g)d g T g D(g)d P   g T g      accordion in 7

T   T g d P   g d g D g d g      untitled
```

Experimental duets, ensemble patterns and mini-sequences

2/4:

```
| | | | | | | |
D g d g d G d g      Golden Mean
x   x   x x   x      Earth Tribe
```

```
| | | | | | | |
  g d g D   d g      Samba part
  x   x   x x x      Santana: Milagro
```

```
| | | | | | | |
d g T g D G T G      Airto: Batucada
G   g d   d g d      Olatunji: KiyaKiya
T g   g D     g      untitled
x   x   x x   x      Earth Tribe
```

4/4:

```
| | | | | | | | | | | | | | | |
G   g   g d g d G   g d   d g d     Primitive Fire
      x x         x x     x         fast Af-Lat rock
x   x       x x       x
```

```
| | | | | | | | | | | | | | | |
x   x   x   x   x x   x x     x     percussion: Amazonia
x   x         x   x     x x         untitled (hi-lo):
      x   x                   x
```

```
| | | | | | | | | | | | | | | |
G   g d   d g d G   g   P           dance warmup
G   g d   d g d G   g d   d g d     untitled
```

```
| | | | | | | | | | | | | | | |     Samba roll I:
D g D g(D)P   P(D)g D g   P T        1.
        (P T)             (P T P)

D g d P   P d g D   D   d g d g       2.
                    (d g T P T P)
```

```
| | | | | | | | | | | | | | | |     Samba roll II:
D g d P   P d g D   D   d g d g       8-bar:
D g d P   P d g D   d g T P T P

G   P T g   P T G   P T g   P T       accompaniment
```

```
| | | | | | | | | | | | | | |       Samba turnaround
D   D g   g d   G   G   T   g
    (d)                 (g d g)

T   d g   g d   G   G  : X4 = break
```

```
| | | | | | | | | | | | | | | |     Swing high reggae:
D(g)d g D g d g D g d g   g d g       w/ Latin/triplet feel
(variations: alt. or selective g>G)
D   P       g     P     g g g
D   g g     g g D   g g   T g g
D   d g     d g D   d     P T P       reggae

  x x x   x x x   x x x   x   x       bell 1.
```

```
| | | | | | | | | | | | | | | |     bell 2.
x x     x x x x
    x x       x x
```

```
| | | | | | | | | | | | | | | |     misc. percussion
x x o o x x o o x x o o x x o o
  x x   x x   x x   x x
x x x x x x x x x x x x x x
    x   x   x   x
      x       x
```

```
| | | |   | | | |   | | | |   | | | |      shake me
d g T     T g D G(d)g d g d g D G          part 1 = 8 bars:
d)g T     d g D G     g d g d G   (G)
D)                              (g/D)
        d g T G D G T g T                  part 2. or sequence
```

```
| | | |   | | | |   | | | |   | | | |      Ethiopian variations
D   g d G     d g D   G     d g d g         Ethiopian walking rhythm
D   D G d     d g D   D G d g d g           King Sunny live
D   g d G     d g D g d G d g T g           Ethiopian variation
```

```
| | | |   | | | |   | | | |   | | | |
D - d g T - d g D - d g T P T P            1. (8-bar)
D - d g T - d g D G d g D G d(g)

D - d g T - d g D - d g D - - -            2.
T P T P T - d g T P T P - - - -            2. alt.
```

```
| | | |   | | | |   | | | |   | | | |      Sunjam:
D     d g d g D     P       P     g d g     1.
D       G T     P D     D     g d g         2.
```

```
| | | |   | | | |   | | | |   | | | |      Lamba Rock:
D g d g T     d g D g d g D     D
D     d g D     d g D   d g D G
G     P T g d P T G     P T d g P T
G     P T g d P T G     P         G
P       D P     g d P     D P     g d
```

```
| | | |   | | | |   | | | |   | | | |      jun-jun (8-bar):
X   X   X         X   X   X
X   X   X     X     X   X
```

```
| | | |   | | | |                          
X   X x X x X x          shaker
x     x     x     x      bell/clave
```

```
| | | | | | | | | | | | | | | |   untitled:
D    d g D g T g D g d P    g d g   Yelle
D G    g D G    g D G    P    T     Pan Logo
D    d g    g d g D    d g    g d g 2/4 accompaniment
D g d P D g T g D g d P D g T g     Middle East 2/4
D    D    d g d g D    D g    g d g Samba turnaround
```

proto-Samba *<try by itself or with basic hi-lo>*

```
| | | | | | | | | | | | | | | |
g    P T G    G T    d P T G    G T   ashiko style
g    P T G    P T g    P T G    P T   accomp.

| | | | | | | | | | | | | | | |       basic Samba hi-lo
d g d g D    D g    g d g D    D       1.
P    P d G    G D P    P d G    G D    2.
                                   (other variations):
| | | | | | | | | | | | | | | |
T    T    D G    P    P    P D    D     djembe/conga
T    T    D    P    P    g D g d g      basic hi-lo
T    T g D(G)D P    P d g D    D g      S.G. Wilson version

| | | | | | | | | | | | | | | |    (2/4 accomp.:)
d g T g D G T g d g T g D G T g     Batucada
D g T    G d g D g T    G d g       rock variation
   d g D G T P    d g D G T P        variation
```

basic Samba lo-hi version 1. (bossa nova feel)

```
| | | | | | | | | | | | | | | |
D    P D G    P D    D P D G    P      1.
D    g T    D    D g T    T            2.
        (G - G -)
```

basic samb lo-hi version 2.

```
| | | | | | | | | | | | | | | |
D    D    T    d G    G    g d g d g   Duncan
D    d g T    d g D    d g T(g)d g     accomp.
G    P T g    P T G    P T g    P T    variation
```

```
| | | |  | | | |  | | | |  | | | |      reggae Samba:
D     g T      G      G     g T g d g     djembe 1
D   D   d      G      G     g d g T g     djembe 2
  x x x    x x x    x x x    x x x        bell or shaker
    x x      x x      x x      x x        shaker or bell
  g d g    g d g    g d g    g d g        conga/drum 1
    P T      P T      P T      P T        conga/drum 2


| | | |  | | | |  | | | |  | | | |      untitled
T   d g d g T    P        D   G           Bakongo
x     x     x     x     x x    x x     x  percussion: Amazonia
```

3/4

```
| | | |  | | | |  | | | |
D   d      G d g D P T g       First dance jam 1.
d g T    d g T g d g D G       2.


| | | |  | | | |  | | | |
D G D    D G d G d G D         Safari
x     x    x       x   x       clave


| | | |  | | | |  | | | |
D G   g d(g)D    d g d g       Gbogbo'ara-le nko (Olatunji)
T   G    D   G    d g d g      Bo Conlan
x x   x x      x               right hand--stick
              X     X k        left hand--bell (k=both)
D   d    T g D P    g T g      jogging Samba
  (G) (d)         (d)

x x   x   x x   x   x          Bakongo 1
x x   x   x x x x       x      --part 2 or sequence


| | | |  | | | |  | | | |  | | | |  | | | |  | | | |
D       G     d g d g d G     D   g     d   G   d   g     drum
x     x   x x   x     x     x   x   x   x     x   x     junjun
H     H               L   H       L   H       L          bell
G d g D g    G d g D    d G d g D g    G d g D   d        drum
```

5/4

```
| | | | | | | | | | | | | | | | | | | |
D(g)T g D G T g D P D(g)T g D G T g D P     batu-pumpa
D   d g T G d g T g ...                      untitled
D   d G   g d g T g ...                      untitled
```

```
| | | | | | | | | | | | | | | | | | | |
  g d g D   d g D P   g d g D   d g D P      untitled
D   d g d g   g d g ...                      untitled
```

6/8

```
| | | | | | | | | | | |
d G d g D g d G d G d G      6/8 bomba
d G d g D g   G d g D        untitled
                             and/or:
d g D G d g D g D g D g      yin-yang (8-bar):
D G d g D G d G d G d G
```

```
| | | | | | | | | | | |
d g d P   g d g d G   g      Julie's house I
g D   d G d g D   d G d
```

```
| | | | | | | | | | | |
D   d P   P d g T g T g      Julie's house II
D   D P d g D   D P d g
```

```
| | | | | | | | | | | | | | | | | | | |    Julie's House III
T g d g T - d g T - d g T G D G D -        (X2)
P - P d G - P d P d G T/...                (X3)
```

9/8

```
| | | | | | | | | | | | | | | | | | | | |
D g d G d g D g d G d g D g D G D G         jam groove
D g d G d g D g d G d   d   G   G          accomp.
```

7/8

```
| | | |  | | |  | | | | | | |
d g T g  T g d  G d g d g D G    untitled
T   T    T        g d g   g d g
```

```
| | | |  | | |  | | | | | | |
D   d g  d g d  g D   d g d g    untitled
D   d g  d g D  G   G D   T G
```

```
| | | |  | | |  | | | | | | |
D     P  g T g  D   D g d g      untitled
        (d)
D   d g  d g D  g d g d
```

```
| | | |  | | |  | | | | | | |
g d g d  G   g      d g   G      1.
D   d g  T   d g D    d g T g    2.
```

```
| | | |  | | |  | | | | | | |
x   x    x      x x x   x x x    African clave
T   T    T        g d g   g d g  drum version
D g   G d        g D g   G D g   Airto: Samba funk
D     P  g T g  D   D g d g      untitled
G d g T  g T g  d G d g d g D    untitled
```

3/5/7--*played together as round...*

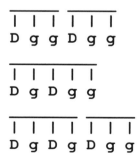

```
| | | | | |
D g g D g g
```

```
| | | | |
D g D g g
```

```
| | | | | | |
D g D g D g g
```

<u>Sequences:</u>

<u>untitled</u>

```
___ ___ ___ ___
| | | | | | | | | | | | | | | |
D   D G T(g D)
D   D G d g d g D P     D P
d g d g T   T P   P T P D   d
D   d   d g d g T   T P   P T P
```

<u>untitled</u>

```
_____ _____ _____ _____
| | | | | | | | | | | | | | | |
D     G T     P T   P   d g d g
D G d g T g T g D G d g T g T g
T   T g D G d g d g d g D G d G
D     G T     P T   P   T P T P
D     G d   g d   g   d g d g
```

Thursday night jam: wiggle (8-bar)

```
____ ____ ____ ____
| | | | | | | | | | | | | | | |
d   d         d     g            1.
d   d T       d   T g D g T g

D   D         D     G   g d g    2.
D   D   d   d g D   d g D g T g
```

<u>Untitled</u>

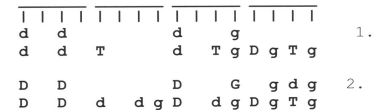

```
____ ____ ____ ____
| | | | | | | | | | | | | | | |
d)g T   d g D G   g d g d G  (G)   1. (8-bar)
D)                        (g/D)
    (d g T G D G T g T)             2. (or play along w/ 1.)
```

<u>Untitled</u>

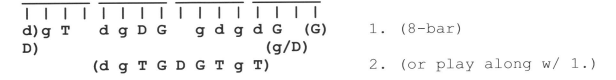

```
____ ____ ____ ____
| | | | | | | | | | | | | | | |
d)g T   d g D G   g d g d G  (G)   1.
D)                        (g/D)
    (d g T G D G T g T)             2.
```

Untitled

```
|  |  |  |  |  |  |  |  |  |  |  |  |  |  |  |  |  |  |
D        P     g T g D     D g d g          D G d g g    1.
D        P     g T g       D G d g g D     D g d g       2.
```

Amazonian sequence:

```
|  |  |  |  |  |  |  |
D G    g d    d
D G(D)G T    T
D G d P    g T
D G D g    g d g
  G D G d g d g
  g T g T P T P
T g    g d g d g
```

```
|  |  |  |  |  |  |  |  |  |  |  |  |  |  |      Amazonia
D G D g    g d g D G(D)G T    T
      "          D G    g d    d
      "          G D G d g d g
D G d P    g T   D G(D)G T    T          then return, rpt....
```

Resources

Practice Exercises

BREATHING: 40 bpm: 10 times counting: 1-2 (inbreath), 1-2 (out), 5 times counting: 1 2 3 4 (in), 1 2 3 4 (out)

HAND DRILLS:

• Paradiddles (176 bpm):

a. **R**LRR **L**RLL   b. **R**LRLRR **L**RLRLL   c. **R**LRLRLRR **L**RLRLRLL

• Rumba (D - g g): 108 bpm. Switch hands.

• rR lL rR lL : 116 bpm.

• 4 + 3 (Pepe): play four notes, then three in same time span; then both together. Switch hands, vary loudness

```
 | | | |
 R R R R
 L   L   L
```

• **TIMING:** 176 bpm.

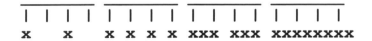

```
 | | | | | | | | | | | | | | | |
 x   x   x x x x xxx xxx xxxxxxxx
```

• **YIN-YANG:**

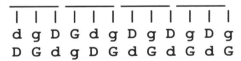

```
 | | | | | | | | | | | |
 d g D G d g D g D g D g
 D G d g D G d G d G d G
```

• **KIDI VARIATIONS** (Chernoff), both hands, @ 208 bpm:

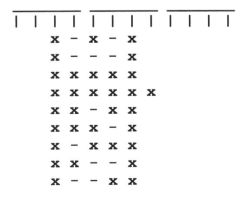

```
 | | | | | | | | | | | |
     x - x - x
     x - - - x
     x x x x
     x x x x x x
     x x - x x
     x x x - x
     x - x x x
     x x - - x
     x - - x x
```

Basic Drumming Exercises and Rhythms

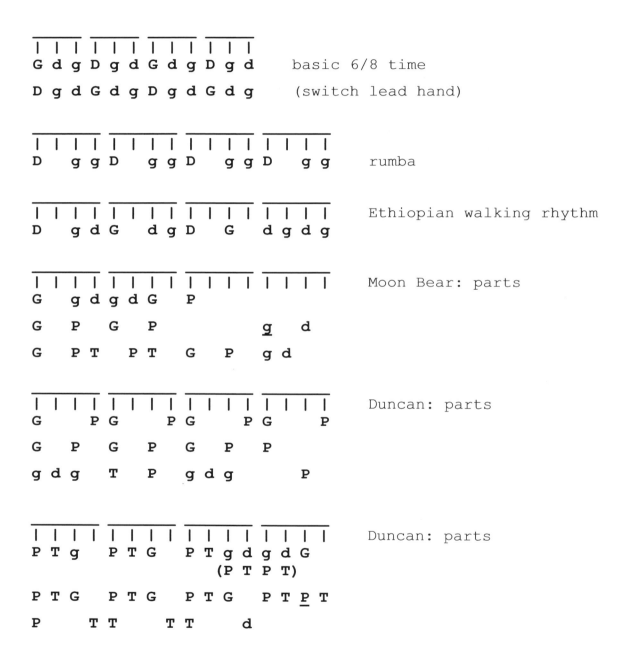

```
| | | | | | | | | | | |
G d g D g d G d g D g d       basic 6/8 time

D g d G d g D g d G d g       (switch lead hand)


| | | | | | | | | | | |
D   g g D   g g D   g g D   g g    rumba


| | | | | | | | | | | | | | | |
D   g d G   d g D   G   d g d g    Ethiopian walking rhythm


| | | | | | | | | | | | | | | |
G   g d g d G   P
G   P   G   P                 g   d
G   P T   P T   G   P   g d    Moon Bear: parts


| | | | | | | | | | | | | | | |
G       P G       P G       P G       P    Duncan: parts
G   P   G   P   G   P   P
g d g   T   P   g d g           P


| | | | | | | | | | | | | | | |
P T g     P T G     P T g d g d G    Duncan: parts
                (P T P T)
P T G     P T G     P T G     P T P T
P     T T     T T     d
```

Of Drum Groups and All-Night Jams (*from Cougar WebWorks website*)

Starting a Drum Group	24-Hour Drumming
Friday Night Jam	Trance Dance

Starting a Drum Group

A bunch of us where I live have been playing African drums now for six years. This is nothing by African standards; but you do what you can. The first workshop happened here, sparking our engagement ever since, and a number of excellent teachers have passed through the area boosting our skills periodically: notably Fatala and Alpha Yaya Diallo. Three of us have taken Olatunji's week-long workshop at Hollyhock: for me providing the biggest jump in skill and understanding.

Gradually we've learned to work with multi-part rhythms. Each part by itself is easy to learn, in these traditional African and Latin pieces. But the timing between the parts creates the dynamic tension which drives them, and the difficulty in mastering as a group. Still, four or five of us through regular weekly practices brought a half-dozen selections up to performance level over the course of three or four years. After a public performance at the local fall faire in September 1994, and a studio taping session soon after, we finally lost steam and fell apart, and have met only sporadically since, with turnover of half the core group. Why?

Part of it has to do with individual energies and priorities, but part of it has to do with the nature of what we were attempting. A month of intensive twice-a-week practices before that fall faire, and the attendant pressure to perform well at the time, caused some of us enormous anxiety that carried over afterward. I flubbed a couple of notes in my own part once or twice, and felt terrible about it--even though people in the crowd (you could hardly even call them an audience, wandering around the fair grounds doing their own thing) never noticed. Our subsequent studio session came off perfectly. A local guitarist, probably the best musician around, had the best advice to offer: mere proficiency at the rhythms is not enough to engage an audience. We played, at best, like machines. That kind of music would work okay for trance or ritual but for a contemporary crowd, whether listening or dancing, you need the added dynamism of a soloist, which we lacked with our inexperience.

The Friday Night Jam

During the last six years a number of the local neophyte drummers have attempted to breathe life into and out of that longer-lived institution, the Friday Night Jam. Haven of Elvis officionados and Credence Clearwater hacks, Willie Nelson impersonators and would-be-Dead-heads, the Friday Night Jam has lived by one rule: anything goes. Unfortunately for my taste, the "any" part of it sometimes gets lost in the Standards shuffle. Which is to say, group improvisation is hard to do well. When it works, however, it's dynamite, true inspiration, golden. It can even redeem the most tired of oldies, given an injection of altered lyrics, rhythms, and original solos.

The chronic problem at the Friday Night Jam has been to amalgamate the Afro-Latin drums and percussion with the western guitars, accordion, piano, harmonica, and their associated forms: primarily straight-ahead four-four. The drummers generally want to lean the beat over to the offbeat, the syncopated, the reggae. Reggae has been a convenient meeting ground because the compromise is simply found in the regular upbeat. But more than that is the issue of a controlled, recognizable "song" versus an extended, authentic and moveable jam.

Drum energy works best in waves, without restrictions of straightjacket lyrics, measures, predetermined chord changes. You can put it all together in a great package, if you're Santana or Olatunji. For us amateurs, that challenge takes work and practice as a group, and these are not appropriate to the looser anarchy of the jam. Even the oft-attempted "Let's take turns and go around the circle for starting something" is hard to maintain consistently in that venue. So success is left to chance, to who shows up and the mood they're in, to the phase of the moon or the health of the crop or the status of one's lovelife, to how many drums can support each other for the occasional detour down Africa lane. It's all about listening, and sharing leadership, and these are qualities that don't come to us easily or automatically.

The biggest obstacle in this culture comes from the worship of the guitar god. The lead guitar calls the shots: sets the melody and mood, determines the volume (easily overpowering drums with a twist of the amp button, or toning them down if there's no amp until the life goes out of them). It's true that rhythm is fundamental and so a single percussionist can take any song and shift its character, ruin it or drive it to new life. But in terms of group dynamics, the guitarist is generally preeminent, by default. Everyone looks to them for the next song, waits for them to retune, and depends on the structures that they have memorized and are offering as a well-furnished boat for everyone to ride in. What the drummer offers is support: this is what is expected. For a drummer to share or take the lead is not expected or easily allowed. Conversely, it's hard for other musicians used to taking lead melodic parts to learn to settle for supportive, truly rhythmic roles.

So lately the jam is in decline. Lately there haven't been many drummers showing up, because when we do, we're held back by the inertia of low energy, low volume, and low creativity. We, like the other musicians, are aging, or have a lot of distractions on our minds, or are afraid to boldly take the loose reins, or have simply given up trying--for now. But as always, it's different every week. Who knows what stranger or visitor will show up this time, or what random collection of hideaways will decide to come out and celebrate this full moon? When it fails it's deadly dull, and a Friday night wasted. But when it clicks, and moves into magic, there's nothing like it in the world.

ALL-NIGHT DRUMMING AND TRANCE DANCING

We had our fifth annual All-Night Drum this year. Different every year: and always a special event, a highlight. February: when everyone needs a boost of some kind, a rift in the cold gray routine, and this does it like nothing else. Here the drums have reign for a full 24 hours. One rule: keep the beat going. Whoever shows up, by word of mouth or friendly notice, shows up. It's a jam all the way....

Notes from the first annual 24-hour drum:

We arrived at the hall, called in the four directions, chanted, beat the steady 210 of the shaman's drum, Michael and Walkin and Jane and Rowena and I, and a guy from New Denver: gettin in the mood. Then began a good rolling rock in the forming circle, with a jazz beat offset by Ken. Julie, Lars, Doug all showed up and joined.

From there, a pastiche, a roller-coaster, a trading of percussion toys, a sharing of drums, ongoing beat. Peter, Michael M. show up, go like crazy. Later, Julie and Jane with Peter, Doug and New Denver, cohesive and driving.

Sometimes it didn't always "work." During the most high-energy jamming, as between Michael and me, or me on the good djembe and Nigel on the yew, I'd be self-centered, loud and improvisational. Julie and Nigel later would say they'd look for the quietest drum, to play to that; or that the loud "stuff" was overbearing, impenetrable, lost on a jag. Lars remarked that traditionally African drummers didn't play free of the forms until age 30, after fifteen years of practice. "Yeah," I replied, "but we've been listening to jazz for twenty years."

Miles Davis said, "There are no mistakes."

Walkin said, "It's all good."

Into the night, the evening and night.

Michael lays down, Julie and I take it up. Me on the big bass, her on the djembe, steady, slow, and powerful. Michael says, "that was the best music I've heard in Argenta." I say, "that's what I thought hearing you guys play when I lay down to sleep."

Of course I didn't sleep.

When we lay out in the circle on the mats and benches, we took rattles and shakers in our hands, to keep the beat. At one point only I was up, with the sticks. Then New Denver relieved me, and he took up the slow bass djembe.

Toward morning we made strong black coffee and got into some grooved jamming. Alternating with slow breathers. At one sparse point Doug said "It feels like some Buddhist colony."

Okay, I thought, and set up a sustained 210 on the yew drum, chanting Om with New Denver beside me, Doug cross-legged on the mat opposite. Jane nearby; Julie wandering, Lars and Michael gone, Ken asleep or out. It took off--the rolling drumstick beats, the billowing group voice.

Nigel walked in, dumbstruck. Later he said, "It felt like a church, a sacred space. You guys were egoless, totally spaced out. You'd gotten rid of everything, burned it all away." He took over the driving force on the yew drum, eyes closed and grooving from then on, the last four hours. "I figured you'd need the energy boost by then."

When it's over, we drift outside in the sun on bright morning snow. And the ravens pick it up and carry it on: quork, a quork-quork…qu-qu-qu-qu-quork…

Trance Dance:

It began as a one-time event, intended to create "community ritual."

But we immediately scheduled another one three months later; and after that one, realized we really needed to do this every three months, at each midpoint between solstice and equinox.

There is a minimum of preparation and instruction beforehand: learning the steps, from a West African dance; and the rhythms, locally generated by drummers experienced with West African patterns. The key for both dancers and drummers is consistency: to go all night with the same steps, the same rhythms. In this repetition and commitment comes the opportunity for trance. Forgetting oneself in the power of the whole.

Even with solos, which are permitted a single dancer and drummer at a time when the dancer feels moved by a pitch of excitement to break free and go into the circle, the impulse and flight is guided not by ego but by sheer union with the high energy created: the gathering vortex released.

We go eight hours, breaking bread together at dawn, or sharing fruit. There has been an amazing display of endurance by all involved, with everyone going at it steadily, hardly any breaks, a little snack or drink of water, a brief loosening up and then back in. Afterwards there is sharing of how it was, what happened, how it might be better next time.

In February we had thirty-five dancers, eleven drummers, and three digeridoo players miked to match the volume of the drummers' sound--calling back and forth from opposite ends of the hall, with the dancers circling in between. The low frequencies and voiced tones of the diges gave us all an added dimension of transport to other realms.

But ultimately the experience is not one of escape or exotic adventure. There are no drugs involved. It's more a grounding, a bonding, a building of community energy. Personal transcendence comes in the form of union with group spirit and with the spirit of rhythm itself. Stretching personal boundaries to the limits of the sacred space. Leaving the banks to ride the river.

References

Books

Brown, Thomas A. <u>Afro-Latin Rhythm Dictionary: A Complete Dictionary for all Musicians.</u> Van Nuys, CA: Alfred Publishing, 1984.

Chernoff, John Miller. <u>African Rhythm and Sensibility</u>.

Davis, Wade. "The Art of Shamanic Healing." Shadows in the Sun: Essays on the Spirit of Place. Edmonton: Lone Pine, 1992.

Hart, Mickey, with Jay Stevens. <u>Drumming at the Edge of Magic: A Journey into the Spirit of Percussion.</u> San Francisco: HarperSanFrancisco, 1990.

Moreira, Airto. Airto: The Spirit of Percussion. [Ed. Rick Mattingly]. Wayne, N.J.: 21st Century Music Productions, 1985.

Moses, Bob. <u>Drum Wisdom</u>. [Ed. Rick Mattingly]. Cedar Grove, NJ: Modern Drummer Publications, 1984.

Olatunji, Babatunde. <u>Drums of Passion Songbook</u>. [Transcribed and Edited by Doug Lebow]. New York: Olatunji Music, 1993. 2109 Broadway, Suite 477, New York, NY 10023. (212) 580-7737.

Reed, Ted. <u>Latin Rhythms for Drums and Timbales</u>. Clearwater, FL: Ted Reed, 1960.

Wilson, Sule Greg. <u>The Drummer's Path: Moving the Spirit with Ritual and Traditional Drumming.</u> Rochester, VT: Destiny, 1992. [companion tape available]

Wollner, Ruth. <u>Improvisation in Music</u>.

Audio

Abdel Kabirr	Fatala
Alpha Yaya Diallo	Gabrielle Roth
Anugana and Sebastiano	Guam
Baaba Maal	Ken Shorley
Babatunde Olatunji	King Sunny Ade
Baka Beyond	Mickey Hart
Bakongo	Santana
Diga Rhythm Band	Themba Tana
Edwina Lee Tyler	Youssou N'Dour

Video

Paulo Mattioli

Internet

http://djemberhythms.com

Index

About the Author

My first favorite music was Elvis's "Hound Dog." I was eight. I also liked Louis Armstrong and so learned to play the trumpet. Unlike some of my peers, I outgrew Elvis and moved on to the Beach Boys, Cream, Marvin Gaye and Jimi Hendrix, through moves between Atlanta, New York, Baltimore and Chicago. Along the way some James Brown and Chicago blues also crept under my skin, and Santana got the inner drums rolling. I studied a little music improvisation at Dartmouth College and from there not much happened for twenty years, until my first drum workshop. There was no turning back.

I've made my living as a teacher, carpenter and treeplanter, and also worked as a homesteader and nonviolence trainer. Since 1972 I've written and edited numerous pieces of publication in a variety of fields, and currently operate an eclectic e-mag called Cougar WebWorks, in which a some of this material has appeared. I've made a number of drums and play them with other drummers and dancers at every opportunity.

--Nowick Gray

Order the Newest Book in the Roots Jam Series

- Dive deep into African drumming styles from around the world.
- Find simple notation for djembe, dunun, conga, tabla and batucada parts from Guinea, Mali, Cuba, Brazil, Belize, India.
- Groove on tribal beats for hip hop and DJ mixes, samba bands, kirtan, dance classes, or drum circles.
- Explore archetypal music patterns, polyrhythm, improvisation, and drum culture.

DjembeRhythms.com

Roots Jam 2

West African and Afro-Latin Drum Rhythms

by

Nowick Gray

Cougar WebWorks
© 2002 by Nowick Gray

email: now@djemberhythms.com
web: http://www.djemberhythms.com

Recording: Kyra Soko (j_and_k@direct.ca, 250-366-0054). Parts played by Nowick Gray and Carol Ross.

Acknowledgements

Thanks to all those who have shared their live drum knowledge with me; especially Chris Berry, Bo Conlan, Michel Coté, Joseph (Pepe) Danza, Alpha Yaya Diallo, Thione Diop, Duncan Johnston, Mamady Keita, Greg Kozak, Michael Moon Bear, Dido Morris, Robert (Ah) Northern, Babatunde Olatunji, Zave Reinhart, Nii Tettey Tetteh, and David Thiaw.

Thanks also to those whose written and recorded material has provided inspiration and sources of rhythms for this collection, in particular Larry Morris, Michael Wall, Doug Falconer, and a number of other high-quality online sources of rhythm notation (see **Rhythm References**).

Finally, thanks go to the Columbia Kootenay Cultural Alliance (North Kootenay Lake Arts and Heritage Council) and Columbia Basin Trust for supportive funding for this project.

National Library of Canada Cataloguing in Publication

Gray, William N., 1950-
    Roots jam 2 : West African and Afro-Latin drum rhythms / by Nowick Gray.

Also available in an electronic version
Includes bibliographical references and index.
ISBN 0-9682033-3-7

        1. Percussion instruments--Studies and exercises. 2. Drum--Studies and
exercises. 3. Musical meter and rhythm--Africa, West--Studies and exercises.
4. Percussion music--Teaching pieces. 5. Percussion ensembles--Teaching pieces.
I. Title.

MT655.3.G784 2002a   786.8'1224'076   C2002-902772-1

Roots Jam 2 - Table of Contents

1. Rhythm Culture: Where We Begin

Struck sound gives pleasure, whereas unstruck sound leads to liberation.
--the Narada Purana

Rhythm is everywhere. All of Nature, whether the natural rhythms familiar to us on our whirling Earth, or the deepest and most distant cosmic impulses, breathes with a regularity as identifiable as our own heartbeat. To drum is to connect more fully with this universal pulse, leaving the rest of our temporary divisions behind.

At the same time, to give ourselves to the power of the drum is not merely to dissolve into the cosmic soup. The power of rhythm is both unifying and freeing. There is room for infinite creativity, made possible by the strength of the deep foundation. The common pulse gives us permission to partake of a dynamic dance that celebrates the richness of diversity within wholeness.

The African homeland of the human race has been from time immemorial a living rhythm workshop. It is here that we can find the oldest and richest musical tradition on the planet. In particular, the countries of West Africa, from Senegal and Mali down through Nigeria and the Congo, provide us to this day with a sophisticated and powerful body of rhythms that can fuel the dancing spirit like no other.

The present collection also pays special homage to the New World lineage, the rhythmic legacy brought by slaves and kept alive through centuries of unimaginable suffering. The Afro-Latin tradition blends the musical and cultural roots of Africa with non-African elements in a vibrant and life-affirming style that has universal appeal. In addition, the body of rhythms known as "Middle Eastern" is represented with a small selection; here African roots are blended with wider Mediterranean and Arabian influences.

This now-widespread body of African-based rhythms comes to us from a variety of historical and cultural contexts that still hold specific and sacred meanings for the people living within those settings. Outsiders (like myself) can only give respect for the gift of this music which has gone out from the regions of its birth and development. And while our intentions cannot be identical to those of the originators of this music, we can yet commit ourselves to the sacred power of its instruments and rhythms which we have received, and to give our own best energy to its continuing evolution.

One of music's greatest gifts is its age-old ability to flow across cultural boundaries, fostering both unity and healthy diversity, appreciation and understanding. Let us honor the traditions reflected here as contemporary vehicles for human freedom, as living channels of greater connection with nature and spirit.

The present collection begins with an introduction to Rhythm Notation, time signatures, and hand drum technique, followed by a more in-depth exploration of the foundations of polyrhythmic percussion. The main body of the book consists of Collected Rhythms for ensemble, from the African, Afro-Latin, and Middle Eastern traditions. Chapter 4 is a virtual Rhythm Workshop, which distills from the actual rhythms an essential toolkit for drummers, with a wide variety of generic and standard patterns and exercises. Chapter 5 takes us beyond the rhythms to the qualitative side of Rhythm Culture: Where We Go with this music. Finally, a selected list of Resources and references (with online links) serves as a guide for further enjoyment and study.

2. Rhythm Notation

"How do you climb this mountain?"
"Ask the deer."
"How do you find one?"
"Just follow their tracks."

Why Notation?

Written notation is not part of the ancient African musical tradition. To learn a traditional African rhythm in the traditional way, means to grow up in the culture where the music is a living part of you, or to study for years with a master drummer (or both).

Written notation--like writing itself--is a tool that newcomers to the tradition can use to access and learn the music more quickly. Audio recording is another useful tool. Both are simply aids to memory in recalling a rhythm you may have heard or learned only once. Notation can also aid learning and communication between drummers, whether or not you're in the same room.

"The map is not the territory"...but having a map to follow is better than being lost--or not going on the journey at all.

The following three sections might be considered most appropriate for the basic, intermediate, and advanced drummer, respectively. Please refer to the **"Basic Guide"** below to become familiar with the notation used throughout this book. "Further Considerations" includes a more in-depth look at time signatures, the order of using right and left hands, and African vs. Afro-Latin drumming styles. Finally, for an optional excursion into the theory and practice of playing polyrhythms, you are invited to proceed through the third section on "Polyrhythmic Percussion." (Or, simply delve into the collected rhythms that come later, whenever you're ready!)

The Rhythm Notation: A Basic Guide

Instrument terms:

Djembe (or jembe) -- Standard West African bell-shaped hand drum

Junjun (or dunun, dundun) -- Large double-headed drum played with sticks, often with attached bell. Or, the largest (dundunba) of the family of double-headed drums.

Songba (or sangba, sangban) -- Medium-sized double-headed drum

Kenkeni -- Smallest double-headed drum

Like the junjun, the songba and kenkeni can have attached bells.

Basic notation for djembe:

The primary notation in this book, as in the first edition of *Roots Jam* (1996), is based on the traditional Yoruba "oral notation" terminology as taught by Babatunde Olatunji. It mimics the standard range of sounds produced by the West African djembe.

G: Gun ("Goon") = bass beat with lead/strong hand
D: Dun ("Doon") = bass beat with other hand <1-GD.mp3>

g: go = rim beat with lead/strong hand: tip half of fingers
d: do ("doe") = rim beat with other hand <2-gd.mp3>

P: Pa = slap beat with lead/strong hand: sharp glancing stroke with fingers
T: Ta = slap beat with other hand <3-PT.mp3>

- : = one-beat rest

Audio file links in the text point to .mp3 audio files to demonstrate the rhythms. You can purchase the full set of 29 audio files for only $6.99 from my website at:
http://djemberhythms.com/books/order-roots-jam-drum-rhythm-books/ See full index on p. 85 of this book.

Additional notes, for other drums and percussion:

x = bell or percussion note; on cowbell, note struck at center of bell body

x = underlined (or bold, or capitalized) note means stressed or accented

X = junjun and bell notes struck simultaneously

O = normal open note on junjun (usually played along with bell)

o = higher/unaccented note on junjun/bell; on cowbell, note struck at edge of mouth

k = stick on wood or metal rim of drum

M = muted note on junjun, with stick pressed to drum head (includes bell note)

H = high note on two-tone bell (or substitute **x**, center note, with cowbell)

L = low note on two-tone bell (or substitute **o**, mouth note, with cowbell)

d = down-stroke, on guiro or shaker

u = up-stroke, on guiro or shaker

(G) = parentheses indicate optional or "ghost" note(s), or muted note

[x x x] = triplet: in 4/4 time, three beats played in place of normal two

[x - x] = in 4/4 time, two notes "expanded" slightly and played with "swing feel": as if they were the two ends of a triplet
x- = note played just "ahead of the beat"

F or **Gd, Gt, Pt, gf** = flams. (Gt=GT, Pt=PT, gf=gd) Play two notes almost as one single beat, in the order written.
RH / LH = play with right hand / left hand

> = continue on to play next bar or phrase

:| = return to start of bar or phrase

X3 = repeat bar or phrase a given number of times

Map of Notes on Drum Head:

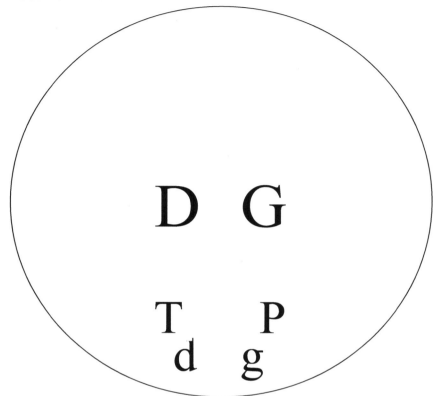

Additional tips on using the notation:

Use or visualize the above map when reading the rhythms in this book. Since different people learn best in different ways, here are some other ideas for learning the notation.

1. **Sing the rhythms.** As you read G - D - g d g d, say silently or aloud, *Goon, Doon, godo godo* <4-sing.mp3>

2. **Repeat slowly** (with visual and voiced cues) until your hands remember a rhythm.

3. **Don't worry too much about Left vs. Right at first.** When learning a rhythm, if the left and right handing seems too complicated, focus on the basic three sounds, with whichever hands you like: bass **(G/D)**, slap **(P/T),** and rim-tone **(g/d).** As your speed increases it will become more important to find a fluid left-right balance for each rhythm.

Notation Format

The layout of written notation is modified here from the format used in the first edition of Roots Jam. A typical 4/4 rhythm in the earlier book would look like this:

```
 _____   _____   _____   _____
 | | | | |   | | | | |   | | | | |   | | | | |
 D - d g - g d g D - D - d g d g    <5-Zungo.mp3>
```

This method has several advantages for the djembe player, compared to conventional music notation or other drum notation systems:

- Because drum and percussion notes aren't sustained but struck once, it makes sense to show the timing for these beats as single and equal. Rests are measured by the same, single-beat units. With this single-letter shorthand, each note or rest occupies an equal visual place in the pattern.

- The six-note system (G D g d P T) follows traditional terminology (Dun Gun go do Pa Ta), which covers aurally both the range of standard djembe sounds (bass, rim, slap) and the order of handing (right/left). All of these, along with the rests and overall timing, can be found within a single line of notation.

- It's clear and direct to see where the beats and rests from different parts line up relative to each other, when each part is a single line and these are aligned in a polyrhythmic ensemble arrangement. In four or five lines you can see all the necessary information at a glance.

- A pattern can be composed, transcribed and transmitted easily with hand-lettering or standard typed keyboard characters.

The same 4/4 rhythm notated above would appear in the present book as follows:

4/4

[4 pulses]	1	.	*	.	2	.	*	.	3	.	*	.	4	.	*	.
[16 beats]	G	-	g	d	-	d	g	d	G	-	G	-	g	d	g	d

This form of "box notation" has increasingly become a standard published form for hand drummers, because of the visual ease of lining up multiple parts with each other and with the main 4-pulse structure of most rhythms. (For handwritten notes or email, the earlier format--or simply writing the letters and dashes in a line without the grid structure--remains the most efficient).

The other basic change from *Roots Jam* is a default lead with the "strong-hand" (formerly "right-hand") notes, G / g / P. While I still recommend the fluid use of both hands as "lead," the notation reads more clearly with the consistency of just one: in this case, the hand playing G, g, and P (more on handing later).

The use of the terms "**beat**" and "**pulse**" is somewhat interchangeable, depending on which authority you choose to take sides with. Eric Charry, for instance, in his comprehensive study, Mande Music, calls the quarter-notes "beats" and the sixteenth notes "pulses." But despite the scholarly authority of Charry and others, I find the popular terminology favored by hand drum teachers such as Rebeca Mauleón, Arthur Hull, and Michael Wall more intuitively appropriate.

The pulse, according to Hull, "is where you tap your foot." The pulses represent the primary beats and connote the inner pulse or feel of the music, while the individual beats are synonymous with the individual notes of the pattern. (Be aware, then, that the conventional term "beats per minute," or "bpm," in this book refers to "pulses per minute.")

Time Signatures

The total 16-beat, 4-pulse **phrase** notated above comprises one "**bar**," in the standard Western time signature **4/4**. The 4/4 bar contains four pulses or quarter notes, each containing four beats, or sixteenth notes. **2/4** time simply marks a phrase half as long: two pulses or quarter notes:

2/4

	1	.	*	.	2	.	*	.
	G	-	D	-	g	d	g	d

The beats beginning each of the pulses are the primary **downbeats**. Note the use of asterisks (*) for the beats halfway between the primary pulses. In some cases (e.g., a reggae rhythm) these in-between beats would be called **upbeats**. But a dance in two or four will generally count all the even-numbered beats as downbeats. There are eight to a bar in 4/4 time, and these will generally be marked in a dance by an "eight-count":

pulse	1	.	*	.	2	.	*	.	3	.	*	.	4	.	*	.
downbeat	1	+	2	+	3	+	4	+	5	+	6	+	7	+	8	+

Bars divided into beats in groups of three pose an additional challenge. Consider the following pattern, which carries the auspicious title, "Mother Rhythm." The pulse is signaled by the bass notes on 1 and 2, which we'll strengthen with a junjun. Generally in Western notation such a phrase would be marked "**6/8**," meaning six eighth notes.

6/8 <6-68poly.mp3>

	1	.	.	2	.	.
djembe	G	d	g	D	g	d
junjun	O	-	-	O	-	-
bell	x	-	x	-	x	-

A phrase comprising twelve beats carries the time signature "**12/8**":

12/8

	1	.	.	2	.	.	3	.	.	4	.	.
short bell	x	-	x	-	x	x	-	x	-	x	-	x

Further Considerations

More about Time Signatures

Confusion arises if we compare the division of notes in a **ternary** bar (6/8 or 12/8) with the layout of a **quaternary** bar (2/4 or 4/4). In the latter, we've identified each beat as a sixteenth note; while in the ternary rhythms the single note carries a name with twice the weight: an eighth note.

It could be argued that in a rhythm of three beats to the pulse, calling the notes eighths or sixteenths is equally absurd. I would agree; it's pretty arbitrary. I use the conventional time signatures here as a convenient bridge between this notation and standard music notation.

As for deciding which timing to choose, I look mainly to the length of the phrase. If a basic repeating pattern fills two bars of 2/4 time (sixteen beats total), I prefer to call it one bar in 4/4. Likewise, a definable phrase filling two bars of 6/8 time (twelve beats total) will be written here as 12/8.

Handing

The question of which hand or note to lead with is also problematical. The earlier *Roots Jam* book began out of personal need for learning, remembering, and comparing rhythms. And while I'm right-handed, I usually felt most comfortable playing drum rhythms with a left-hand lead. Thus, most of the rhythms in *Roots Jam* begin with D / d / T. The issue is complicated, though, because D - G could just as arbitrarily be learned as right - left, or stronger - weaker. And the very nature of African rhythms moves us away from a strict even-numbered downbeat, toward a greater reliance on offbeats, upbeats, "swing," and 12/8 timing...in which the "other" hand's beats are equally "dominant." Some rhythms are taught with a certain handing pattern that seems important to their particular "feel." And still another consideration is the physical need for balance, to alternate or change the lead hand from time to time just to avoid overuse, fatigue, bruising, and tendonitis.

Out of all this confusion of priorities, the present volume opts for a standardized form, where the default lead is G, g, or P, and these notes are played by the stronger hand. The order of handing in a given pattern then proceeds according to various considerations:

- the way the rhythm was taught to me or how I found it written
- following a strict alternation of hands, beat by beat
- finding overall balance between the hands
- achieving a certain desirable feel

The advantage of strict alternation is that it's easier to keep time during rests, as the hands can keep moving with a regular alternating motion even when not playing. Some of these silent notes can even be voiced as "**ghost**" notes, though a cleaner sound results without them. This method can be helpful, however, when first learning the timing of a rhythm.

The disadvantage of strict alternation is that a rhythm with a constant emphasis on the downbeats--as in many doumbek (Middle Eastern drum) rhythms and other straight-ahead 4/4 patterns--will quickly cause fatigue in the lead hand. If you experience fatigue when playing such a rhythm, try varying the handing for a better right-left balance. Here are two examples: <7-Ethiopian.mp3>

	1	.	*	.	2	.	*	.	3	.	*	.	4	.	*	.
Ethiopian walking rhythm (before)	G	-	g	d	G	-	g	d	G	-	G	-	g	d	g	d
Ethiopian walking rhythm (after)	G	-	d	g	D	-	g	d	G	-	D	-	g	d	g	d
Akiwowo (before)	G	-	P	T	G	-	g	d	G	-	P	T	G	-	g	d
Akiwowo (after)	G	-	T	P	D	-	g	d	G	-	T	P	D	-	g	d

The bottom line is that the order of handing in a given rhythm is presented here as a suggestion. I encourage you to adapt the written notation to your own needs. This may be easier if you learn a rhythm first as written, and then once you start to own the basic feel of it, vary it according to your taste.

Here's a basic exercise you can use to balance the emphasis of your two hands. It's also a good exercise to use for focusing on your technique in distinguishing between the bass, rim, and slap sounds on the djembe. Last but not least, it'll give you a feel for playing polyrhythms, if you're not familiar with them already (more on this subject in a minute). Once you're comfortable playing version 1, try version 2. Note that the box with [>] in it means to continue playing the next line.

	1	.	*	.	2	.	*	.	3	.	*	.	4	.	*	.	
version 1	G	-	D	-	P	-	T	-	G	D	-	g	-	d	g	-	>
<8-ver1.mp3>	D	-	G	-	T	-	P	-	D	G	-	d	-	g	d	-	
version 2	G	-	D	-	P	T	d	g	G	D	-	P	-	T	g	-	>
<9-ver2.mp3>	D	-	G	-	T	P	g	d	D	G	-	T	-	P	d	-	

Afro-Latin Hand Drum Techniques

All three of the standard djembe beats notated here are open beats. Play them with a light touch, as lifting sound from the drum instead of pounding your hands onto the drum. The result will be easier on your ears and on your hands (not to mention the drum).

This style of open notes is unlike the style conga players use, with heel-and-finger placements resting on the drum head, and closed slaps. I have, however, transcribed some conga rhythms for djembe, especially when the source notation indicates a more open style. Normally I translate heel and other muffled notes as bass notes, in parentheses (G, D).

When the drums indicated are **tumba**, **conga**, and **quinto** (ranging from low to high tone range), you can approximate the desired sound by substituting djembes of different sizes. The same goes for playing **surdo** rhythms on the junjun. Likewise, many African rhythms here call for congas but may be played with the given beats on djembe (or ashiko or other drums).

As for authenticity, I consider that "Latin" rhythms are generally "Afro-Latin"--in other words, originating in African roots. But it's really just a matter of naming rhythms and being honest about our intentions. We can play a given rhythm--say, Guaguanco--with any instrumentation or variation we choose. Meanwhile we need to be aware that the result will likely depart (both musically and culturally) from what other people think of or expect from a Guaguanco.

Polyrhythmic Percussion: What's Going On?

The Clave: Beyond the Binary Pulse

The clave (*clah'-vay*: a pair of short, hardwood sticks struck together) is perhaps the most ancient rhythm instrument. Perhaps because of its antiquity, and also for its ability to cut sonically over and through the deeper pounding of accompanying drumbeats, it has acquired the status of the core of the polyrhythmic framework.

In contemporary Latin music, whether Afro-Cuban or Brazilian, the clave pattern is so integral to the whole body of rhythmic development that it's often not even played. The other patterns are built around the pulse of the clave so well that the pulse is felt even when it's not literally heard. Therein lies the power of its name: clave in Spanish means key, code, or keystone. (Anyone who has ever been to rockwall-covered Spain knows the importance of the keystone.) Or sometimes the word is written as clavé, meaning "fixed" or "nailed"--just as appropriate to the role of its rhythm.

For the origin of the Afro-Latin clave rhythms we can go back to the African sacred traditions, where the 6/8 clave pattern (which came to be played on an iron bell) might be well considered "the mother of all polyrhythms." To this day it continues to power the trance-producing Voudoun rhythms of Haiti, as well as 6/8 dance rhythms in Afro/Latin night clubs around the globe.

In contemporary rhythm circles we give this ancient sacred rhythm the pedestrian nickname, "the short bell"--though like most of its derivatives, it can be played with sticks or on a bell, depending on the rhythm and the instruments at hand. The pattern fills two bars of 6/8 time, or one bar in 12/8: <10-shortbell.mp3>

	1	.	.	**2**	.	.	**3**	.	.	**4**	.	.
short bell	x	-	x	-	x	x	-	x	-	x	-	x

When the pattern is repeated, the last beat of the phrase serves as a "**pickup**" note to carry the momentum directly to the starting beat again. This way of cycling energy forward, reinforcing itself with fresh momentum, is probably the closest humans will ever get to inventing (or discovering) a perpetual motion machine.

In establishing a rhythm foundation, of course, we can go back even further to a simple clave pattern marking the pulse. Striking every beat, x x x x , or every other beat on a **binary** pulse, x - x - x - x - , is the simplest rhythm of all. It goes on an on, indefinitely, the heartbeat of the cosmos. And indeed, such a pulse forms the foundation of rhythms everywhere, from aboriginal Australia to North and South America, through marches and popular Western tunes. This straight-ahead, binary pulse also continues to serve as the basic measure of many African polyrhythms.

But while simplicity is helpful, simply marking the pulse with downbeats can be monotonous. One improvement can be made by accenting every other note: from 1/1 is born 2/4. Four downbeats, two pulses:

	1	.	*	.	2	.	*	.
	x	-	(x)	-	x	-	(x)	-

Another solution, if playing with other instruments tuned into the basic downbeat pulse, is to use the clave to accent the in-between beats as upbeats (and perhaps not even striking the downbeats):

	1	.	*	.	2	.	*	.
	(x)	-	x	-	(x)	-	x	-

In simplest terms, this emphasis on the "upbeat" defines the feel of what we know today as reggae.

Another solution to the potential monotony of the binary pattern is to stretch the beats apart slightly. If we simply stretch the intervals between the beats by adding a rest, we get 6/8 time: x - - x - - . But without anything else going on, the effect is the same as the binary x - x - , only perhaps slower. So rather than just stretching, let's *nudge* the beats slightly.

Beginning with x x x x, we get x - x x - x. This single subtle shift in timing gives us the dynamic effect of anticipation before every downbeat: the pickup note is born. It gives roundness and depth to the binary pulse, giving it what's called a **swing** feel. The effect can be quite subtle; but once you're attuned to it, you'll notice it driving the beat and motivating your feet in all kinds of places--the Celtic reel for instance:

	1	.	*	.	2	.	*	.
straight reel	x	x	x	x	x	x	x	x
swung reel	x	-	x	x	-	x	x	-	x

<11-straight.mp3> <12-swung.mp3> The swung version gives us the fundamental character of 6/8 timing. In this case, however, the simple ternary pulse (**x** - -) takes on extra energy and texture, via the pickup note, to fuel the dance.

	1	.	.	2	.	.
swing feel	x	-	x	x	-	x
Dununba 1	P	-	g	T	-	d

The Dununba part for djembe notated here <13-Dununba.mp3> is virtually a universal accompaniment part for African polyrhythms in 6/8 or 12/8. With this kind of rhythm the downbeat is heavily accented; but the feel of the piece is also rounded through the anticipation of the rest and the pickup note which follows it. The dancer's body follows this rounded motion through to its dependable and inevitable conclusion with each successive downbeat.

This whole exercise in notation is merely academic to the indigenous percussionist, who may interpret a rhythm by traditional feel, or by improvisational texture, to ride on a sweet bubble poised somewhere indefinably between 2 and 3 (or, we might say, between 4 and 6, 8 and 12, or 12 and 16).

For instance, if we nudge a little further, we can go from six to eight beats, back to an even-numbered pattern, while still maintaining the more rounded, swinging feel: x - x x - x (in 6/8) becomes x - - x x - - x (in 2/4).   <14-stretch.mp3>

Two Across Three, Three Across Four

Returning to the short bell, notice its pattern of single and double beats. The pickup note at the end is in the unique position of being the first of a double beat whose partner, just around the corner at the "one" pulse, establishes the sense of the downbeat, a single struck beat followed by a rest. A basic variation, also of great antiquity, simply shifts the pattern to start at a different point in the looping cycle, to the fourth struck beat of the short bell's bar. This is called the "long bell." Note here the same pickup note at the end. The main difference in feel when playing the long bell, compared to the short bell, is the longer phrase--"one, two, three..." instead of "one, two...) before the first doubled beat. <15-longbell.mp3> <16-jazzbell.mp3>

	1	.	.	2	.	.	3	.	.	4	.	.
short bell	x	-	x	-	x	x	-	x	-	x	-	x
long bell	x	-	x	-	x	-	x	x	-	x	-	x
jazz bell	x	x	-	x	-	x	x	-	x	-	x	-

The "jazz bell" is simply the long bell pattern reversed--or started halfway through the cycle. Another, more common variation is to drop a couple of the beats from the basic phrase. The result is the two-bar "6/8 Son clave," a rhythm from Ghana which has become a core pattern in Latin music (shown here in one bar of 12/8):

	1	.	.	2	.	.	3	.	.	4	.	.
short bell	x	-	x	-	x	x	-	x	-	x	-	x
long bell	x	-	x	-	x	-	x	x	-	x	-	x
6/8 Son clave	x	-	x	-	x	-	-	x	-	x	-	-

Stretching this rhythm out, to fill a phrase of sixteen instead of twelve beats, produces the most standard Latin clave pattern of all, the "Son Clave" in four. This evolution can be seen to represent the transition from the sacred African dances to more conventional Western arrangements. (Traditional Latin timing would give the Son clave two bars in 2/4; here it appears in one bar of 4/4): <17-44Son.mp3>

	1	.	*	.	2	.	*	.	3	.	*	.	4	.	*	.
Son clave	x	-	-	x	-	-	x	-	-	-	x	-	x	-	-	-
6/8 Son clave	x	-		x	-		x	-	-		x	-	x	-	-	

To see how closely the 6/8 version <18-68Son.mp3> relates to the 4/4 version, it appears in the second line with the extra notes grayed out. Note that the places where the played notes line up with the pulses (pulse one and four, in bold) are the same, whether in 4/4 or 12/8 time. The last of these, on the four, is of special importance in marking the end of the phrase and is given the name "ponché" (punch). It serves as the resolution point for the tension of the phrase--a tension which has been heightened (in the case of either timing) by the sequence of beats moving "across the grain" of the foundation pulse. In both timings, the underlying pulse is re-established and realigned at this point, on the four. In both cases this emphasis is prepared by the preceding beat with its short rest, following the anticipatory longer rest.

The ponché also serves to set up the beginning of the phrase again, the downbeat on the "one." If both versions of the Son clave were distilled to align with the basic four-pulse underlying both 4/4 and 12/8, we would notice a familiar pattern:

	1	2	3	4	1	2	3	4
	x	-	-	x	x	-	-	x

The other note of special interest in the 4/4 Son clave is the second note in the phrase (marked by the ▼ symbol in the pulse).

	1	.	*	▼	2	.	*	.	3	.	*	.	4	.	*	.
Son clave	x	-	-	x	-	-	x	-	-	-	x	-	x	-	-	-

This is the only note not played on a downbeat. Given the name "bombo" (bass drum) in Spanish-speaking countries, it offers the key to the dynamic tension of the phrase-- and I would go so far as to say, in the general body of African, Latin, and "World Beat" music. It also offers us the key to working with polyrhythm.

Let's take another look at the three rudimentary patterns "in three" to see what they have in common. Oddly enough, it's a binary pulse.

	1	.	.	2	.	.	3	.	.	4	.	.
short bell	x	-	x	-	x	x	-	x	-	x	-	x
long bell	x	-	x	-	x	-	x	x	-	x	-	x
6/8 Son clave	x	-	x	-	x	-	-	x	-	x	-	-

All three of these basic ternary rhythms present a succession of beats predominantly in the binary forms [x -] and [x x]. Especially at the beginning, this binary structure gives us an impression of downbeats working across the grain of the fundamental ternary pulse, which might be expressed by an accompanying junjun or shaker.

The effect of the short bell is to switch from (binary) downbeats to upbeats, halfway through the bar. The effect of the long bell is similar, but the beats at "3" and "4" also signify a switch from a binary to a ternary feel. The 6/8 Son clave is not so symmetrical; it produces a mixed effect in the order, 2-2-3-2-3.

In the above examples we have a two-pulse running alongside a three-pulse. A polyrhythmic effect can also be achieved by playing a four over a three, as in Tiriba. The ternary pulse is established by the three junjun and bell parts. The three djembe parts all suggest a counter-rhythm in four, with their emphasis on the fifth beat (grayed, below).

	1	.	.	**2**	.	.	**3**	.	.	**4**	.	.
djembe 1	G	T	g	-	T	-	G	T	-	G	T	-
djembe 2	G	-	-	d	P	-	G	-	-	d	P	-
djembe 3	G	-	P	D	g	d	G	T	-	D	g	d
junjun bells	x	x	-	x	x	-	x	x	-	x	x	-
junjun	O	-	-	-	O	-	O	-	-	-	-	-
songba	M	-	-	O	-	-	M	-	-	O	-	-
kenkeni	O	O	-	M	-	-	O	O	-	M	-	-

The low junjun part ties everything together by playing only that fifth beat and the primary pulses ("1" and "3").

Summary

In the ternary pattern, the dynamic tension of polyrhythm is achieved with the binary feel of the bell or clave (and perhaps reinforced as well with other quaternary parts), contrasting with the foundation pulse. In the quaternary pattern, the same kind of musical interest can be achieved by even one key note struck in the right place--the bombo--giving us the more rounded feel of three against the underlying march of the two or four. Another, more subtle and subjective means of rounding out the feel is by the nudging apart of binary notes with additional rests, creating pickup notes which anticipate and accentuate the downbeats that follow, and resulting in a rhythm that "swings."

So far this discussion of polyrhythm has been strictly technical, and mainly limited to the polyrhythmic elements within a single key part, played by the clave or bell. But it should be reiterated that the foundation of any polyrhythmic ensemble will be established and maintained all the while by the primary pulse--whether in a junjun part, a shaker or guiro, or simply the common structure of the multi-part rhythm.

In addition, those of us who are relative newcomers to African music should be aware of the deeper cultural and philosophical context of polyrhythmic percussion. One of African music's foremost ambassadors in the West, C. K. Ladzekpo of the University of California (http://www.cnmat.berkeley.edu/~ladzekpo/), puts it this way:

> In the cultural understanding, the *technique of polyrhythm* simply asserts the highly unpredictable occurrences of obstacles in human life. They occur without a warning. It reinforces the need for the development of a strong and productive purpose built on a foundation of adequate preparation for life....It is by this strength that ordinary people become heroes, by maintaining themselves in a tranquil state of mind and preserving the free use of their reason under most surprising and terrible circumstances.

Timing Exercises

Son and Reverse Son

The standard 4/4 or 2/4 Son clave is also referred to as the 3-2 Son clave. "3-2" can be confusing because it sounds like a time signature, when really it's just a snapshot of the number of beats in the two bars of 2/4 time--three in the first, two in the second.

2/4 time	1	.	*	.	2	.	*	.	1	.	*	.	2	.	*	.
3-2 Son	x	-	-	x	-	-	x	-	-	-	x	-	x	-	-	-
2-3 (reverse) Son	-	-	x	-	x	-	-	-	x	-	-	x	-	-	x	-

Play and compare the feel of these two mirror-image rhythms.

The 2-3 or reverse Son has two beats in the first bar, three in the second. It's the same 16-beat pattern; it just starts in a different place. Many Latin rhythms use the 2-3 instead of the 3-2 clave; some use either one. Rebeca Mauleón stresses the importance, however, of sticking to one or the other throughout the piece, and not switching back and forth. That way the ensemble can rely on a consistent sense of where the "one" is.

Clave Claps

1. Take any clave pattern such as those notated above.

2. Keep the downbeat pulse with your foot tapping (toe or heel is fine; we won't be picky with that!).

3. Play the clave pattern with hand claps.

4. Experiment to get the feel of both 4/4 and 12/8 clave patterns.

2 vs. 3

Here's a simple yet profound exercise to demonstrate the difference between a two-feel and a three-feel.

1. Play the following rhythm: G - g d g d . Play it over and over for a while until you get into a groove with it.

2. Choose which notation best describes the feel of your playing. Is it like this, with three beats per pulse... <19-68pulse.mp3>

6/8	1	.	.	2	.	.
	G	-	g	d	g	d

or like this, with two beats per pulse? <20-34pulse.mp3>

3/4	1	.	2	.	3	.
	G	-	g	d	g	d

3. Let the bold notes be more accented to match the pulse...then less.

4. Finally, let your hands and ears find that tenuous place where the notes are coming with equal weight, wavering to neither side (the two or the three), but somewhere in between...in the sweet center of the moving moment.

Time the Gaps

Compare the feel of the following two rhythms, one in 4/4 and the other in 12/8. Try feeling each unplayed beat. Here are two ways to count rests while playing:

1. Keep alternate hands moving by playing "ghost notes" on the rim of the drum, off the head.

2. Voice the rests silently: "**Pa** uh uh do **pa** uh uh do **pa**..." or "**Pa** uh go **ta** uh do **pa**..."

	1	.	*	.	**2**	.	*	.	**3**	.	*	.	**4**	.	*	.
4/4	P	-	-	d	P	-	-	d	P	-	-	d	P	-	-	d

	1	.	.	**2**	.	.	**3**	.	.	**4**	.	.
12/8	P	-	g	T	-	d	P	-	g	T	-	d

Extending the previous pattern into an ensemble arrangement, we take on the challenge of layering the effects of different timings. Try the following exercise for three or four players (from Luis Nunez):

	1	.	.	**2**	.	.	**3**	.	.	**4**	.	.
djembe 1	P	-	g	T	-	d	P	-	g	T	-	d
djembe 2	(G)	-	d	-	d	-	(G)	-	d	(G)	-	d
junjun bell	x	x	-	x	x	-	x	x	-	x	x	-
junjun	M	-	O	-	M	-	O	-	M	-	O	-
--variation	O	-	-	-	O	-	-	-	O	-	-	-

Junjun and Bell Patterns

Playing polyrhythms yourself, as with a bell and junjun combination, or drum kit, can be intimidating at first. Here's an example that's tricky at first, but with methodical learning and practice, becomes second nature: <21-Zepaule.mp3>

Zepaule	**1**	.	.	**2**	.	.	**3**	.	.	**4**	.	.
junjun bell	x	-	x	-	x	-	x	x	-	x	-	x
junjun	-	O	O	-	O	O	-	O	O	-	O	O

Kim Plainfield, in teaching rhythms for the drum kit, advises learning to play one part at normal speed first, then adding an additional part, just one note at a time. In the example above, you would first learn the bell part, then play it with only the first junjun beat (O) added in. Next add the second beat. With the initial rest included, you'd now be playing only the first [- O O] of the junjun part. Add more notes in the same manner, keeping to normal tempo all the while. (Alternatively, start with the whole junjun part at normal speed, and add the bell part to it, one note at a time).

I prefer to learn different parts in combination right from the beginning. The key is to take it as slowly as necessary, one step at a time. By referencing each hand with what the other is doing, beat by beat, you'll have constant cues as to what to do next. Gradually your hands, ears, and brain learn the sequence of interlocking patterns until the combined result flows automatically. As you gain facility with higher tempos, the rhythm will approach its proper feel. And the more rhythms you learn in this way, the faster the learning curve becomes for new ones. This method is also effective for learning polyrhythms with two or more drummers.

> Music is my religion, my politics. While making music together people surpass invisible frontiers--as music is the only language which reaches from the heart to heart without words or aggression...
>
> --Yacoub "Bruno" Camara

3. Rhythm Collection

Tradition and Improvisation

I play the basic form of a rhythmic figure until it varies itself.
--Correa Djalma, in Flatischler

The question of departing from strict rhythmical forms (as with other aspects of traditional cultures) is a sensitive one. Many drummers, drum teachers, and others who identify with a certain cultural form take issue with "cultural appropriation" when rhythms are taken out of context and changed.

I try to hold to the middle path that includes, on the one side, respectful acknowledgement, and on the other side, freedom to adapt to the situation at hand-- ultimately to the spirit of the moving moment.

This marriage of traditional pattern and creative freedom is the essence of my philosophy in *Roots Jam* (1 and 2), as reflected in the title. In both collections I have tried to be thorough and accurate in my research and transcription of traditional rhythms. I also recognize the inevitable mutation worked by the various translations along the way, as a pattern migrates from the cultural time and place it calls home. To memory's lapses are added creative patches; the ear plays tricks and the recorder's pencil errs. When we end up, in North America in 2002, with a dozen "traditional" arrangements of "Kuku," how can we say which one is "authentic"?

In compiling and arranging traditional rhythms here, I've tried to identify common elements in order to arrive at the essence of a given rhythm. In many cases that job starts with associating rhythms that come with slightly different names--whether from migration between African cultures, evolution into Afro-Latin forms, or transcription into English (often via French or Spanish spelling). Then there is the matter of identifying parts. I've tried to be comprehensive here rather than simple--presenting a maximum of options and variations to choose from. Where sources disagree--as they almost always do--I've attempted to distinguish parts (e.g., djembe 1, djembe 2, djembe 3) by a number of factors including agreement of sources, reputation of sources, and intrinsic differences in feel between parts.

The result is a large collection of variations that gives you the flexibility--and responsibility--to choose and arrange parts according to your own circumstances. Choose according to level of difficulty, number of players, or fullness and complexity of the desired sound. I encourage also creative substitutions of available instruments-- congas and djembes, different kinds of bass drums, shakers and bells.

It's useful also to recognize that just as a pattern will evolve over time and geography, even in the traditional setting it will be subject to spontaneous interpretation, by dancers and drummers who are also responding to each other. In the heat of the moment, the solo drummer relies on a body of "licks" he or she has previously mastered, which may even be rooted in a traditional verbal language. Yet there is still room to be carried away, into where the music wants to go, into new places.

Arrangement List

This list is rather arbitrary and is assembled for convenience. If you have less players than a full ensemble, just select key parts for the number of players you have. Conversely, if you have more players than parts, some parts can be doubled up. Or, it usually works to add a simple shaker or clave on the pulse, even if they are not notated in the rhythms. Both of these latter strategies are effective for incorporating players whose skills are less advanced than others.

4/4

for two players

Mombassa

for three players

Ekonga
Gota
Mané
Village Dance

Comparsa
Eleggua
Ijexa

for four players

Akiwowo
Boushay
Bwanga
Frekoba
Jondon
Kpatsa
Nokobe
Soli
Timini
Wollosidon
Yembela

Banda
Merengue
Mozambique
Oggun

for five players

Bolon
Dalah
Dennadon
Fanga
Fankani
Kakilambe
Kebendo
Kurubi
Lafé
Makuru
Moribayassa
Sunu
Uffunu

Comparsa
Guaguanco
Ra Ra
Samba (Batucada)

for six or more players

Aconcon
Balakulania
Diansa
Gahu
Gumbe
Highlife
Kassa
Kpanlogo
Kuku
Lamba
Masacote
Shiko
Tordo

Bossa Nova
Baião
Bomba
Calypso
Comparsa
Conga
Guaguanco
Ibo
Mambo
Pilon
Rumba
Rumba Yesa
Samba
Tumbao

12/8

for two players

Mami Wata
Palo

for three players

Adowa
N'kisi
Sofa

for four players

Batakato
Etumba Nambuaka
Sedeba

Chango
Daome
Ibo

for five players

Abondan
Basikolo
Baye
Bintin
Djabara
Jewe
Linjen
Maraka
Nantaloma

Camberto
Eleggua

for six or more players

Abioueka
Djaa
Dununba
Fume Fume
Kakilambe
Mandjani
Nañigo
Soli
Sorsornet
Tiriba
Yankadi
Zebolah

Abakua
Bahavento
Bembe
Mahi
Yanvalou
Zepaule

Collected Rhythms

4/4 - African

Aconcon (Senegal--play with Timini)

	1	.	*	.	2	.	*	.	3	.	*	.	4	.	*	.
low djembe	G	–	g	d	–	T	P	–	G	–	g	d	–	T	P	–
high djembe	P	(T)	–	T	P	–	g	d	P	(T)	–	T	P	–	g	d
mid djembe	P	(T)	–	d	P	(T)	G	–	P	(T)	–	d	P	(T)	G	–
							(g)								(g)	
shaker	d	u	–	d	u	–	d	u	d	u	–	d	u	–	d	u
junjun bell	x	–	x	x	–	x	x	–	x	–	x	x	–	x	x	–
junjun	O	–	–	–	–	–	–	–	–	–	O	(O)	–	O	–	–
	O	–	–	–	–	–	–	–	–	–	–	–	–	–	–	–
junjun/bell (var.)	X	–	–	–	X	–	–	–	X	X	–	X	X	–	–	–
faster:	X	–	–	–	X	–	X	–	X	–	–	–	X	–	X	–

Akiwowo (Yoruba--folk song)

	1	.	*	.	2	.	*	.	3	.	*	.	4	.	*	.
low djembe	G	–	g	d	P	–	g	d	G	–	g	d	G	d	g	d
mid djembe	G	–	P	T	G	–	g	d	G	–	P	T	G	–	g	d
high djembe	P	–	P	–	g	d	–	T	–	T	–	T	g	d	g	–
junjun bell	–	–	x	x	–	–	x	x	–	x	–	x	–	–	x	x
junjun	O	–	–	–	M	–	–	–	O	–	–	–	M	–	–	–

Balakulania (weddings, or circumcision)

	1	.	*	.	2	.	*	.	3	.	*	.	4	.	*	.
djembe 1	P	–	–	T	P	–	g	d	P	–	–	T	P	–	g	d
djembe 2	G	–	g	d	–	–	P	–	G	–	g	d	–	–	P	–
--variation	G	–	g	d	–	–	P	d	g	–	G	T	–	–	P	–
djembe 3	–	–	P	T	–	–	P	T	–	–	g	T	g	d	P	T
junjun bell	x	–	x	x	–	x	x	–	x	–	x	x	–	x	x	–
junjun	O	–	–	–	–	–	O	–	O	–	–	–	–	–	O	–
--variation	O	–	–	–	O	–	–	–	O	–	o	–	O	–	–	–
songba bell	x	–	x	x	–	x	x	–	x	–	x	–	x	x	–	x
songba	–	–	–	–	–	–	–	–	–	–	O	–	O	–	–	–
--variation	M	–	(O)	O	–	(O)	–	(O)	–	–	O	–	O	–	–	–
kenkeni bell	x	–	x	–	x	–	x	–	x	–	x	–	x	–	x	–

kenkeni	O	-	-	-	O	-	-	-	O	-	-	-	O	-	-	-

Bolon (Malinke)

	1	.	*	.	**2**	.	*	.	**3**	.	*	.	**4**	.	*	.
djembe 1	P	-	-	T	P	-	g	d	P	-	-	T	P	-	g	d
djembe 2	g	d	-	T	-	-	P	-	g	d	G	-	D	-	G	-
djembe 3	g	d	P	T	-	-	P	D	g	d	P	T	G	-	P	D
kenkeni bell	x	x	-	x	-	x	x	-	x	x	-	x	-	x	x	-
kenkeni	O	O	-	M	-	-	M	-	O	O	-	M	-	-	M	-
junjun bell	x	-	x	x	-	x	x	-	x	-	x	-	x	-	x	-
junjun	O	-	-	-	-	-	-	-	-	-	O	-	O	-	O	-

Boushay (Congo)

[play swung]	**1**	.	*	.	**2**	.	*	.	**3**	.	*	.	**4**	.	*	.
high djembe	P	-	g	d	P	-	g	d	P	-	P	T	-	-	g	d
mid djembe	-	-	g	d	-	-	P	-	-	-	g	d	-	-	P	-
low djembe	G	-	G	-	g	d	-	-	G	-	G	-	g	d	-	-
songba/bell	x	-	-	-	x	-	-	-	x	-	-	o	x	-	o	-

Bwanga (Congo--power)

	1	.	*	.	**2**	.	*	.	**3**	.	*	.	**4**	.	*	.
low djembe	G	-	d	-	G	-	d	-	G	-	d	-	G	-	d	-
mid djembe 1	g	-	T	g	-	g	T	-	g	-	T	-	G	G	T	-
mid djembe 2	g	-	d	-	G	-	T	g	-	g	d	-	G	-	T	-
high djembe 1	-	-	P	T	-	-	g	d	-	-	P	T	-	-	g	d
high djembe 2	g	d	-	-	P	T	-	-	g	d	-	-	P	T	-	-

Dalah (Guinea--women's fishing song)

	1	.	*	.	**2**	.	*	.	**3**	.	*	.	**4**	.	*	.	
djembe 1	P	-	-	T	P	-	g	d	P	-	-	T	P	-	g	d	
djembe 2	G	-	g	d	-	-	P	T	G	-	g	d	-	-	P	T	
kenkeni bell	x	-	x	-	x	-	x	-	x	-	x	-	x	-	x	-	
kenkeni	O	-	-	-	O	-	-	-	O	-	-	-	O	-	-	-	
songba bell	x	-	x	x	-	x	x	-	x	-	x	-	x	-	x	-	
songba	O	-	O	O	-	-	-	-	M	-	-	-	O	-	O	-	>
	O	-	O	O	-	-	-	-	M	-	-	-	M	-	-	-	
junjun bell	x	-	x	x	-	x	x	-	x	-	x	x	-	x	x	-	
junjun	O	-	-	-	-	-	O	-	O	-	-	-	-	-	O	-	

Dennadon (Guinea--introduces Mandjani 12/8)

	1	.	*	.	2	.	*	.	3	.	*	.	4	.	*	.
djembe 1	P	T	-	D	g	-	d	-	P	T	-	D	g	-	d	-
djembe 2	P	-	-	T	P	-	g	d	P	-	-	T	P	-	g	d
kenkeni bell	x	-	x	-	x	-	x	-	x	-	x	-	x	-	x	-
kenkeni	O	-	-	-	O	-	-	-	O	-	-	-	O	-	-	-
songba bell	x	-	x	x	-	x	x	-	x	-	x	x	-	x	x	-
songba	-	-	-	M	-	-	M	-	-	-	O	O	-	-	O	-
songba (faster)	O	-	O	O	-	O	O	-	O	-	O	O	-	-	O	-
junjun bell	x	x	-	x	x	-	x	-	x	-	x	-	x	-	x	-
junjun	O	O	-	-	o	-	-	-	O	-	O	-	o	-	-	-
--variation	-	-	-	o	-	-	o	-	-	-	O	O	-	-	O	-

Diansa (Mali--celebration)

	1	.	*	.	2	.	*	.	3	.	*	.	4	.	*	.
djembe 1	P	-	-	T	P	-	g	d	P	-	-	T	P	-	g	d
djembe 2	G	d	-	d	G	-	P	-	G	-	g	d	G	-	P	-
--variation	P	T	-	D	g	-	d	-	P	T	-	D	g	-	d	-
djembe 3	P	-	g	d	P	-	G	-	P	-	g	d	P	-	G	-
--variation	P	T	-	T	P	-	g	d	P	-	G	-	P	D	g	d
bell	x	-	x	-	x	-	x	-	x	-	x	-	x	-	x	-
kenkeni	O	-	-	-	-	O	O	-	O	-	-	-	-	O	O	-
--variation			(x	M)							(x	M)				
songba	O	-	-	O	-	-	O	-	-	-	-	-	-	-	O	-
--variation	O	-	x	O	-	x	O	-	x	-	M	-	x	-	O	-
junjun	-	-	-	-	-	-	-	-	-	-	-	O	-	-	-	-
--variation	o	-	-	o	-	-	o	-	-	-	O	-	-	-	o	-
junjun (fast)	O	-	-	M	-	-	O	-	O	-	-	M	-	-	O	-
junjun/bell (var.)	M	-	x	-	x	-	x	-	M	-	O	-	x	-	x	-
	M	-	x	-	x	-	O	O	-	O	O	-	x	-	x	-

Ekonga (Congo) [note similarity of name and parts to Conga (Cuba)]

	1	.	*	.	2	.	*	.	3	.	*	.	4	.	*	.
djembe 1	G	-	g	d	G	-	g	d	G	-	g	d	G	-	g	d
djembe 2	P	-	P	d	P	-	P	d	P	-	P	d	P	-	P	d
djembe 3	G	-	d	-	P	T	-	-	G	-	d	-	P	T	-	-

Fanga (Guinea/Liberia--welcome) <22-Fanga.mp3>

	1	.	*	.	2	.	*	.	3	.	*	.	4	.	*	.
high djembe	P	T	-	-	P	T	-	-	P	T	-	-	g	d	-	-
--variations...	P	T	-	-	g	d	-	-	g	d	-	-	g	d	-	-
	-	-	P	T	-	-	P	T	-	-	P	T	g	d	P	T
lead djembe	G	-	-	d	-	g	d	-	D	-	D	-	d	g	-	-
--variation	G	-	-	d	-	g	d	-	-	g	d	-	G	-	D	-
low djembe	G	-	(G)	D	-	D	g	d	G	-	-	(D)	G	-	g	d
--variations...	G	-	G	D	-	D	g	d	G	-	G	D	-	D	g	d
	G	-	G	D	-	-	P	-	G	-	-	D	G	-	P	-
	G	-	-	D	G	-	g	d	G	-	D	-	G	-	g	d
	G	-	-	-	G	-	g	d	G	-	G	-	-	-	g	d
low bell	-	-	x	x	-	-	x	x	-	-	x	x	-	-	x	x
junjun bell	x	x	-	-	x	x	-	-	x	x	-	-	x	x	-	-
junjun	O	-	-	-	(M)	-	-	-	O	-	O	-	(M)	-	-	-
--variation	O	-	-	O	-	(O)	O	-	O	-	(O)	-	o	O	-	-
shaker	x	-	x	x	x	-	x	x	x	-	x	x	x	-	x	x

Fankani (Guinea-feast days)

	1	.	*	.	2	.	*	.	3	.	*	.	4	.	*	.	
djembe 1	P	-	-	T	P	-	g	d	P	-	-	T	P	-	g	d	
djembe 2	P	-	-	T	P	-	G	-	P	-	g	d	P	-	G	-	>
	F	d	g	d	g	-	P	-	F	d	g	d	g	-	P	-	
kenkeni bell	x	-	x	-	x	-	x	-	x	-	x	-	x	-	x	-	
--variation	x	x	-	x	-	x	x	-	x	x	-	x	-	x	x	-	
kenkeni	O	O	-	M	-	-	-	-	O	O	-	M	-	-	-	-	
songba/junjun bell	x	-	x	x	-	x	x	-	x	-	x	x	-	x	x	-	
songba	-	-	-	-	-	-	-	-	-	-	O	O	-	-	-	-	>
	-	-	-	-	-	-	O	-	O	-	O	O	-	-	-	-	
junjun	-	-	-	-	-	-	O	-	-	-	-	-	-	-	O	-	>
	-	-	-	-	-	-	-	-	-	-	-	-	-	-	O		

Frekoba

	1	.	*	.	2	.	*	.	3	.	*	.	4	.	*	.	
djembe 1	G	-	-	d	G	-	d	-	G	-	-	d	G	-	d	-	>
	G	-	-	d	G	-	d	-	G	d	-	d	G	-	T	-	
--variation	P	-	-	T	g	-	P	-	G	-	-	T	g	-	P	-	>
	G	T	-	T	g	-	P	-	G	-	-	T	g	-	P	-	
djembe 2	P	(T)	-	d	P	-	G	-	P	-	-	d	P	-	G	-	
djembe 3	g	d	P	T	-	P	T	-	g	d	P	T	-	P	T	-	
junjun bell	x	-	-	-	-	-	x	-	-	-	x	-	x	-	-	-	
junjun	O	-	-	O	-	-	O	-	O	-	-	O	-	-	O	-	
junjun/bell --variations...	O	-	O	O	-	-	-	-	O	-	O	O	-	-	x	-	
	O	-	O	O	-	O	-	O	O	-	-	-	O	O	-	O	>
	O	-	-	-	-	-	x	-	-	-	x	-	x	-	-	-	

Gahu (Ghana/Ewe)

	1	.	*	.	2	.	*	.	3	.	*	.	4	.	*	.	
bell	x	-	-	-	x	-	-	-	x	-	-	-	x	-	-	-	
--variations...	L	-	-	H	(L)	-	H	-	(L)	-	H	-	(L)	-	H	-	
	L	-	H	-	H	H	H	-	L	-	H	-	H	H	H	-	
					(-	L)											
	L	-	H	-	H	-	H	-	L	-	H	-	H	-	H	-	>
	L	-	H	-	L	-	H	-	L	L	-	L	L	-	H	-	
	H	-	H	H	-	-	L	-	H	-	H	H	-	L	-	-	
shaker	d	-	-	d	u	-	d	-	u	-	d	-	u	-	d	-	
high drum	-	-	g	d	-	-	g	d	-	-	g	d	-	-	g	d	
mid drum	g	d	-	P	T	-	g	d	g	d	P	-	T	-	g	d	
--variations...			(P	T	-)												
	g	-	-	d	g	-	P	T	P	T	g	-	g	-	P	T	>
	P	T	-	d	g	-	P	T	P	T	g	-	g	-	P	T	
	g	d	g	d	-	T	P	-	g	d	g	d	-	T	P	-	
low drum	g	(D)	-	g	D	-	g	-	D	-	g	-	D	-	g	-	
--variations...	G	-	-	-	G	-	d	-	G	-	-	-	G	-	d	-	
	G	-	-	-	d	-	G	-	G	-	-	-	d	-	G	-	
	G	-	d	-	G	-	d	-	G	-	d	-	g	D	-	d	
	G	-	G	D	g	d	G	D	G	-	G	D	g	d	-	d	
junjun	O	O	-	O	O	-	-	-	M	-	-	-	M	-	-	-	

Gota (Benin)

	1	.	*	.	2	.	*	.	3	.	*	.	4	.	*	.
bell	L	-	H	-	L	-	H	-	L	-	H	-	L	-	H	-
--variation	L	-	L	-	H	H	H	H	L	-	L	-	H	H	H	H
djembe 1	G	-	-	-	-	-	g	d	P	-	-	-	G	D	G	D
--variation	G	-	g	d	G	D	g	d	G	-	g	d	G	D	g	d
djembe 2	-	T	-	T	G	-	g	d	-	T	-	T	G	-	g	d

Gumbe

	1	.	*	.	2	.	*	.	3	.	*	.	4	.	*	.
djembe 1	g	d	-	-	G	-	T	-	G	-	T	-	G	-	T	-
djembe 2	g	d	-	-	g	d	-	-	g	d	-	-	g	d	-	-
djembe 3	-	T	-	d	P	-	-	d	P	-	g	T	-	d	-	d
djembe 4	P	T	P	T	-	T	g	d	-	T	-	-	P	T	g	d
djembe 5	g	T	-	d	P	-	g	T	-	d	P	-	g	d	-	-
junjun/bell	x	O	-	-	x	-	O	-	x	-	O	-	x	-	O	-

Highlife (W. Africa)

	1	.	*	.	2	.	*	.	3	.	*	.	4	.	*	.
clave	-	-	-	x	-	-	-	x	-	-	-	-	-	-	-	x
bell	x	-	x	x	-	x	x	-	x	-	x	x	-	x	x	-
low drum	G	-	-	d	G	-	g	d	G	-	-	d	G	-	g	d
--variation	G	-	-	D	G	-	G	D	G	-	-	D	G	-	G	D
mid drum	g	-	d	-	G	-	D	-	g	-	-	T-	-	-	g	d
--variation	G	-	T	-	P	-	g	d	G	-	-	T-	-	-	g	d
high drum	g	-	-	d	g	-	-	d	g	-	-	d	g	T	-	d
--variation	g	-	g	d	g	d	-	-	g	d	g	d	-	d	g	-
junjun bell	-	-	x	x	-	-	x	x	-	-	x	x	-	-	x	x
junjun	O	-	-	-	M	-	-	-	O	-	-	M	-	-	-	-

Jondon (Mail--royal servants; play with Wollosidon)

[swung]	1	.	*	.	2	.	*	.	3	.	*	.	4	.	*	.
high drum	g	-	d	-	P	T	P	T	g	d	-	T	P	T	P	-
mid drum	g	d	P	T	G	T	P	T	g	d	P	T	G	T	P	T
--variation	P	T	-	g	P	T	-	d	P	T	(F)	d	P	T	-	d
low drum	g	-	g	D	P	P	-	F	g	g	-	D	P	P	-	F
junjun	O	-	O	-	-	-	-	-	O	O	-	-	-	-	-	-
junjun/bell	x	x	-	O	x	x	-	O	O	-	O	-	O	O	-	O

Kakilambe (Senegal--harvest; see also 12/8 version from Guinea)

<23-Kaki.mp3>	1	.	*	.	2	.	*	.	3	.	*	.	4	.	*	.	
break	P	T	P	T	P	-	T	-	-	-	g	d	g	-	T	-	>
	P	-	-	-	-	-	g	d	g	-	d	-	g	-	-	-	
djembe 1	g	d	-	d	g	-	D	-	g	-	d	-	G	-	D	-	
			(G)										(G	D	G)		
djembe 2	G	-	-	d	g	-	T	-	G	-	d	-	g	-	T	-	
--variations...			(G)										(g	d	g)		
												(D	-	g	d	P)	
high drum	G	-	d	g	d	-	P	T	G	-	d	g	d	-	P	T	
shaker	X	-	-	-	X	-	-	-	X	-	-	-	X	-	-	-	
junjun bell	-	-	-	x	-	-	x	-	-	-	-	-	x	-	x	-	
junjun	O	-	-	O	-	-	-	-	O	-	O	-	-	-	-	-	
junjun bell --variations...	-	-	x	x	-	-	x	x	-	-	x	x	-	-	x	x	
	x	-	-	x	x	-	x	-	x	-	x	-	x	-	x	-	>
	x	-	-	x	x	-	x	-	x	-	x	-	x	-	-	-	
junjun --variation	O	-	-	O	-	-	O	-	-	-	-	-	-	-	-	-	>
	O	-	-	O	-	-	-	-	O	-	O	-	-	-	-	-	
junjun (faster)	O	-	-	O	-	-	O	-	-	-	-	-	-	-	-	-	>
	O	-	-	-	-	-	-	-	-	-	-	-	-	-	-	-	

Kassa (Guinea--workers' harvest)

[swung]	1	.	*	.	2	.	*	.	3	.	*	.	4	.	*	.
djembe 1	P	T	-	T	P	-	g	d	P	T	-	T	P	-	g	d
	g	d	-	-	P	-	-	-	g	d	-	-	P	-	(D)	-
djembe 2	P	-	-	T	P	-	g	d	P	-	(G)	T	P	-	g	d
	P	-	-	T	P	-	D	-	P	-	g	d	P	-	D	-
djembe 3	(G)	-	g	d	-	-	P	-	(G)	-	g	d	-	-	P	-
--variations...	G	-	P	T	g	d	P	T	G	-	P	T	g	d	P	T
	G	-	P	T	-	-	P	d	g	-	P	T	G	-	P	d
	(g)															
	P	T	-	-	P	T	g	d	P	T	G	-	P	T	g	d
	g	d	P	T´	-	D	P	T	g	d	P	T	-	D	P	T
shaker	x	-	-	-	x	-	-	-	x	-	-	-	x	-	-	-
cowbell	x	-	-	x	-	-	x	-	-	-	x	-	x	-	-	-
--variation	x	-	-	x	x	-	x	-	x	-	x	-	x	-	x	-
junjun bell	x	x	-	x	-	x	x	-	x	-	x	-	x	-	x	-
--variation	x	-	x	x	-	x	x	-	x	-	x	-	x	-	x	-
junjun	O	O	-	O	-	-	-	-	-	-	O	-	O	-	O	-

...Kassa...	1	.	*	.	2	.	*	.	3	.	*	.	4	.	*	.
junjun variations...	O	-	O	O	-	-	(M)	-	-	-	O	-	O	-	O	-
	o	-	-	O	O	-	-	-	o	-	o	-	-	-	-	-
songba	-	-	-	O	-	-	-	-	-	-	-	-	O	-	-	-
--variation	O	-	-	-	-	-	-	-	-	O	-	-	-	-	-	-
kenkeni	O	-	-	M	-	-	O	-	O	-	-	M	-	-	O	-
--variation	o	o	-	o	-	o	o	-	o	o	-	o	-	o	o	-

Kebendo (Guinea--faithfulness)

	1	.	*	.	2	.	*	.	3	.	*	.	4	.	*	.
djembe 1	g	d	-	T	G	-	P	-	G	-	-	T	G	-	P	-
djembe 2	G	-	P	T	G	-	g	d	G	-	P	T	G	-	g	d
kenkeni bell	x	-	x	-	x	-	x	-	x	-	x	-	x	-	x	-
kenkeni	O	-	-	-	O	-	-	-	O	-	-	-	O	-	-	-
songba/junjun bell	x	-	x	x	-	x	x	-	x	-	x	x	-	x	x	-
songba	-	-	O	O	-	-	-	-	-	-	O	(O)	-	-	-	-
junjun	-	-	-	-	-	-	O	-	-	-	-	-	-	-	O	-

Kpanlogo (Ghana--street rhythm)

	1	.	*	.	2	.	*	.	3	.	*	.	4	.	*	.
clave	x	-	-	x	-	-	x	-	-	-	x	-	x	-	-	-
--variation	-	-	x	-	-	-	x	-	-	-	x	-	-	-	x	-
shaker	d	-	d	u	d	-	d	u	d	-	d	u	d	-	d	u
tumba	g	d	g	d	G	-	P	T	g	-	P	T	G	-	P	T
--variation			(-	T)							(-	D	G	d	g	-)
conga	G	-	P	T	g	-	P	T	G	-	P	T	g	-	-	d
--variations...	G	-	P	T	G	-	P	T	G	-	g	d	G	-	P	T
													(g)			
	G	-	P	T	g	-	P	T	G	d	P	-	g	d	-	d
	g	-	P	T	-	-	g	d	g	-	P	T	-	-	g	d
quinto	P	T	G	-	P	-	g	d	G	-	P	d	-	-	g	-
bell 1	L	L	L	L	L	-	H	-	-	-	H	-	-	-	H	-
bell 2a	H	-	-	H	-	-	H	-	-	-	H	-	H	-	-	-
bell 2b	-	-	-	-	-	-	L	-	-	-	L	-	-	-	L	-
bell 3	H	H	-	-	H	H	-	-	H	H	-	-	H	H	-	-
bell 4	L	L	-	H	-	L	-	H	L	-	H	-	L	-	-	-
drum 1	G	D	P	T	-	P	T	-	-	-	P	T	-	-	P	T
drum 2	G	D	-	d	G	D	-	d	G	D	-	T	-	-	P	-
djembe 1	g	(d)	(g)	-	P	-	(D)	-	G	-	-	-	G	d	g	-
djembe 2	-	-	P	T	-	-	P	T	-	-	g	(d)	g	-	P	T

Kpatsa (Ghana)

	1	.	*	.	2	.	*	.	3	.	*	.	4	.	*	.
djembe	G	-	G	D	g	d	g	d	G	-	g	d	-	d	g	d
junjun	O	-	-	-	O	O	O	O	O	-	-	-	-	-	-	-
bell 1	L	-	-	-	-	-	L	-	L	-	-	-	H	-	H	-
bell 2	H	-	L	-	L	-	H	-	H	-	-	-	-	-	-	-

Kuku (Guinea--celebration)

	1	.	*	.	2	.	*	.	3	.	*	.	4	.	*	.	
basic djembe	G	-	g	d	G	-	P	-	g	d	g	d	G	-	P	-	
djembe 1	P	T	-	d	g	d	P	-	P	T	-	d	g	d	P	-	
--variations...			(g)				(T)				(g)				(T)		
	g	d	-	(T)	g	d	P	-	g	d	-	(T)	g	d	P	-	
	Gd	-	g	d	G	T	P	-	Gd	-	g	d	G	T	P	-	
djembe 2	G	-	g	d	-	-	P	-	G	-	g	d	-	-	gf	-	
--variations...	g	-	d	g	-	-	Pt	-	P	-	T	P	-	-	P	-	>
	P	-	P	T	-	T	g	d	P	-	P	-	P	T	g	T	
djembe 3	G	-	-	-	G	-	-	-	P	-	T	-	g	d	-	-	
--variations...	g	d	-	-	g	d	-	-	g	d	-	-	g	d	-	-	
	P	-	T	-	g	d	-	-	P	-	T	-	g	d	-	-	
djembe 4	-	-	P	-	T	-	g	d	-	-	P	-	T	-	g	d	
--variation	-	-	g	d	-	-	P	-	-	-	g	d	-	-	P	-	
shaker	-	x	X	x	-	x	X	x	-	x	X	x	-	x	X	x	
bell	-	-	x	x	-	-	x	x	-	-	x	x	-	-	x	x	
--variations...	x	-	x	x	-	x	x	x	-	x	-	x	-	x	-	x	
	x	-	x	x	-	x	x	x	-	x	-	x	x	-	x	x	
	x	-	(x)	-	x	-	(x)	-	x	-	(x)	-	x	-	(x)	-	
junjun	O	-	O	-	O	-	-	-	M	-	-	M	-	-	-	-	
--variations...	M	-	-	O	-	-	-	-	M	-	-	-	O	-	O	-	>
	O	-	-	O	-	-	-	-	M	-	-	-	-	-	-	-	
	-	-	O	O	-	-	M	-	-	-	-	M	-	-	O	-	
	O	-	-	-	-	-	o	-	O	-	-	o	-	-	o	-	X3
(>)	O	-	-	-	-	-	O	-	O	-	-	O	-	-	O	-	
	o	-	-	O	-	-	o	-	o	-	-	-	-	-	o	-	
songba	M	-	M	-	M	-	-	-	O	-	-	O	-	-	-	-	
--variations...	O	-	-	M	-	-	O	-	(O)	-	-	-	-	-	(O)	-	
	O	-	-	M	-	-	O	-	O	-	-	M	-	O	-	-	
	O	-	-	-	-	-	O	-	O	-	-	-	-	-	-	-	>
	-	-	-	-	-	-	O	-	O	-	-	-	-	-	-	O	
kenkeni	O	-	-	O	O	-	-	O	O	-	-	O	O	O	-	O	
--variation	O	O	-	-	O	O	-	-	O	O	-	-	O	O	-	-	

Kurubi (Ivory Coast--women, last year before marriage)

	1	.	*	.	**2**	.	*	.	**3**	.	*	.	**4**	.	*	.
djembe 1	g	d	-	T	g	d	P	-	g	d	-	T	g	d	P	-
djembe 2	G	-	g	d	G	-	P	T	G	-	g	d	G	-	P	T
kenkeni bell	x	-	x	-	x	-	x	-	x	-	x	-	x	-	x	-
kenkeni	O	-	-	-	-	-	O	-	O	-	-	-	-	-	O	-
songba/junjun bell	x	-	x	x	-	x	-	x	x	-	x	-	x	x	-	x
songba	O	-	-	O	-	O	-	-	-	-	-	-	-	-	-	-
junjun	-	-	-	-	-	-	-	o	O	-	O	-	O	O	-	-

Lafé (Guinea--female dancer outside circle)

	1	.	*	.	**2**	.	*	.	**3**	.	*	.	**4**	.	*	.
djembe 1	P	-	-	T	P	-	g	d	P	-	-	T	P	-	g	d
djembe 2	G	-	g	d	-	-	P	-	G	-	g	d	-	-	P	-
kenkeni bell	x	-	-	-	x	-	-	-	x	-	-	-	x	-	-	-
kenkeni	-	-	O	O	-	-	O	O	-	-	O	O	-	-	O	O
kenkeni bell (var.)	x	-	x	-	x	-	x	-	x	-	x	-	x	-	x	-
kenkeni (var.)	O	-	-	-	O	-	-	-	O	-	-	-	O	-	-	-
songba/junjun bell	x	-	x	x	-	x	-	x	x	-	x	-	x	x	-	x
songba	M	-	-	M	-	M	-	-	O	-	O	-	O	O	-	-
junjun	-	-	-	-	-	-	-	O	O	-	O	-	O	O	-	-

Lamba (Mali/Guinea--healing, thanks) <24-Lamba.mp3>

[can be swung]	**1**	.	*	.	**2**	.	*	.	**3**	.	*	.	**4**	.	*	.
low djembe	g	d	P	T	G	(T)	P	T	g	d	P	T	G	(T)	P	T
--variations...	G	-	P	T	g	d	P	T	G	-	P	T	g	d	P	T
	g	-	d	-	g	-	(P)	D	G	-	-	D	G	-	-	-
mid djembe	g	d	P	-	-	D	P	-	g	d	P	-	-	D	P	-
--variation	g	d	P	d	g	T	g	d	P	-	-	-	F	-	F	-
high djembe	P	-	-	d	P	-	g	d	P	-	-	d	P	-	g	d
shaker	X	-	X	x	X	x	X	x	X	-	X	x	X	x	X	x
--variation	x	-	x	x	x	-	x	x	x	-	x	x	x	-	x	x
junjun/bell	X	-	X	-	X	-	-	-	X	-	X	-	X	-	-	-
	X	-	X	-	X	-	-	X	-	(X)	X	-	X	-	-	-
junjun bell	x	-	x	-	x	-	x	-	x	-	x	-	x	-	x	-
junjun	O	-	O	O	O	-	O	-	O	-	O	O	O	-	O	-
songba	-	-	-	-	-	-	O	-	O	-	O	O	-	-	-	-

>

Makuru (Guinea--celebration; play with Yankadi)

	1	.	*	.	2	.	*	.	3	.	*	.	4	.	*	.	
junjun: intro	O	O	-	O	O	-	O	O	O	-	O	O	-	O	-	O	>
	O	-	-	O	O	-	O	O	O	-	O	O	-	O	-	O	
junjun	O	-	-	O	O	-	O	-	O	-	O	O	-	-	-	-	
--variation	O	-	-	O	O	-	-	-	o	-	o	-	o	-	-	O	
kenkeni	O	-	O	O	-	-	O	-	-	-	-	-	-	-	O	-	>
	-	-	-	-	-	-	O	-	-	-	-	-	-	-	O	-	
djembe 1	G	d	-	d	G	-	T	-	G	-	d	-	G	-	d	-	
--variations...															(T)		
	G	-	-	d	g	-	d	-	G	-	d	-	g	-	d	-	
	G	-	-	d	g	-	G	-	-	d	g	-	G	-	-	-	
	G	-	-	T	G	-	d	-	g	-	g	d	-	-	-	-	
djembe 2	G	-	-	T	-	d	g	-	G	-	P	-	g	d	P	-	
--variations...													(-	d	g)		
	G	-	-	T	-	d	g	-	G	-	-	T	-	d	g	-	
djembe 3	g	-	-	T	-	-	-	d	g	-	P	-	T	-	-	d	

Mané (Guinea--women: weddings, baptism)

	1	.	*	.	2	.	*	.	3	.	*	.	4	.	*	.
djembe 1	P	-	g	T	-	d	P	-	g	-	P	-	g	d	g	-
djembe 2	G	-	d	-	G	-	T	-	G	-	d	-	G	-	T	-
djembe 3	G	-	-	d	G	-	-	-	G	-	g	-	G	-	-	-

Masacote

	1	.	*	.	2	.	*	.	3	.	*	.	4	.	*	.
clave	-	-	x	-	x	-	-	-	x	-	-	x	-	-	x	-
cowbell	x	-	x	-	x	x	-	x	-	x	x	x	-	x	-	x
									(x	-)						
guiro	d	-	d	u	d	-	d	u	d	-	d	u	d	-	d	u
djembe	g	-	G	d	g	-	-	d	G	d	-	d	g	-	-	d
conga	g	(d)	P	-	-	g	-	d	-	T	P	-	-	-	-	-
tumba	-	-	-	d	g	-	-	-	-	-	-	D	G	-	g	d
junjun	O	-	o	-	O	-	o	-	O	-	o	-	O	-	o	-

Mombassa (Ghana)

	1	.	*	.	2	.	*	.	3	.	*	.	4	.	*	.
djembe 1	P	T	G	-	P	T	-	D	P	T	G	-	P	T	-	D
djembe 2	G	-	g	d	G	-	g	d	-	-	P	T	-	T	g	d

Moribayassa (Guinea--women, return of absent person or good fortune)

	1	.	*	.	2	.	*	.	3	.	*	.	4	.	*	.
low djembe	G	-	g	d	G	-	T	-	G	-	g	d	G	-	T	-
high djembe	P	-	-	T	P	-	g	d	P	-	-	T	P	-	g	d
kenkeni bell	x	-	x	-	x	-	x	-	x	-	x	-	x	-	x	-
kenkeni	O	-	-	-	O	-	-	-	O	-	-	-	O	-	-	-
songba bell	x	-	x	-	x	-	x	-	x	-	x	-	x	-	x	-
songba	O	-	-	-	M	-	-	-	M	-	O	-	O	-	O	-
junjun bell	x	-	x	x	-	x	x	-	x	-	x	x	-	x	x	-
junjun	O	-	-	-	-	-	O	-	O	-	-	-	-	-	O	-

Nokobe (Ghana/Ewe)

	1	.	*	.	2	.	*	.	3	.	*	.	4	.	*	.
drum	g	-	g	d	G	-	d	-	G	-	P	T	-	T	P	-
drum w/ stick	-	-	x	x	-	-	x	x	-	-	x	x	-	-	x	x
bell	L	-	H	H	-	H	H	-	L	-	H	-	H	-	H	-
shaker	d	-	-	d	u	-	d	-	d	-	-	d	u	-	d	-

Shiko (Nigeria)

	1	.	*	.	2	.	*	.	3	.	*	.	4	.	*	.
clave	x	-	-	x	-	-	x	-	-	-	x	-	x	-	-	-
bell 1	L	L	H	H	L	L	H	H	L	L	H	H	L	L	H	H
bell 2	x	-	x	x	-	x	x	-	x	-	x	x	-	x	x	-
tumba	g	-	d	-	G	-	D	-	g	-	d	-	G	D	-	-
conga 1	G	-	-	-	G	-	d	-	G	-	-	-	G	-	d	-
conga 2	G	-	P	T	G	-	P	T	G	-	P	T	g	d	-	-
--variation	g	-	P	T	G	-	G	T	-	d	P	T	G	-	G	T
quinto	g	-	g	d	-	d	g	-	P	-	P	T	-	T	P	-
junjun	O	-	o	-	o	-	-	-	O	-	o	-	o	-	-	-
--variation	O	-	O	-	-	-	-	-	O	-	O	-	-	-	-	-

Soli [slow; see 12/8 for fast] (Guinea--circumcision)

	1	.	*	.	2	.	*	.	3	.	*	.	4	.	*	.	
djembe	P	-	P	T	-	-	g	d	P	-	-	P	T	-	g	d	
kenkeni	O	-	O	-	O	-	x	-	x	-	O	-	O	-	x	-	
songba	O	-	-	-	O	-	-	-	O	-	-	-	O	-	x	-	>
	O	-	x	-	O	-	x	-	O	-	x	-	O	-	x	-	
junjun/bell	x	-	x	x	-	x	-	x	x	-	O	-	O	-	x	-	
--variation	x	-	x	O	-	O	-	O	O	-	O	-	O	-	x	-	>
	x	-	x	x	-	x	-	x	x	-	O	-	O	-	x	-	

Sunu (Mali--harvest celebration)

	1	.	*	.	2	.	*	.	3	.	*	.	4	.	*	.	
djembe 1	P	-	g	d	P	-	-	T	P	-	g	d	P	-	-	T	
--variation	P	-	-	T	P	-	g	d	P	-	-	T	P	-	g	d	
djembe 2	g	-	P	T	-	D	P	d	g	-	P	T	-	D	P	d	
--variation	g	d	-	T	P	-	-	T	g	d	-	T	P	D	-	T	
djembe 3	P	-	g	d	g	T	-	-	P	-	g	d	g	T	-	-	
kenkeni bell	x	-	x	x	-	x	x	-	x	-	x	x	-	x	x	-	
kenkeni	O	-	-	M	-	-	O	-	O	-	-	M	-	-	O	-	
junjun	O	-	-	-	-	-	-	-	-	-	-	-	-	-	-	O	>
	O	-	-	-	-	-	-	-	-	-	-	-	O	-	-	O	>
	O	-	-	O	O	-	O	-	O	-	O	-	O	-	-	O	
--variation	O	-	-	O	-	-	-	o	O	-	-	O	-	-	-	o	

Timini (Senegal--play with Aconcon)

	1	.	*	.	2	.	*	.	3	.	*	.	4	.	*	.
djembe 1	P	T	-	T	P	(T)	g	d	P	T	-	T	P	(T)	g	d
--variation	g	d	-	d	P	-	g	d	g	d	-	d	P	-	G	-
djembe 2	-	T	G	d	g	T	P	-	-	T	G	d	g	T	P	-
--variation	T	G	d	g	T	P	-	-	T	G	d	g	T	P	-	-
djembe 3	G	-	P	T	G	-	g	d	G	-	P	T	G	-	g	d
junjun bell	x	x	-	x	x	-	x	-	x	x	-	x	x	-	x	-
junjun	O	O	-	O	O	-	-	-	O	O	-	O	O	-	-	-
junjun bell (var.)	x	-	-	x	-	-	x	-	x	-	-	x	-	-	x	-
junjun (var.)	o	-	-	o	-	-	O	-	o	-	-	o	-	-	O	-
--fast variation 1:	-	-	x	-	-	-	x	x	x	-	x	-	x	-	x	x
	O	O	-	O	O	-	-	-	-	-	-	-	-	-	-	-
--fast variation 2:	x	-	x	-	x	-	x	x	-	-	x	-	x	-	x	x
	-	-	-	-	-	-	-	-	O	O	-	O	O	-	-	-
junjun/bell (var.)	X	-	-	-	X	-	X	-	X	-	-	-	X	-	X	-

Tordo (Guinea--male initiation)

	1	.	*	.	2	.	*	.	3	.	*	.	4	.	*	.
djembe 1	g	d	-	D	P	-	T	-	P	-	-	D	P	-	T	-
djembe 2	P	-	-	T	P	-	g	d	P	-	-	T	P	-	g	d
bell	x	x	-	x	x	-	x	-	x	-	x	x	-	x	x	-
kenkeni, songba bell	x	x	-	x	x	-	x	-	x	-	(x)	-	x	-	x	-
kenkeni	-	-	O	O	-	-	M	-	-	-	O	O	-	-	M	-
songba	O	O	-	-	M	-	M	-	M	-	-	-	O	-	O	-
junjun bell	x	x	-	x	x	-	x	-	x	-	x	-	x	-	x	-
junjun	O	O	-	-	-	-	-	-	-	-	O	O	-	O	O	-
	O	O	-	-	-	-	-	-	-	-	-	-	-	-	-	-
--variation	O	O	-	-	o	-	o	-	o	-	-	-	O	-	O	-

(>)

Uffunu (Ewe)

	1	.	*	.	2	.	*	.	3	.	*	.	4	.	*	.
tumba	g	d	g	d	P	T	-	T	P	-	P	T	-	T	P	-
--variation	g	d	g	d	G	-	-	-	D	-	-	-	G	-	-	-
conga 1	-	T	P	-	g	d	g	d	P	T	-	T	P	-	P	T
conga 2	P	-	P	T	-	T	P	-	g	d	g	d	P	T	-	T
quinto	P	T	-	T	P	-	P	T	-	T	P	-	g	d	g	d
junjun bell	x	-	x	-	x	-	x	-	x	-	x	-	x	-	x	-
junjun	O	-	-	O	-	-	O	-	O	-	-	O	-	-	O	-

Note: This piece functions as a kind of round. With the exception of the tumba variation, each successive conga part begins the tumba's phrase one primary downbeat later: conga 1 on the "2," conga 2 on the "3," and the quinto on the "4."

Village Dance (West Africa)

	1	.	*	.	2	.	*	.	3	.	*	.	4	.	*	.
djembe 1	G	-	-	d	-	-	g	-	G	d	g	-	g	d	P	T
djembe 2	g	-	g	d	-	-	-	D	g	-	g	d	P	-	P	T
bell (*son clave*)	x	-	-	x	-	-	x	-	-	-	x	-	x	-	-	-
									^ start							

Wollosidon (Mali--royal servants, dance of freedom; play with Jondon)

	1	.	*	.	2	.	*	.	3	.	*	.	4	.	*	.
djembe 1	G	-	G	-	P	T	P	T	g	d	-	d	-	d	g	-
--variation	G	D	-	D	P	-	T	-	G	D	-	D	-	d	g	
djembe 2	g	-	d	-	P	-	-	T	-	g	-	d	-	g	-	-
djembe 3	g	d	P	T	-	-	P	T	g	d	P	T	-	-	P	T
junjun/bell	O	-	O	-	x	-	-	-	O	O	-	-	x	-	-	-

Yembela (rain song)

	1	.	*	.	2	.	*	.	3	.	*	.	4	.	*	.
low drum	G	-	T	-	g	-	T	-	G	-	T	-	g	d	P	-
mid drum	G	-	g	d	-	-	P	-	G	-	g	d	-	-	P	-
high drum	g	-	P	T	g	-	P	T	g	-	P	T	g	-	P	T
junjun bell	-	-	x	x	-	-	x	x	-	-	x	x	-	-	x	x
junjun	O	-	O	O	-	-	-	-	O	-	O	O	-	-	-	-

4/4 - Afro-Latin

Banda (Haiti)

	1	.	*	.	2	.	*	.	3	.	*	.	4	.	*	.
bell	x	-	-	x	-	-	x	-	x	-	-	x	-	-	x	-
drum	G	-	-	-	G	-	T	-	P	-	T	-	G	-	-	-
kenkeni bell/stick	x	-	x	x	-	x	x	-	x	-	x	x	-	x	x	-
kenkeni	-	O	-	O	O	-	-	-	-	O	-	O	O	-	-	-
junjun bell/stick	x	-	-	x	-	-	x	-	x	-	-	x	-	-	x	-
junjun	O	-	-	-	-	-	O	-	O	-	-	-	-	-	O	-

Bossa Nova (Brazil)

	1	.	*	.	2	.	*	.	3	.	*	.	4	.	*	.
clave	x	-	-	x	-	-	x	-	-	-	x	-	x	-	-	-
junjun	O	-	x	O	O	-	x	O	O	-	x	O	O	(O)	x	O
drum rim	k	-	-	k	-	-	k	-	-	-	k	-	k	-	-	-
conga 1	P	-	-	d	G	-	-	-	P	-	-	d	G	-	-	-
conga 2	G	(d)	g	d	G	d	-	T	-	T	(g)	d	G	d	g	(d)
conga 3	G	-	g	D	G	-	g	-	G	-	g	D	G	-	g	-
--variation	G	-	g	D	G	-	g	D	-	D	g	d	G	-	g	d
percussion	x	x	x	x	x	x	x	x	x	x	x	x	x	x	x	x

Baião (Brazil) [note similarity of name and parts to Baye (Congo)]

	1	.	*	.	**2**	.	*	.	**3**	.	*	.	**4**	.	*	.
bell 1	-	-	H	-	L	-	H	-	-	H	-	H	L	-	H	-
bell 2	o	-	x	-	o	-	x	-	o	-	x	-	o	-	x	-
triangle	-	-	x	x	-	-	x	x	-	-	x	x	-	-	x	x
cabasa	x	-	x̲	x	x	-	x̲	x	x	-	x̲	x	x	-	x̲	x
maracas	x	-	-	x	x	-	-	-	x	-	-	x	x	-	-	-
snare (r = roll)	X	x	x	X	x	x	X	r	X	x	x	X	x	x	X	x
pandeiro	G	d	-	D	g	-	P	-	G	d	-	D	g	-	P	-
bongos	g	d	g	d	G̲	-	-	-	g	-	-	d	G̲	-	-	-
conga	P	-	d	P	T	-	G	-	P	-	d	P	T	-	G	-
basic drum	O	-	-	O	-	-	O̲	-	O	-	-	O	-	-	O̲	-
			(o̲	-	-	O)						(o̲	-	-	O)	
high drum	(G)	-	P	d	P	d	P	T	(G)	-	P	d	P	d	P	T
	(G)	-	P	d	P	d	P	T	g	T	P	d	P	d	P	T
low drum	(G)	-	P	d	g	-	T	-	(G)	-	P	d	g	-	T	-
drum variations...	P	-	g	d	g	-	G	-	P	-	g	d	g	-	G	-
	g	-	P	d	g	-	g	-	g	-	P	d	g	-	g	-
	P	-	g	d	g	d	-	d	P	-	g	d	g	d	-	d
	gd	gd	g	d	g	d	-	d	gd	gd	g	d	g	d	-	d
	g	d	-	d	g	d	-	d	g	d	-	d	g	d	-	d
	g	d	g	T	g	d	P	d	g	d	g	T	g	d	P	d

Bomba (Puerto Rico)

	1	.	*	.	**2**	.	*	.	**3**	.	*	.	**4**	.	*	.
clave	x	-	-	x	-	-	x	-	-	-	x	-	x	-	-	-
bell	x	-	x	-	x	-	x	-	x	-	x	-	x	-	x	-
small bell	-	-	x	x	-	-	x	x	-	-	x	x	-	-	x	x
large bell	x̲	x̲	-	x	-	x	x	-	x	x	-	x	x	x	x	-
shaker	x	-	x̲	-	x	-	x̲	-	x	-	x̲	-	x	-	x̲	-
guiro	d	-	d	u	d	-	d	u	d	-	d	u	d	-	d	u
drum (sticks)	x	-	x	-	x	x	x	x	x	-	x	x	x	-	-	x
drum	-	-	P T	-	-	-	G D	-	-	-	P T	-	-	-	g d	-
quinto/bongo	-	-	-	g	-	g	d	-	-	-	-	g	-	g	d	-
conga/djembe	G	T	-	T	-	d	g	-	G	T	-	T	-	d	g	-
low conga	g	d	G	T	P	-	g	-	-	-	T	g	T	P	-	g	-
--variation	g	d	g	T	-	D	G	-	g	d	g	T	-	D	G	-
junjun	-	-	O	-	-	-	O	-	-	-	O	-	-	-	O	-

Calypso (Trinidad)

	1	.	*	.	2	.	*	.	3	.	*	.	4	.	*	.	
clave	-	-	x	-	x	-	-	-	x	-	-	x	-	-	x	-	
bell	-	-	x	x	-	-	x	x	-	-	x	x	-	-	x	x	
high bell	x	x	-	x	x	x	x	-	x	x	-	x	x	x	x	-	
tumba	G	(D)	-	D	(G)	d	P	-	G	(D)	-	D	(G)	d	P	-	
--variations...	g	d	-	T	g	d	G	-	g	d	-	T	g	d	G	-	
	g	-	D	-	-	g	D	-	g	-	D	-	-	g	D	-	
	-	-	-	-	-	-	g	-	-	-	-	-	g	-	-	-	
low conga	G	-	-	D	G	-	-	-	-	D	-	D	G	D	-	-	
mid conga	P	-	-	g	T	-	D	-	P	-	-	g	T	-	D	-	
--variations...	g	-	-	d	g	-	D	-	g	-	-	d	g	-	G	-	
	G	-	-	D	G	-	g	-	G	-	-	D	G	-	g	-	
			(d)								(d)						
	P	-	d	P	-	d	P	-	d	P	-	d	P	-	d	P	>
	-	d	P	-	d	P	-	d	:|								
high conga	g	d	-	-	g	d	-	-	g	d	-	-	g	d	-	-	
quinto	P	-	-	-	-	-	-	-	g	-	-	-	-	-	-	-	>
	g	-	g	-	-	-	-	-	g	-	g	-	-	-	-	-	
bongos	g	-	g	D	-	D	P	D	g	D	g	d	g	D	G	d	

Comparsa (Cuba--Carnaval)

version1:	1	.	*	.	2	.	*	.	3	.	*	.	4	.	*	.
clave	-	-	x	-	x	-	-	-	x	-	-	x	-	-	-	x
bell	L	-	L	-	H	H	-	L	-	L	L	-	H	-	H	-
--variation	H	-	H	-	L	L	-	-	H	H	-	-	L	-	H	L
surdo	o	-	-	o	-	-	o	-	o	-	-	O	-	-	o	-
--variation	O	-	-	-	-	-	-	-	-	-	-	-	O	-	-	-
tumba	g	-	-	T	P	-	-	T	P	-	-	T	g	-	g	-
			(D)				(D)				(D)					
conga	-	-	P	T	-	-	g	d	-	-	P	T	-	-	g	d
quinto	-	T	P	-	d	g	-	T	-	P	-	-	-	d	-	g
--variation	G	D	g	-	g	d	g	-	G	D	g	-	g	d	g	-
version 2:																
clave	x	-	-	x	-	-	-	x	-	-	x	-	x	-	-	-
bell	H	H	H	H	L	-	-	H	H	-	H	-	L	-	-	H
tumba	G	-	-	-	G	-	d	-	G	-	-	-	G	-	d	-
--variation	G	-	d	-	G	-	d	-	G	-	d	P	-	-	d	-
conga	g	-	-	-	d	-	g	-	D	-	-	-	D	-	-	d
quinto	-	T	P	-	d	-	g	-	d	-	g	-	T	P	-	P
Comparsa,	1	.	*	.	2	.	*	.	3	.	*	.	4	.	*	.

version 3:																
clave	x	-	-	x	-	-	x	-	-	-	x	-	x	-	-	-
conga	-	-	-	-	g	-	d	-	-	-	-	-	g	d	-	-
tumba	-	g	d	-	-	-	-	-	g	-	d	-	-	-	-	g

Conga (Cuba) [note similarity of name and parts to Ekonga (Congo)]

	1	.	*	.	2	.	*	.	3	.	*	.	4	.	*	.
clave	x	-	x	-	-	-	x	-	-	x	-	-	x	-	-	-
--variation	-	-	-	x	x	-	x	-	-	-	-	x	x	-	x	-
cowbell 1	o	-	-	-	x	x	x	x	o	-	-	o	-	x	-	x
cowbell 2	x	-	x	-	o	-	-	x	-	x	-	-	o	-	o	-
djembe	G	-	g	D	g	D	g	D	g	-	-	D	-	-	g	-
--variation	g	-	G	D	g	-	G	D	g	-	-	T	-	-	g	d
quinto	G	-	P	T	-	-	g	d	-	-	P	T	G	-	g	-
conga	G	-	d	-	P	-	d	-	P	-	-	D	-	-	-	-
--variation	G	-	d	-	(G)	-	d	-	G	-	d	P	-	-	(d)	-
tumba	-	-	-	D	G	-	P	-	-	-	-	D	G	-	P	-
tamboura	G	D	G	D	G	D	G	D	G	-	G	D	-	-	G	-
junjun bell	x	-	x	-	x	x	-	-	x	x	-	x	x	-	-	-
junjun	-	-	O	-	-	-	O	-	O	-	-	O	O	-	-	-
percussion	-	-	x	-	-	-	x	-	-	-	x	-	-	-	x	-
percussion	x	-	-	-	x	-	-	-	x	-	-	x	-	-	-	-

Eleggua (Santeria; see also in 12/8)

	1	.	*	.	2	.	*	.	3	.	*	.	4	.	*	.
drum 1	G	-	-	d	G	-	d	-	G	-	P	-	-	d	-	-
drum 2	g	d	g	D	-	-	-	-	g	-	d	-	P	-	-	-
junjun bell	-	-	x	-	x	-	-	-	x	-	-	-	x	-	x	-
junjun	O	-	-	O	-	-	O	-	-	-	O	-	O	-	-	-

Guaguanco (Cuba)

	1	.	*	.	2	.	*	.	3	.	*	.	4	.	*	.
bell	x	-	x	x	-	x	-	x	x	-	x	-	x	x	-	x
clave	-	-	x	-	x	-	-	-	x	-	-	x	-	-	x	-
--variations...	x	-	-	x	-	-	x	-	-	-	x	-	x	-	-	-
	x	-	x	x	-	x	-	x	x	-	x	-	x	x	-	x
mid conga	G	-	-	D	-	-	P	-	-	-	-	D	G	-	P	-
--variation	P	-	-	T	-	-	g	-	G	-	-	D	(G)	(d)	g	-
tumba	G	-	-	D	G	-	d	-	G	-	-	D	G	-	d	-
--variations...													(T)			
	G	-	d	G	-	G	T	-	G	-	d	-	G	-	T	-
...Guaguanco...	1	.	*	.	2	.	*	.	3	.	*	.	4	.	*	.

conga 1	G	D	g	d	G	D	G	D	G	D	g	d	G	D	G	D
conga 2	G	-	D	-	G	d	-	-	G	D	G	D	G	d	-	-
--variation	G	-	T	-	T	P	-	T	P	-	T	-	T	-	g	d
quinto	G	-	g	D	-	d	P	-	(G)	d	P	-	g	T	-	d
drum variations...	G	-	d	G	d	-	G	d	g	-	d	g	d	-	G	d
	(P)			(P)												
	G	-	D	G	D	-	G	D	g	-	D	g	D	-	G	D
	-	g	d	-	-	-	-	P	-	-	-	g	-	-	-	-
	-	P	T	-	-	g	-	g	-	-	-	P	-	-	-	-
junjun	-	-	-	-	-	-	o	-	o	-	-	o	o	-	O	-

Ibo (Haiti; see also in 12/8)

	1	.	*	.	2	.	*	.	3	.	*	.	4	.	*	.
clave	x	-	-	x	-	-	x	-	-	-	x	-	x	-	-	-
sticks	x	-	x	x	-	-	x	x	x	-	x	x	-	-	x	x
--variation	x	-	x	-	x	-	-	-	x	-	x	-	x	-	-	-
sticks on drum	x	-	x	x	-	x	x	-	x	-	x	x	-	x	x	-
bell	x	x	-	x	x	-	x	-	x	-	x	-	x	-	x	-
--variation	x	-	x	-	x	x	-	x	x	-	x	-	x	x	-	x
tumba	G	-	d	-	G	-	d	-	G	-	d	-	g	d	-	-
conga	g	d	-	d	G	-	g	d	G	-	g	d	G	-	g	-
--variation	g	d	-	d	g	-	(g)	D	g	-	g	(d)	g	-	(g)	D
quinto	g	-	g	d	-	d	g	-	P	-	P	T	-	T	P	-
--variation	g	-	g	d	g	-	g	d	g	-	g	d	g	-	g	d
junjun	M	-	O	-	M	-	-	-	M	-	-	-	M	-	-	-

Ijexa (Brazil)

[Play bass notes to muffle slaps]	1	.	*	.	2	.	*	.	3	.	*	.	4	.	*	.	
conga	P	-	-	D	P	-	g	D	P	-	-	D	P	-	g	D	>|
	P	-	-	D	P	-	g	-	g	d	-	D	P	-	g	D	
tumba	P	-	-	d	g	-	G	-	P	-	-	d	g	-	G	-	>
	P	-	-	d	g	-	G	-	g	d	g	d	g	-	G	-	
bell	H	-	H	-	L	-	L	-	H	H	-	L	-	L	L	-	
--variations...	H	H	H	-	L	L	-	H	-	H	H	-	L	-	L	-	
	-	-	H	H	H	-	L	L	-	H	-	L	-	L	L	-	
(or rev. HL)	H	-	H	-	L	L	-	H	-	H	H	-	L	-	L	-	
(or rev. HL)	H	H	-	L	-	L	L	-	H	-	H	-	L	-	L	-	

Mambo (Cuba)

	1	.	*	.	**2**	.	*	.	**3**	.	*	.	**4**	.	*	.
clave	-	-	x	-	x	-	-	-	x	-	-	x	-	-	x	-
--variation	x	-	-	x	-	-	x	-	-	-	x	-	x	-	-	-
cowbell (fast)	-	-	x	-	-	-	x	x	-	-	x	-	-	-	x	x
--variation	x	-	x	x	-	x	-	x	x	-	x	-	x	x	-	x
quinto (fast)	G	-	T	-	g	-	g	d	G	-	T	-	g	(d)	g	d
bell	L	-	H	H	L	-	H	H	L	-	H	-	L	-	H	H
--slow variation 1	x	-	x	-	x	x	-	x	x	-	x	-	-	x	-	x
--slow variation 2	x	-	x	-	x	x	-	x	-	x	x	x	-	x	x	x
conga (slow)	g	D	P	-	G	d	g	d	G	d	P	-	G	d	g	d
junjun	O	-	o	O	o	-	-	-	o	-	-	O	-	-	-	o
--variation	O	-	O	-	-	-	-	-	-	-	o	-	-	-	-	-

Merengue (Dominican Republic)

	1	.	*	.	**2**	.	*	.	**3**	.	*	.	**4**	.	*	.
clave	-	-	-	x	x	-	x	x	x	-	x	-	-	-	-	-
bell	-	-	-	-	x	-	-	-	x	-	-	-	-	-	-	-
drum 1	G	D	G	D	G	-	d	P	d	-	G	-	d	-	P	-
--variation	G	D	G	D	G	-	-	d	g	-	d	-	g	-	d	-
drum 2	O	-	-	-	-	-	-	-	-	-	-	-	O	O	O	O
--variation	g	-	-	D	P	-	g	-	G	-	T	-	g	d	g	d

Mozambique (Cuba)

	1	.	*	.	**2**	.	*	.	**3**	.	*	.	**4**	.	*	.
clave	x	-	-	x	-	-	-	x	-	-	x	-	x	-	-	-
--variation	-	-	x	-	x	-	-	-	x	-	-	x	-	-	x	-
bell	o	-	o	-	x	-	-	o	-	o	-	x	-	-	x	-
--variations...	o	-	o	-	o	o	-	o	-	o	o	-	o	o	-	o
					(x	x)							(x	x)		
	o	-	x	-	o	-	x	o	-	x	x	x	o	-	x	x
	o	-	o	-	x	x	x	x	o	o	-	x	x	x	x	x
	L	-	L	-	H	H	-	L	-	L	-	-	H	-	H	-
tumba	G	-	-	D	-	-	G	-	-	-	-	D	-	-	G	-
--variations...	-	-	-	T	-	-	P	-	-	-	-	D	-	-	P	-
	G	-	T	G	d	g	D	P	D	-	-	-	g	-	-	-
	G	-	g	d	G	D	-	D	-	D	g	d	g	-	P	d
conga	-	-	P	-	-	T	-	P	-	T	P		g	d	-	T
--variation	G	-	-	-	d	-	-	-	G	T	P	d	g	d	G	T
quinto	-	-	g	d	-	-	P	T	-	-	g	d	-	-	P	T
bass/junjun	O	-	-	O	-	-	O	-	O	-	-	O	-	-	O	-

Oggun (Santeria)

	1	.	*	.	2	.	*	.	3	.	*	.	4	.	*	.
bell	x	-	-	x	-	-	-	x	-	-	x	-	x	-	-	-
high drum	P	-	-	d	P	-	-	-	P	-	d	-	P	-	-	-
mid drum	P	-	-	-	T	-	-	-	P	-	-	-	gf	-	-	-
low drum	P	-	-	-	g	-	T	-	g	-	D	-	g	-	-	-

Pilon (Cuba)

	1	.	*	.	2	.	*	.	3	.	*	.	4	.	*	.	
clave	x	-	-	x	-	-	x	-	-	-	x	-	x	-	-	-	
bell	H	-	L	L	H	-	L	L	H	-	-	-	-	-	-	-	
conga	G	d	P	d	(G)	d	G	D	g	-	P	T	g	d	G	-	
junjun	-	-	-	-	-	-	-	(O)	O)	-	-	O	-	-	O	O	
quinto (*mute bass*)	G	-	D	-	G	-	D	-	G	-	D	-	G	-	-	-	>
	-	-	D	-	P	-	-	-	G	-	d	-	g	-	D	-	
tumba	-	-	-	-	-	-	-	-	-	-	-	-	-	D	-		>
	g	-	-	-	-	-	D	-	-	-	-	-	-	-	-	-	

Ra Ra (Haiti)

	1	.	*	.	2	.	*	.	3	.	*	.	4	.	*	.	
bell	x	-	x	x	-	-	x	-	x	-	x	x	-	-	x	-	
high drum	g	d	g	d	g	d	P	d	g	d	g	d	g	d	P	d	
mid drum	g	d	-	P	D	g	T	-	G	-	T	-	G	-	T	-	
low drum	G	-	-	-	D	-	-	-	G	-	-	-	G	-	D	-	>
	G	-	-	-	G	-	d	-	g	-	D	-	g	-	d	-	
junjun	O	-	-	-	o	-	-	-	M	-	M	-	o	-	-	-	

Rumba (Cuba)

	1	.	*	.	2	.	*	.	3	.	*	.	4	.	*	.
clave	x	-	-	x	-	-	x	-	-	-	x	-	x	-	-	-
cowbell	o	-	-	-	x	-	-	-	o	-	-	-	x	-	-	-
guiro	d	-	d	u	d	-	d	u	d	-	d	u	d	-	d	u
sticks	X	-	x	X	-	x	-	X	x	-	X	-	X	x	-	x
conga	G	-	T	-	(g)	-	g	d	G	-	T	-	(g)	-	g	d
tumba	G	-	-	D	G	-	g	-	G	(d)	-	D	G	-	g	-
quinto	G	-	G	D	G	-	G	D	g	-	G	d	G	-	G	D

Rumba Yesa (Cuba)

	1	.	*	.	2	.	*	.	3	.	*	.	4	.	*	.
high bell	X	-	X	-	o	o	-	-	X	-	X	-	o	o	-	-
low bell	-	-	X	X	-	-	X	X	-	o	-	o	-	-	X	X
bell variation	-	L	-	L	-	-	H	H	-	-	H	H	-	-	H	H
quinto (stick)	O	O	-	-	O	O	-	-	O	O	-	-	O	O	-	-
conga (stick)	-	-	-	-	-	-	O	O	-	-	-	-	-	-	O	-
conga 1	G	-	-	-	g	-	G	D	-	d	g	d	-	-	G	-
conga 2	G	-	-	D	(G)	-	g	-	G	-	-	D	(G)	-	g	-
--variation												(-	g	d	g	d)
conga 3	G	-	d	d	G	-	d	d	G	-	d	d	G	-	d	d
conga 4	P	T	-	-	P	T	-	-	P	T	-	-	P	T	-	-
tumba	P	-	-	D	g	-	g	(D)	P	-	-	D	g	-	g	(D)
--variation	g	-	-	T	-	-	P	-	-	D	G	D	-	-	g	d
junjun bell	-	-	X	X	-	-	X	X	-	-	X	X	-	-	X	X
	(-	X	-)													
junjun	O	-	-	O	-	-	O	-	-	-	-	-	-	-	O	-

Samba (Brazil)

	1	.	*	.	2	.	*	.	3	.	*	.	4	.	*	.
surdo	M	-	-	-	O	-	-	M	M	-	-	-	O	-	-	M
basic bell	H	-	H	-	L	L	-	H	-	H	-	L	L	-	L	-
basic drum	g	-	g	-	G	-	-	d	-	d	-	T	G	-	G	-
				(d)									(D	-	D	G)
accompaniment	G	d	P	d	-	-	d	G	d	P	d	-	-	d	-	d
--variation	G	-	P	T	G	-	g	d	G	-	P	T	G	-	g	d
djembe	g	-	g	d	P	-	(G)	d	-	d	-	d	P	-	G	-
--variation 1	g	-	P	D	G	-	P	d	-	d	P	D	G	-	P	-
--variation 2	P	-	G	D	g	-	P	T	-	d	G	D	g	-	P	-
conga 1	P	-	-	d	G	-	(P)	-	P	-	-	d	G	-	(P)	-
conga 2	P	-	P	d	G	-	G	D	P	-	P	d	G	-	G	D
conga 3	G	-	g	-	T	-	-	G	T	-	-	g	D	-	D	-
tumba	G	-	-	-	g	-	-	-	G	-	-	d	g	d	-	-
			(D)										(-	g)		
guiro	d	u	d	u	d	u	d	u	d	u	d	u	d	u	d	u
shaker	X	-	X	X	X	-	X	X	X	-	X	X	X	-	X	X
clave/stick on rim	k	-	k	-	-	k	-	k	-	k	-	-	k	-	k	-
bell/cymbal	-	x	-	-	x	-	x	-	x	-	x	-	-	x	-	x
junjun	O	-	x	O	O	-	x	O	O	-	x	O	O	-	x	O
													(O)			

...Samba...	1	.	*	.	2	.	*	.	3	.	*	.	4	.	*	.
bell variations...	H	-	H	-	L	L	-	H	-	H	-	L	-	L	L	-
	H	-	H	-	L	L	-	H	-	H	-	H	L	-	L	-
	L	-	L	-	H	H	-	L	-	L	-	H	-	H	H	-
	L	-	H	-	H	-	L	L	-	H	-	H	H	-	L	-
	H	-	H	-	L	-	L	-	H	H	-	L	-	L	L	-
	H	-	L	L	-	H	-	H	-	-	-	L	L	-	H	-
	H	-	L	L	L	H	-	H	-	-	-	L	L	-	H	-

>

Samba--Batucada [note similarity of name and parts to Batakato (Nigeria)]

	1	.	*	.	2	.	*	.	3	.	*	.	4	.	*	.
surdo	O	-	-	-	O	-	-	-	O	-	-	-	O	-	(O)	-
shaker	x	-	x	x	x	-	x	x	x	-	x	x	x	-	x	x
bongos	-	O	-	O	-	O	O	-	O	-	O	-	O	O	-	O
timbales	O	-	-	O	O	-	-	O	O	-	-	O	O	-	-	O
conga	P	-	-	-	d	-	-	-	P	-	-	-	d	-	-	-
--variation	g	d	P	d	G	D	P	D	g	d	P	d	G	D	P	D

Tumbao

	1	.	*	.	2	.	*	.	3	.	*	.	4	.	*	.
Son style...																
clave	x	-	-	x	-	-	x	-	-	-	x	-	x	-	-	-
tumba	G	-	-	d	-	-	P	-	(P)	-	-	d	-	-	G	-
conga	g	-	P	D	(G)	-	P	(T)	g	-	P	D	(G)	-	P	-
Tango style...																
cowbell	o	-	o	-	x	x	-	o	-	o	-	x	-	x	x	-
tumba	g	-	-	T	G	-	P	-	g	-	-	T	G	-	P	-
conga 1	-	-	P	-	-	-	g	d	-	-	P	D	G	D	g	d
conga 2	g	-	P	d	-	T	g	T	-	T	P	-	g	d	-	T
junjun	-	-	-	O	-	-	O	-	-	-	-	O	-	-	O	-

4/4 - Middle Eastern

Beledi

	1	.	*	.	2	.	*	.	3	.	*	.	4	.	*	.
low drum	G	-	G	-	g	d	g	d	G	-	g	d	g	-	-	-
high drum	G	-	G	-	g	(d)	P	-	G	-	g	(d)	P	-	(g	d)
--variations...	G	d	g	-	-	-	d	d	G	-	d	d	g	-	d	d
	G	-	d	g	-	d	g	-	G	-	G	-	.P	-	-	-
junjun/bell	O	-	O	-	x	o	x	-	O	-	-	-	o	x	-	x

Falahi/Raqs Bambi (Egypt)

	1	.	*	.	2	.	*	.	3	.	*	.	4	.	*	.
drum 1	G	d	-	d	G	-	d	-	G	d	-	d	G	-	d	-
drum 2	P	-	g	d	g	-	P	-	P	-	g	d	g	-	P	-
Falahi (half-time)	G	-	P	-	-	-	P	-	G	-	(g	d)	P	-	(g	d)

Raqs Skandarai (Egypt)

	1	.	*	.	2	.	*	.	3	.	*	.	4	.	*	.	
drum 1	G	-	g	d	G	-	g	d	G	-	g	d	G	-	g	d	>
	G	-	g	d	G	-	g	d	P	-	g	d	g	-	d	-	
drum 2	P	-	g	d	P	-	g	d	P	-	g	d	P	-	g	d	>
	P	-	g	d	P	-	g	d	P	-	-	-	-	-	-	-	

[various]

	1	.	*	.	2	.	*	.	3	.	*	.	4	.	*	.	
Chiftateli	G	-	(g	d)	g	-	P	-	(g	d)	G	-	P	-	(g	d)	>
	G	-	(g	d)	G	-	(g	d)	P	-	-	-	-	-	-	-	
					(G	-)											
Guwazi (Egypt)	G	-	(g	d)	G	-	G	-	(g	d	g)	-	P	-	-	-	
--variation	G	-	P	-	(g	d)	G	-	G	-	(g	d)	P	-	(g	d)	
--variation	G	d	P	-	g	d	G	D	G	-	g	d	P	-	g	d	
Sombati	G	-	-	(d)	P	(d)	P	-	G	-	(d	d)	P	-	(g	d)	
Serto	G	-	g	D	-	d	g	d	G	-	g	T	-	d	g	d	
Masmoudi (Morocco)	G	-	g	d	G	-	g	d	P	(d)	g	d	P	-	g	d	>
	G	-	g	d	g	d	P	-	g	d	g	d	P	-	g	d	
--variations...	G	-	-	-	G	-	-	-	(P)	-	-	-	P	-	-	-	>
	G	-	g	d	g	-	P	-	g	d	g	-	P	-	-	-	
	G	-	g	d	G	-	-	-	g	d	g	d	P	-	g	-	>
	G	-	g	d	P	d	g	-	g	d	g	d	g	-	P	d	

12/8 - African

Abioueka (Guinea--small children)

	1	.	.	2	.	.	3	.	.	4	.	.	
djembe 1 (a)	G	-	D	-	P	T	-	T	-	d	g	-	X3
(>) (b)	G	d	g	D	g	d	G	d	g	D	g	d	
(b) variation	(G)	-	G	-	g	d	g	T	-	d	g	d	
djembe 2	P	-	T	-	g	d	-	T	-	d	g	-	
djembe 3	G	-	-	D	g	d	G	-	-	D	g	d	
djembe 4	P	T	P	-	g	d	P	T	P	-	g	d	
junjun bell	x	-	x	-	x	-	x	-	x	-	x	-	
junjun	O	-	O	-	-	-	-	-	-	-	-	-	
songba bell	x	-	x	-	x	x	-	x	-	x	x	-	
songba	-	-	-	-	O	O	-	M	-	O	O	-	
kenkeni bell	x	x	-	x	x	-	x	x	-	x	x	-	
--variation	x	-	x	x	-	x	x	-	x	x	-	x	
kenkeni	O	-	-	O	-	-	O	-	-	O	-	-	

Abondan (Guinea/Ivory Coast--welcome; played with Tiriba)

	1	.	.	2	.	.	3	.	.	4	.	.	
break	F	g	-	g	-	g	-	g	d	-	d	-	>
	-	F	-	F	-	F	-	-	-	-	P	-	
djembe 1	G	-	-	d	-	T	G	-	-	-	P	-	>
	G	d	g	d	g	T	G	-	-	-	P	-	
djembe 2	G	-	-	d	-	T	G	-	g	d	g	d	
												(T)	
kenkeni/bell	x	O	O	x	O	O	x	O	O	x	O	O	
songba/bell	M	-	x	O	-	O	x	-	M	-	M	-	>
	x	O	-	O	-	O	x	-	M	-	M	-	
junjun/bell	O	-	-	x	-	-	O	-	-	x	-	-	
junjun variation	O	-	-	o	-	o	-	-	O	-	O	-	>
	-	o	-	o	-	o	-	-	O	-	O	-	

Adowa (Ghana)

	1	.	.	2	.	.	3	.	.	4	.	.
bell	x	-	-	-	x	-	-	x	x	-	-	x
drum	g	-	g	d	P	-	g	T	g	d	P	
clap	-	-	-	-	x	-	-	x	-	-	x	-

Basikolo

	1	.	.	**2**	.	.	**3**	.	.	**4**	.	.
djembe 1	G	T	g	(d)	P	-	G	T	g	(d)	P	(T)
djembe 2	P	-	d	g	-	-	P	d	g	T	-	-
--variation	g	-	P	D	P	-	G	T	-	D	(g)	d
djembe 3	P	-	-	P	d	g	T	-	-	-	g	d
--variation	G	-	-	d	g	-	G	-	-	d	g	-
junjun bell	x	-	x	-	x	-	x	-	x	x	-	x
junjun	O	-	-	o	O	-	O	-	-	o	-	-
shaker	x	-	x	x	-	x	x	-	x	x	-	x

Batakato (Nigeria) [note similarity of name, parts to Batucada Samba (Brazil)]

	1	.	.	**2**	.	.	**3**	.	.	**4**	.	.
djembe 1	g	-	P	-	P	-	g	d	-	T	-	d
djembe 2	g	T	P	D	G	d	g	T	P	D	G	d
djembe 3	G	T	P	d	g	D	G	T	P	d	g	D
junjun	O	o	o	O	o	o	O	o	o	O	o	o
--or: ashiko	M	k	k	M	k	k	M	k	k	M	-	O

Baye (Congo) [note similarity of name and parts to Baião (Brazil)]

	1	.	.	**2**	.	.	**3**	.	.	**4**	.	.		
bell	x	-	x	-	x	x	-	x	-	x	-	x		
high drum	P	-	d	P	-	-	P	T	-	Pt	g	d		
high-mid drum	g	d	-	(D)	P	T	g	d	-	(D)	P	T	>	
	g	d	-	Pt	g	d	g	d	-	(D)	P	T		
low-mid drum	G	-	d	-	P	-	G	T	g	d	P	-		
junjun	o	-	O	-	M	-	O	-	-	O	-	o		
--or: low drum	d	-	G	-	P	-	D	-	-	D	-	g	>	
	-	-	T	G	-	-	D	-	-	D	-	g		

Bintin (Ghana)

	1	.	.	**2**	.	.	**3**	.	.	**4**	.	.
bell	x	-	x	-	x	x	-	x	-	x	-	x
low drum	g	d	g	d	g	-	G	D	G	D	G	-
songba	O	-	-	M	-	-	O	-	-	M	-	-
songba w/ stick	-	O	O	-	O	O	-	O	O	-	O	O
mid drum	-	-	G	-	g	-	-	-	G	-	g	-
mid drum w/ stick	O	-	-	O	-	-	O	-	-	O	-	-
high drum	G	-	g	T	P	-	g	d	g	T	P	-

Djaa (Guinea--victory, wealth, success)

	1	.	.	**2**	.	.	**3**	.	.	**4**	.	.	
djembe 1	P	-	g	T	-	-	P	-	g	T	-	-	
djembe 2	P	-	P	T	g	d	P	-	P	T	g	d	
bell	x	-	-	x	-	-	x	-	-	x	-	-	
songba bell	x	-	x	-	x	-	x	x	-	x	-	x	
songba	O	-	O	-	O	-	-	M	-	M	-	-	
kenkeni bell	x	x	-	x	x	-	x	x	-	x	x	-	
kenkeni	O	O	-	M	-	-	O	O	-	M	-	-	
junjun bell	x	-	x	x	-	x	x	-	x	x	-	x	
junjun	O	-	O	O	-	-	-	-	(O	O)	-	O	
--variation	o	-	O	-	o	-	O	O	-	o	o	O	>
	O	-	-	o	-	-	o	-	-	-	-	O	

Djabara

	1	.	.	**2**	.	.	**3**	.	.	**4**	.	.	
djembe 1	g	T	-	D	P	-	g	T	-	D	P	-	
djembe 2	P	-	g	d	-	-	P	-	g	d	-	-	
kenkeni bell	x	x	-	x	x	-	x	x	-	x	x	-	
kenkeni	M	-	-	O	O	-	M	-	-	O	O	-	
songba bell	x	-	x	-	x	-	x	-	x	x	-	x	
songba	O	-	M	-	M	-	M	-	O	O	-	O	
junjun bell	x	-	x	-	x	-	x	-	x	x	-	x	
junjun	O	-	-	-	-	-	O	-	-	-	-	-	
--variation	O	-	o	-	o	-	o	-	O	O	-	O	
break	PT	P	T	-	g	-	d	-	T	P	-	T	>
	P	-	-	-	-	T	P	-	T	P	-	-	
(break: ensemble)	-	-	-	-	-	x	x	-	x	x	-	-	

[Dununba--see next page]

Etumba Nambuaka (Congo)

	1	.	.	**2**	.	.	**3**	.	.	**4**	.	.	
bell	x	-	x	-	x	x	-	x	-	x	-	x	
tumba	G	-	G	-	g	d	-	T	-	T	g	d	
conga	g	-	P	d	P	T	g	-	P	d	P	T	
quinto	g	d	g	-	g	d	g	-	g	d	g	-	
mid break	P	T	P	-	P	T	P	-	gf	d	g	-	
end break	P	T	P	-	P	T	P	-	P	T	P	-	>
	P	T	P	-	gf	d	g	-	g	d	g	-	Pt

Dununba (Guinea--strong men, disputes)

	1	.	.	2	.	.	3	.	.	4	.	.	
djembe 1	P	(d)	g	T	-	-	P	(d)	g	T	-	-	
--variations...	g	d	g	T	-	-	g	d	g	T	-	-	
	P	-	g	T	g	d	P	-	g	T	-	-	
	P	-	g	T	-	D	P	-	g	T	-	D	
			(P)						(P)				
	P	d	G	T	(g)	D	P	d	G	T	(g)	D	
	P	-	G	T	g	d	P	-	G	T	g	d	
	P	-	g	d	g	d	P	-	g	d	g	d	
djembe 2	P	-	-	T	g	d	P	-	-	T	g	d	
--variations...	(G)	-	P	-	g	T	-	-	P	-	g	T	
	G	d	g	d	P	-	G	d	g	d	P	-	
djembe 3	-	-	P	-	g	T	-	-	P	-	g	T	
--variations...	-	-	g	-	P	T	-	D	g	-	G	(T)	
	-	g	d	-	P	T	-	G	D	-	G	D	
bell	x	-	x	-	x	x	-	x	-	x	x	-	
kenkeni/bell	(x)	-	O	-	O	O	(x)	(x)	O	-	O	O	
songba/bell	O	-	O	O	-	(x)	-	(x)	O	-	O	-	>
	M	-	(x)	-	(x)	M	-	(x)	M	-	(x)	-	
junjun/bell	x	-	x	x	-	O	O	-	O	O	-	x	
kenkeni bell	-	x	x	-	x	x	-	x	x	-	x	x	
kenkeni	-	O	O	-	O	O	-	O	O	-	O	O	>
	-	O	-	-	-	-	-	-	-	-	-	-	
--variation	-	-	-	-	-	-	-	-	O	-	O	-	>
	O	-	-	-	-	-	-	-	-	-	-	-	
songba bell	x	-	x	x	-	x	-	x	x	-	x	-	>
	x	-	x	-	x	x	-	x	x	-	x	-	
--variation	x	-	x	x	-	x	x	-	x	x	-	x	
songba	O	-	-	M	-	-	O	-	-	M	-	-	
--variations...	M	-	-	-	-	-	-	-	O	O	-	-	>
	M	-	-	-	-	-	O	-	-	-	-	-	
	M	-	-	-	-	-	M	-	-	-	-	-	>
	O	-	-	-	-	-	O	-	O	O	-	-	
junjun bell, shaker	x	-	x	x	-	x	x	-	x	-	x	-	
--variations...	x	-	x	x	-	x	x	-	x	x	-	x	
	-	x	x	-	x	x	-	x	x	-	x	x	
junjun	O	-	-	O	-	-	o	-	o	-	(O)	-	
--variations...	o	-	-	-	-	O	o	-	O	-	-	-	
	-	O	O	-	-	-	-	O	O	-	O	O	>
	-	O	O	-	-	-	-	-	-	-	O	O	

Fume Fume (Ghana)

	1	.	.	2	.	.	3	.	.	4	.	.	
bell	x	-	x	-	x	-	-	x	-	x	-	-	
--variation	L	-	H	-	H	H	-	H	-	H	-	H	
shaker	x	-	-	-	-	-	x	-	-	-	-	-	
djembe 1	g	-	d	-	P	-	D	g	d	-	P	-	
--variation	g	-	d	(G)	P	-	g	D	G	(D)	P	-	
djembe 2	G	-	P	T	P	d	g	-	P	T	P	d	
high drum	G	-	D	-	g	d	G	-	D	-	g	d	
low drum	G	-	-	d	g	-	G	-	-	d	g	-	
--variations...	G	(d	g	d	g)	D	G	(d	g	d	g)	D	
	P	-	-	d	g	(D)	P	-	-	d	g	(D)	
break (Tetteh)	g	-	d	-	P	-							
				start		>	G	T	P	-	T	-	>
	G	-	T	-	P	-	G	T	P	-	T	-	>
	Gt	-	-	(-	-	-)	:|	X3					
	3rd time >			g	d	-	g	d	-	-	Pt	-	>
	g	d	-	g	d	-	g	d	-	-	Pt	-	

Jewe

	1	.	.	2	.	.	3	.	.	4	.	.
bell	x	-	x	-	x	x	-	x	-	x	-	x
low drum	G	-	g	d	-	(D)	G	-	g	d	-	(D)
mid drum	G	d	g	D	g	d	G	d	g	D	g	d
drum w/ stick	D	x	x	D	x	x	D	x	x	D	-	T
high drum	P	-	P	T	g	d	P	-	P	T	g	d
	(G)								(PT	PT)		

Kakilambe (Guinea--masked figure protecting forest; see 4/4 version, Senegal)

	1	.	.	2	.	.	3	.	.	4	.	.	
break	Pt	P	T	P	T	-	gd	g	d	g	d	-	>
	gf	g	d	g	d	-	g	d	-	d	-	-	
--variation	gd	g	d	g	d	-	g	d	-	g	d	-	
bell	L	-	L	-	L	-	H	-	-	H	-	-	
djembe 1	G	-	d	g	T	-	G	d	-	g	T	-	
djembe 2	G	-	G	-	G	-	(G)	d	-	g	T	-	
--variations...	G	-	-	-	P	-	-	d	-	g	d	-	>
	G	-	G	-	G	-	-	d	-	g	T	-	
	G	-	-	-	P	-	-	g	-	d	g	-	>
	P	-	g	d	g	d	P	D	-	D	-	D	

...Kakilambe...	1	.	.	2	.	.	3	.	.	4	.	.	
djembe 3	P	-	d	g	-	T	P	-	d	g	-	T	>|
	P	-	d	g	-	T	G	d	-	g	-	T	
--variation	-	-	P	-	g	T	-	-	P	-	g	T	
djembe 4	g	-	-	D	-	-	G	-	-	D	-	d	
junjun bell	x	-	x	-	x	-	(x)	x	-	(x)	x	-	
--variation	x	-	-	-	x	-	-	x	-	x	x	-	>|
	x	-	x	-	x	-	-	x	-	-	-	-	
junjun	O	-	O	-	O	-	-	-	-	-	-	-	>|
	O	-	-	-	-	-	-	-	-	-	-	-	
--variation	O	-	-	-	o	-	-	-	-	-	-	-	>|
	O	-	O	-	O	-	-	o	-	-	-	-	
junjun/bell	O	-	O	-	O	-	O	o	-	o	-	o	>|
	O	-	-	-	O	o	O	o	O	x	-	x	

Linjen (W. Africa; play with Sedeba)

	1	.	.	2	.	.	3	.	.	4	.	.	
high drum	g	-	g	T	(g	d)	g	-	g	T	(g	d)	
--variation	g	-	P	T	-	d	g	-	P	T	-	d	
mid drum	G	-	G	T	g	d	G	-	G	T	g	d	
--variation	P	-	P	D	g	d	P	-	P	D	g	d	
low drum	-	g	d	-	d	g	-	g	d	-	d	g	
--variation	G	-	D	-	g	-	G	-	D	-	g	d	
shaker	x	-	x	-	x	-	x	-	x	-	x	-	
junjun	O	-	O	x	-	(x)	O	-	O	x	-	(x)	
--variation	O	-	-	-	-	-	O	-	-	-	-	-	
songba	-	-	O	-	-	-	-	-	O	-	-	-	
kenkeni	-	-	-	-	O	-	-	-	-	-	O	-	
break	P	-	P	-	P	-	P	-	-	T	-	-	>|
	P	-	-	-	-	d	g	d	g	d	-	-	

Mandjani (Guinea--virgin girl dancers; introduce with Dennadon)

<25-Man.mp3>	1	.	.	2	.	.	3	.	.	4	.	.
high djembe	P	-	g	T	-	-	P	-	g	T	-	-
--variations...			(G)			(D)			(G)			(D)
	P	-	-	d	g	d	P	-	-	d	g	d
				(T)						(T)		
mid djembe	P	T	-	-	-	-	T	P	-	G	-	D
--variation	P	T	-	-	-	-	P	T	G	-	D	-
low/mid djembe	T	-	P	-	d	g	T	-	P	-	d	g
low djembe	P	-	-	T	P	-	-	D	P	T	g	d
...Mandjani...	1	.	.	2	.	.	3	.	.	4	.	.

kenkeni bell	x	-	x	x	-	x	x	-	x	x	-	x	
kenkeni	O	-	-	-	-	O	O	-	-	-	-	O	
--variations...	-	-	O	-	(o)	O	-	-	O	-	(o)	O	
	x	-	x	x	-	x	x	-	x	-	x	-	
	O	-	-	O	-	-	O	-	-	-	-	-	>
	-	-	-	-	-	-	-	-	-	-	-	O	
	O	-	x	x	-	O	O	-	x	x	-	O	
kenkeni/songba	-	-	O	o	-	o	o	-	-	-	-	-	>
	-	-	O	-	o	-	O	-	-	-	-	-	
songba/bell	O	-	O	-	x	M	-	x	O	-	O	-	
junjun/bell	O	-	x	-	-	O	O	-	x	O	-	x	
--variation	-	x	x	-	x	x	-	O	O	-	O	O	
songba bell	x	-	x	-	x	x	-	x	x	-	x	-	
songba	O	-	O	-	-	M	-	-	M	-	O	-	
junjun bell	x	-	x	-	x	x	-	x	-	x	-	x	
--variations...	x	-	x	x	-	x	x	-	x	-	x	-	
	-	x	x	-	x	x	-	x	x	-	x	x	
junjun	O	-	-	O	-	-	O	-	-	-	-	O	
--variations...	-	-	-	-	-	-	-	-	-	-	-	O	>
	O	-	O	-	O	-	O	-	-	(M)	-	-	
	O	-	-	-	-	-	-	-	-	O	-	-	
	-	O	O	-	-	-	-	-	-	-	O	O	
	O	-	o	-	O	O	O	-	o	-	O	O	

Maraka (Mali--women: marriage and baptism)

	1	.	.	**2**	.	.	**3**	.	.	**4**	.	.
djembe 1	G	-	g	d	P	-	G	-	g	d	P	-
--variations...	G	T	g	d	P	-	G	T	-	G	T	-
	g	d	P	-	P	-	g	T	-	D	P	-
djembe 2	P	-	g	T	-	D	P	-	g	T	-	D
--variation	g	-	T	P	-	d	g	-	T	P	-	d
kenkeni	(M	-	M)	-	O	O	-	O	-	O	-	-
--variation	-	O	-	-	O	-	-	O	-	-	O	-
songba bell	x	-	x	x	-	x	x	x	-	x	-	x
songba	O	(O)	-	M	-	-	O	(O)	-	M	-	-
songba bell (var.)	x	-	x	x	-	x	-	x	-	x	x	-
songba (var.)	O	-	O	-	-	O	-	O	-	O	-	-
junjun bell	x	-	x	-	x	-	x	x	-	x	-	x
junjun	O	-	M	-	M	-	-	O	-	O	-	O
--variation	-	O	-	O	-	O	O	-	M	-	M	-

Nantaloma (Guinea--challenge to youth)

	1	.	.	2	.	.	3	.	.	4	.	.	
high djembe	P	-	-	T	g	d	P	-	-	T	g	d	
low djembe	g	d	-	-	-	-	g	d	-	-	-	-	
junjun bell, kenkeni bell	-	x	x	-	x	x	-	x	x	-	x	x	
kenkeni	-	-	O	-	O	O	-	-	O	-	O	O	
junjun	-	-	-	-	O	O	-	O	O	-	-	-	>
	-	O	O	-	O	O	-	O	O	-	-	-	
songba bell	x	-	x	x	-	x	x	-	x	x	-	x	
songba	M	-	-	-	-	O	-	-	O	-	-	-	>
	O	-	O	-	-	O	-	-	O	-	-	-	

Nañigo

	1	.	.	2	.	.	3	.	.	4	.	.
bell	x	-	x	x	x	-	x	x	-	x	-	x
clave (rev. bell)	x	x	-	x	-	x	x	-	x	x	x	-
maracas	x	x	x	x	x	x	x	x	x	x	x	x
guiro	d	-	u	d	-	u	d	-	u	d	-	u
drum 1	g	-	G	d	-	D	g	D	P	d	G	T
drum 2	P	D	P	D	P	P	D	P	D	P	d	d
bongos (R=bass)	R	L	R	L	R	L	R	L	R	L	R	L
timbales: RH	x	x	x	x	x	x	x	x	x	x	x	x
timbales: LH	x	-	-	x	-	-	x	-	x	-	x	-
junjun and bell	X	-	-	X	-	-	X	-	-	X	-	-
shekere	X	-	-	X	-	-	X	-	-	X	-	-

N'kisi (Congo)

	1	.	.	2	.	.	3	.	.	4	.	.
drum 1	G	-	-	G	d	-	G	-	-	G	d	d
drum 2	g	d	-	d	-	d	g	-	(G	D)	G	D
drum 3	P	-	P	T	-	T	g	d	P	-	g	d

Sedeba (W. Africa; play with Linjen)

	1	.	.	2	.	.	3	.	.	4	.	.	
break	Pt	-	P	T	-	T	P	-	P	T	-	-	>
	Pt	-	-	-	g	d	g	d	g	d	-	-	
djembe 1	P	-	P	-	g	d	-	T	-	T	-	-	
djembe 2	g	-	g	T	-	-	g	-	g	T	-	-	
djembe 3	g	d	-	g	d	-	g	d	-	g	d	-	

...Sedeba...	1	.	.	2	.	.	3	.	.	4	.	.
junjun bell	x	-	x	-	-	-	x	-	x	-	-	-
junjun	O	-	O	-	-	-	O	-	O	-	-	-
junjun bell (var.)	-	-	-	-	x	x	-	x	-	x	-	-
junjun (var.)	O	-	O	-	O	O	-	O	-	O	-	-

Sofa (Guinea--dance of mounted warriors)

	1	.	.	2	.	.	3	.	.	4	.	.
djembe 1	P	-	G	d	g	-	P	-	G	d	g	-
djembe 2	g	d	P	T	G	T	g	d	P	D	P	-
djembe 3	g	d	P	T	P	-	-	-	P	T	P	-	>
	-	-	P	T	P	-	-	-	P	T	P	-

Soli [fast; see 4/4 for slow] (Guinea--circumcision)

	1	.	.	2	.	.	3	.	.	4	.	.
djembe 1	P	-	g	T	-	-	P	-	g	T	-	-
				(d)						(d)		
djembe 2	P	-	-	T	g	d	P	-	-	T	g	d
--variations...	G	d	g	D	P	-	G	d	g	D	P	-
	G	-	-	P	-	D	G	-	d	P	-	F
djembe 3	G	-	G	D	g	d	G	-	G	D	g	d
junjun bell	x	-	x	x	-	x	x	-	x	x	-	x
junjun	-	-	O	O	-	-	-	-	O	-	-	O
--variations...	O	-	-	-	(o)	-	-	-	O	-	(o)	-
	o	-	-	-	O	-	O	-	-	o	-	-
	O	-	-	o	-	-	O	-	-	o	-	-
songba bell	x	-	x	-	x	-	x	-	x	x	-	x
songba	O	-	-	-	M	-	M	-	-	O	-	-
--variation	-	-	-	-	O	-	-	-	-	-	O	-
kenkeni bell	x	-	-	x	-	-	x	-	-	x	-	-
kenkeni	-	-	-	-	O	O	-	-	-	-	O	O
kenkeni/bell	O	-	O	-	x	-	O	-	O	-	x	-
songba/bell	O	-	x	-	M	-	M	-	x	O	-	x
--variations...	O	-	x	-	O	O	-	O	-	O	-	x
	O	-	x	-	O	-	x	-	O	-	O	-
	O	-	x	-	O	-	O	-	x	-	O	-	>
	O	-	x	-	O	-	x	-	O	O	-	x
junjun/bell	O	-	O	-	x	-	x	-	O	O	-	O
--variations...	O	-	O	O	-	O	O	-	O	O	-	O
	O	-	O	O	-	O	-	O	-	O	-	O

Sorsornet (Guinea--girls' respect for mothers) <26-Sorsornet.mp3>

	1	.	.	2	.	.	3	.	.	4	.	.	
intro break	P	T	P	-	P	T	P	-	P	T	P	-	>
	P	T	P	-	g	-	d	-	g	-	d	-	
djembe 1	P	-	g	T	-	-	P	-	g	T	-	-	
djembe 2	P	-	-	T	g	d	P	-	-	T	g	d	>
	P	-	-	P	-	-	T	g	d	P	-	-	
high djembe	P	T	P	-	(G)	-	(D)	-	g	-	-	-	X3
(>)	P	T	P	-	P	T	P	-	P	T	P	-	
mid djembe	g	T	P	T	P	T	g	T	P	T	P	T	
--variation	P	T	P	T	g	d	P	T	P	T	g	d	
low djembe	G	-	D	-	g	d	G	-	D	-	g	d	
kenkeni bell	x	-	x	x	-	x	x	-	x	x	-	x	
kenkeni	-	-	O	-	-	O	-	-	O	-	-	O	
kenkeni/bell	x	O	-	x	O	-	x	O	-	x	O	-	
songba/bell	M	-	x	-	O	-	M	-	x	-	O	-	
junjun	O	O	O	-	-	-	-	-	-	-	-	-	>
	O	O	O	-	-	-	-	-	O	O	O	-	
--variation	O	-	-	o	-	O	-	-	-	-	o	-	
junjun/bell	O	O	O	-	x	-	x	-	x	-	x	-	
--variation	O	O	O	-	x	-	x	-	O	O	O	-	>
	O	O	O	-	x	-	x	-	x	-	x	-	
junjun break	O	O	O	-	O	O	O	-	O	O	O	-	>
	O	O	O	-	O	-	O	-	O	-	O	-	

Tiriba (Guinea--welcome, played with Abondan; or circumcision, medicine men)
      <27-Tiriba.mp3>

	1	.	.	2	.	.	3	.	.	4	.	.
djembe 1	G	T	g	-	T	-	G	T	-	G	T	-
djembe 2	G	-	-	d	P	-	G	-	-	d	P	-
djembe 3	G	-	P	D	g	d	G	T	-	D	g	d
--variation	P	-	g	d	g	d	P	D	-	D	-	-
junjun bells	x	x	-	x	x	-	x	x	-	x	x	-
--variation	x	-	x	-	x	-	x	x	-	x	-	x
junjun	O	-	-	-	O	-	O	-	-	-	-	-
songba	M	-	-	O	-	-	M	-	-	O	-	-
kenkeni	O	O	-	M	-	-	O	O	-	M	-	-

Yankadi (Guinea--appealing place or person; play with Makuru)

	1	.	.	2	.	.	3	.	.	4	.	.	
djembe: intro	G	-	-	-	-	d	g	-	d	g	-	D	>
	G	-	D	G	-	D	g	-	d	g	-	d	>
	G	-	D	-	-	P	-	-	-	-	-	D	>
	G	-	-	P	-	-	P	-	-	-	-	D	>
	G	-	-	-	-	D	G	-	d	g	-	D	>
djembe 1	G	-	-	P	-	D	G	-	d	g	-	(D)	
--variations...							(T)						
	g	d	d	g	d	d	g	d	d	g	-	D	
	G	-	-	-	-	D	G	-	d	g	-	D	>
	G	-	-	P	-	D	G	-	d	g	-	D	
djembe 2	g	-	d	g	-	d	-	-	d	g	-	D	
--variation: (a)	P	-	-	g	-	d	-	-	(P)	-	-	-	>
: (b)	gf	-	-	gf	-	-	P	-	(T)	-	-	-	
or: (b) variation	g	d	g	d	g	d	g	-	-	-	-	-	
djembe 3	G	-	-	-	-	D	G	-	g	d	-	D	
--variations...	P	-	P	d	-	d	P	-	P	-	-	D	
	g	-	d	g	-	d	g	-	d	-	-	D	
junjun bell	x	-	x	x	-	x	x	-	x	x	-	x	
junjun	O	-	-	-	-	-	-	-	-	-	-	O	
--variation	O	-	-	O	-	O	-	-	-	-	-	-	>
	-	-	-	-	-	-	-	-	-	O	-	-	
songba	M	-	-	O	-	O	-	-	-	-	-	-	
kenkeni	-	-	-	-	-	-	O	-	O	-	-	-	

Zebolah (Congo) [note similarity of name and parts to Zepaule (Haiti)]

	1	.	.	2	.	.	3	.	.	4	.	.	
bell 1	x	-	x	-	x	x	-	x	-	x	-	x	
bell 2	-	x	x	-	x	x	-	x	x	-	x	x	
low drum	g	-	-	D	-	-	G	-	-	D	-	d	
--variations	G	-	-	D	-	-	G	(d)	g	d	-	-	
mid drum	G	d	g	D	P	T	G	d	g	D	P	T	
--variations...	g	T	P	d	P	T	g	T	P	d	P	T	
	G	d	g	-	g	D	-	-	P	(T)	P	-	
lead drum	g	-	P	-	g	d	(g)	T	-	T	g	d	
--variation	(G	-	G)										
high drum	Pt	d	g	d	P	-	g	T	-	d	P	-	
--variations...	-	P	T	-	P	T	-	P	T	-	P	T	
	g	d	g	d	g	d	P	-	-	T	-	gd	>
	g	d	g	d	g	d	G	D	-	G	-	gd	

12/8 - Afro-Latin

Abakua (Cuba--secret men's society)

	1	.	.	2	.	.	3	.	.	4	.	.
bell 1	x	x	-	x	x	x	-	x	x	x	-	x
bell 2	x	-	x	-	-	x	-	x	-	x	-	-
shaker	x	-	x	x	x	x	x	x	-	x	-	x
high drum	g	-	-	d	-	-	g	-	-	d	-	-
--variation	G	-	g	d	-	d	G	-	g	d	-	d
mid drum	M	-	O	-	M	-	O	-	M	-	O	-
low drum	-	M	-	-	O	-	-	M	-	-	O	-
--variation	G	-	-	d	-	-	G	-	-	d	-	-

Bahavento (Brazil)

	1	.	.	2	.	.	3	.	.	4	.	.
bell	x	-	x	-	x	x	-	x	-	x	-	x
shaker	-	-	-	x	-	-	-	-	-	x	-	-
clave	x	-	-	x	-	-	x	-	-	x	-	-
surdo/junjun	O	-	-	-	O	O	-	-	-	-	-	O
--variations...	M	-	O	-	O	-	O	O	-	-	-	-
	O	-	-	O	O	O	O	-	-	O	O	O
tumba	T	-	d	g	-	P	T	-	d	g	d	P
conga	g	-	P	T	g	d	g	T	-	T	-	d
--variation	g	D	P	-	P	-	g	d	G	T	-	d
snare [last + first beats = triplet]	x	X	X	X	x x x	X	X	X	X	X	X	x x

Bembe (Cuba) <28-Bembe.mp3>

	1	.	.	2	.	.	3	.	.	4	.	.
clave	x	-	x	-	-	x	-	x	-	x	-	-
high bell	L	-	H	-	H	H	-	H	-	H	-	H
low bell	x	x	-	x	-	x	x	-	x	-	x	-
high drum	g	d	g	d	g	d	g	-	d	-	g	-
--variations...	g	T	P	d	P	T	g	T	P	d	P	T
	P	d	g	T	g	d	P	d	g	T	g	d
	g	T	-	g	T	-	g	T	-	g	T	-
mid drum	P	T	-	T	P	-	g	d	-	d	g	-

...Bembe...	1	.	.	2	.	.	3	.	.	4	.	.
low drum	G	-	P	D	g	(d)	G	-	P	D	g	(d)
--variations...			(G)									
	P	-	g	d	g	-	P	-	g	d	g	-
	P	-	D	P	D	-	P	-	D	P	D	-
	g	d	g	T	G	-	g	d	g	T	G	-
junjun	O	-	-	O	-	-	O	-	O	O	-	-
--variations...	O	-	o	-	-	O	O	-	o	-	-	O
	-	-	O	O	-	-	-	-	O	O	-	O	>
	O	O	-	O	-	-	-	-	O	O	-	-

Camberto (Haiti)

	1	.	.	2	.	.	3	.	.	4	.	.
bell	x	-	x	-	x	-	x	x	-	x	-	x
low drum	g	-	-	D	-	-	G	-	-	D	-	-
tumba	G	-	P	D	g	d	G	-	P	D	g	d
conga	G	-	g	-	P	-	G	d	-	T	-	D
quinto	g	T	P	d	P	T	g	T	P	d	P	T

Chango (Cuba)

	1	.	.	2	.	.	3	.	.	4	.	.
bell	x	-	x	-	x	x	-	x	-	x	-	x
high djembe	P	d	-	Pt	-	d	P	-	d	P	d	d
mid djembe	-	g	-	T	(G)	T	-	g	-	T	(G)	T
low djembe	Pt	-	T	-	T	G	Pt	-	T	-	T	G
low drum starts "1"; others join here >>						*						

Daome

	1	.	.	2	.	.	3	.	.	4	.	.
bell	x	-	x	-	x	-	x	x	-	x	-	x
high drum	-	d	g	-	d	g	-	d	g	-	d	g
mid drum	G	-	P	-	T	-	G	-	P	-	T	-	>
	G	T	-	G	T	-	G	T	-	G	T	-
low drum	-	-	D	-	G	-	D	-	G	-	D	-	>
	G	-	-	d	-	-	g	-	-	d	-	D

Eleggua (Santeria; see also in 4/4)

	1	.	.	2	.	.	3	.	.	4	.	.
bell	x	-	x	-	x	x	-	x	-	x	-	x
clave	x	-	-	x	x	-	x	-	-	x	x	-
high drum	P	(D)	g	T	(G)	d	P	(D)	g	T	(G)	d
mid drum	(G)	T	(G)	d	P	(D)	(G)	T	(G)	d	DP	(D)
--variation	P	-	P	-	g	d	-	T	-	d	g	-
low drum	G	-	P	T	P	d	G	-	P	T	P	-
--variation	G	d	g	D	P	-	G	d	g	D	P	-

Ibo (Haiti; see also in 4/4)

	1	.	.	2	.	.	3	.	.	4	.	.
bell	x	-	x	-	x	x	-	x	-	x	-	x
high drum	P	T	g	T	P	-	P	T	g	T	P	-
mid drum	P	-	-	T	-	-	-	-	-	T	-	-
low drum	-	-	-	-	G	D	-	-	-	-	-	-
--variation	G	-	-	D	-	-	G	-	-	D	-	-

Mahi (Haiti)

	1	.	.	2	.	.	3	.	.	4	.	.
bell	x	-	x	-	x	-	x	x	-	x	-	x
shaker	X	-	-	X	-	-	X	-	-	X	-	-
high drum	o	-	o	-	o	o	-	o	-	o	-	o
conga	-	d	g	-	T	P	-	d	-	T	-	T
--variations...	(T	-)										
	G	-	D	-	P	T	-	G	-	P	-	T
low drum	g	-	g	-	D	-	d	g	-	D	-	d
--variations...	G	-	-	d	-	g	D	-	-	g	-	d
	G	-	-	d	-	d	G	-	-	d	-	d
stick: RH	-	k	k	-	k	-	-	k	-	k	-	k
tumba: LH	o	-	-	-	-	-	o	-	-	-	-	-
break: tumba	g	d	-	-	P	-	-	-	-	-	-	-
break: conga	-	-	-	-	-	gd	g	d	g	d	g	d

Mami Wata (Guinea-Cuba)

	1	.	.	2	.	.	3	.	.	4	.	.
djembe 1	Gt	-	D	-	G	-	Gt	-	D	G	-	-
djembe 2	Pt	d	g	Pt	d	g	Pt	d	g	Pt	d	g

Palo (Cuba)

	1	.	.	2	.	.	3	.	.	4	.	.
bell	X	-	X	-	X	-	X	X	-	X	-	X
--variations...	X	X	X	-	X	X	X	X	-	X	-	X
	X	-	X	X	X	-	X	X	-	X	-	X
drum	G	-	G	D	G	D	g	-	g	d	g	(d)

Yanvalou (Haiti)

	1	.	.	2	.	.	3	.	.	4	.	.
bell	X	-	X	-	X	-	X	X	-	X	-	X
--variation	X	X	-	X	-	X	X	-	X	-	X	-
shaker	X	-	-	-	-	-	X	-	-	X	-	-
--variation	X	-	-	X	-	-	X	-	-	-	-	-
high drum	G	d	g	D	g	d	G	d	g	D	g	d
high drum: sticks	-	o	o	-	o	o	-	o	o	-	o	o
mid drum	G	-	d	-	d	-	G	-	-	d	-	(G)
--variations...										(D	G)	
	G	D	G	-	P	-	g	D	-	-	P	-
	g	d	g	-	P	-	(G)	d	-	-	P	-
low drum	G	-	-	-	T	-	G	-	-	-	T	-
--variation	P	-	-	T	-	-	P	-	g	-	d	-
low drum: stick	k	-	-	k	-	-	k	-	-	k	-	-
low drum: hand	O	-	M	-	-	-	O	o	-	-	-	-
stick on drum	x	x	-	-	x	x	-	-	x	x	-	-
stick and low drum	x	-	-	-	-	-	O	-	-	O	-	-
	x	-	-	-	-	-	x	-	-	-	-	-
low drum repeat break: RH	o	-	-	-	k	-	-	-	-	k	-	-
: LH	-	-	O	-	-	-	o	o	-	-	O	O
return break: RH	O	-	-	-	k	-	-	-	-	-	-	-
: LH	-	-	O	-	-	-	o	o	-	o	-	o

(marker ">" at right of "stick and low drum" row)

Zepaule (Haiti) [note similarity of name and parts to Zebolah (Congo)]

	1	.	.	2	.	.	3	.	.	4	.	.
bell	X	-	X	-	X	-	X	X	-	X	-	X
high drum/kenkeni	-	O	O	-	O	O	-	O	O	-	O	O
--variation	g	k	k	g	k	k	g	k	k	g	k	k
mid drum	G	-	P	D	g	d	G	-	P	D	g	d
--variations...		(T)						(T)				
	g	-	-	d	G	D	g	-	-	d	G	D

...Zepaule...	1	.	.	2	.	.	3	.	.	4	.	.
songba	O	-	M	-	M	-	O	-	M	-	M	-
low drum	P	-	g	d	-	-	P	-	g	d	-	-
--variations...	(G)						(G)					
	P	-	G	D	-	-	P	-	G	D	-	-
	O	-	-	o	-	-	O	-	-	o	-	-
	-	o	o	-	k	-	-	o	-	-	-	k
	k	-	-	k	(k	k)	k	-	-	k	(k	k)
shaker	X	-	-	X	-	-	X	-	-	X	-	-

3/4 and 12/8 - Middle Eastern

While Middle Eastern rhythms appear in a variety of time signatures using threes (3/4, 6/8, 6/4, 12/8), they generally stick to a binary pulse; so most are notated here in 3/4.

3/4	1	.	*	.	2	.	*	.	3	.	*	.	
Basiit	G	-	d	-	G	-	g	d	P	-	d	-	>
	g	-	d	-	G	-	d	-	g	-	d	-	
Chaka	G	-	g	d	g	d	g	-	g	d	g	d	>
	G	-	g	d	g	-	g	d	G	-	g	-	
Darj	G	-	d	g	d	-	G	-	P	-	-	-	
Khlas	G	-	-	-	D	-	-	-	P	-	T	-	
Sheeshtosh	G	-	d	g	d	-	G	-	g	-	-	‥	>
	P	-	d	g	d	-	G	-	g				
Tsamiko	G	-	-	d	P	-	d	-	P	-	d	-	
Yugrig	G	-	-	-	g	-	d	-	P	-	-	-	>
	g	-	G	-	P	-	-	-	-	-	-	-	
Zar	G	-	g	d	g	d	G	-	g	d	g	d	>
	G	-	g	d	g	d	G	-	D	-	P	-	

12/8	1	.	.	2	.	.	3	.	.	4	.	.
Sufi	G	-	-	P	-	d	G	-	-	-	P	-

Moroccan	G	-	(G)	d	-	d	G	-	g	(d)	g	(d)
--bells, shaker	x	-	x	x	-	x	x	-	x	-	x	x
--bass drum	O	-	-	M	-	-	O	-	-	-	M	-

9/8

Giriama Spirit Dance (Haiti)

	1	.	.	2	.	.	3	.	.	
low drum	g	-	D	P	-	d	G	-	T	
mid drum	g	-	T	P	-	d	P	-	T	
high drum	g	d	g	T	P	T	P	-	T	
bell	-	-	-	x	-	-	x	-	-	
stick/bell	x	-	-	x	-	-	x	-	-	>
	x	-	-	x	-	-	-	-	-	

Komodon (Guinea--Dance of the Crazy)

	1	.	.	2	.	.	3	.	.	4	.	.	5	.	.	6	.	.
djembe 1	Gt	-	T	G	d	g	D	P	-	Gt	-	T	G	d	g	D	P	-
djembe 2	g	T	-	g	T	-	g	T	-	g	T	-	g	T	-	g	T	-
--variation	g	d	-	P	T	-	P	T	-	g	d	-	P	T	-	P	T	-
djembe 3	P	-	d	P	-	-	P	-	d	P	-	-	P	-	d	P	-	-
--variations...	g	d	g	d	-	-	g	d	g	d	-	-	g	d	g	d	-	-
	g	-	-	D	-	-	G	-	d	g	-	-	D	-	-	G	-	d
	G	D	-	g	-	d	G	D	-	g	-	d	G	D	-	g	-	d
bell	x	-	x	-	x	-	x	x	-	x	-	x	-	x	-	x	x	-
kenkeni	O	O	-	-	-	-	O	O	-	-	-	-	O	O	-	-	-	-
--variation	O	-	O	-	-	-	-	-	-	O	-	O	-	-	-	-	-	-
songba	O	-	-	O	-	-	O	-	-	O	-	-	O	-	-	O	-	-
--variation	O	-	O	-	O	-	O	-	-	O	-	O	-	O	-	O	-	-
junjun bell	x	-	x	-	x	-	x	-	x	x	-	x	-	x	x	-	x	-
junjun	-	-	-	-	-	-	-	-	O	O	-	-	-	O	O	-	O	-
--variations...	x	-	x	-	O	-	O	O	-	x	-	x	-	-	-	-	-	-
	O	-	O	x	-	-	-	-	O	x	-	-	:|					

Koreduga (Mali--clowns and buffoons)

	1	.	.	2	.	.	3	.	.	
djembe 1	Pt	-	P	D	g	d	G	T	-	
djembe 2	g	d	-	P	T	-	P	T	-	
bell	x	-	x	x	x	-	x	-	x	
junjun 1	O	-	O	-	o	-	o	-	-	
junjun 2	O	-	O	O	O	-	O	-	O	>
	O	-	-	-	o	-	o	-	O	

4. Rhythm Workshop

This chapter presents an all-purpose toolkit for drummers, with a wide variety of generic and standard patterns and exercises which can be adapted for use in solo practice, the drum circle, the dance studio, or the composing room. But first, a brief tale of statistical adventure...

In Search of the "Mother Rhythm"

A couple of years ago during a trip to Spain, I had with me for rhythmic inspiration (besides the ceaseless thrumming of the sea) only a small aluminum drum and a paper copy of Larry Morris' Rhythm Catalog. The Catalog contained a good portion of the traditional rhythms that appear in the present book; and the concept of doing this book arose partly out of the task I set for myself on that sunny Formentera patio, of selecting and converting Larry's notation to my own.

In the course of that work of transcribing dozens of traditional Afro-Latin rhythms, I developed a sense that there was a "Mother Rhythm" (or two) somewhere at the core of it all, which spawned so many intricate variations on just a few fundamental rhythmic forms.

But how to investigate this intuition further? The scientific side of my brain leapt to the challenge. (I was using graph paper, for starters). I decided to "map" the large cross section of available rhythms at my disposal, by simply counting the notes at each location in the rhythmic grid, for both the 12/8 and 4/4 patterns. How many rhythms began by playing the "One," and of these, what was the proportional breakdown of bass notes, rim tones, and slaps?

The result was a number for each of the three kinds of notes for each beat in the twelve- or sixteen-beat phrase. I could then assign an "average" or "most common" type of note played for each beat. If a beat was played relatively sparsely it would be designated with a rest. The same method was extended to bell and junjun parts.

You can use the same approach (just by eyeballing it, if you don't feel like counting) to find the "lowest common denominator" for a traditional rhythm having many variations. See where the primary beats tend to fall most often; be aware of the tonal melody; and above all, keep an ear out for the basic feel. But be sure to include some of the "offbeat" parts in the final mix, for contrast and counterpoint.

In the case of my overall search for generic root patterns, there was considerable leeway for creative decision-making in regard to assigning notes to beats. For example, the primary downbeat of most 12/8 patterns is a bass note, with slaps running a close second. So I scored two main djembe parts--the first beginning with a "G" and the second beginning with a "P." Some of the beat-by-beat decisions were determined by intuitive familiarity with the rhythms I was studying. For instance, a large number of 12/8 rhythms begin with a binary pulse typified by the long bell:
x - x - x - ...
Meanwhile a large number of rhythms often accompanying that one would reinforce the ternary pulse:
X - x X - - ...

So instead of simply arriving at one ultimate "generic" African rhythm, it made sense to keep intact the polyrhythmic integrity of the form, and to score two distinct djembe parts. The same is true in both 12/8 and 4/4 time.

12/8

	1	.	.	2	.	.	3	.	.	4	.	.
bell ("short bell")	X	-	X	-	X	X	-	X	-	X	-	X
(or: "long bell")	X	-	X	-	X	-	X	X	-	X	-	X
junjun 1	O	-	O	-	-	-	O	-	O	-	-	-
junjun 2	-	-	-	-	M	-	-	-	-	-	M	O
djembe 1	G	-	d	-	P	-	G	-	d	G	-	-
djembe 2 (Jewe)	P	-	P	T	g	d	P	-	P	T	g	d

4/4

	1	.	*	.	2	.	*	.	3	.	*	.	4	.	*	.
djembe 1	G	-	-	d	-	-	g	-	G	-	-	d	g	-	d	-
djembe 2	P	-	d	-	G	-	T	-	P	-	P	T	G	-	T	-
junjun	O	-	-	M	-	-	(O)	-	O	-	-	-	M	-	-	-
songba	O	-	-	-	O	-	O	-	O	-	O	O	-	-	O	-
kenkeni	O	-	-	O	M	-	-	-	-	-	-	M	O	-	-	-
bell	H	-	H	H	L	-	H	-	L	-	H	L	H	-	H	-

Interestingly enough, the 12/8 "mother" polyrhythm is virtually a mirror image of its counterpart in 4/4 time. This similarity reinforces the notion that the time-division between 12/8 and 4/4 is really just an arbitrary by-product of the Western analytical approach. The form of the above patterns also suggests that the more meaningful division of timing is the change in feel from the first half to the second half of the bar in both 12/8 and 4/4 time (or, from the first bar to the second bar of 6/8 and 2/4 time). At this midway point the feel changes from binary to ternary, or vice versa--as discussed earlier in the section on clave patterns. See how this works in both timings:

12/8	1	.	.	2	.	.	3	.	.	4	.	.
bell	X	-	X	-	X	-	X	X	-	X	-	X
djembe 1	G	-	d	-	P	-	G	-	d	G	-	-
djembe 2	P	-	P	T	g	d	P	-	P	T	g	d

4/4	1	.	*	.	2	.	*	.	3	.	*	.	4	.	*	.
clave	X	-	-	X	-	-	X	-	-	-	X	-	X	-	-	-
djembe 1	G	-	-	d	-	-	g	-	G	-	-	d	g	-	d	-
djembe 2	P	-	d	-	G	-	T	-	P	-	P	T	G	-	T	-

In both rhythms, djembe 1 marks the shift in feel halfway through the bar, from the offbeat pulse to the downbeat or primary pulse. Djembe 2, in both cases, marks the basic pulse throughout, reinforcing it with the effect of pickup notes.

Thus the "Mother Rhythm" is not some abstract monotheistic figment after all, but a dynamic polarity between pulse and counter-pulse: both odd and even, female and male.

If I were to take this synthesis a step further, it would be simply to overlay the 12/8 grid with the 4/4 grid (as earlier with the 6/8 and 4/4 Son claves), to see that the lead djembe's sixteen-beat phrase is essentially the twelve-beat phrase stretched out with additional rests:

	1	.	*	.	**2**	.	*	.	**3**	.	*	.	**4**	.	*	.
djembe 1	G	-		d	-		g	-	G	-		d	G	-	(g)	
							(P)									

Basic Practice Patterns

6/8

	1	.	.	**2**	.	.
"Mother Rhythm"	G	(d)	(g)	D	g	d
Olatunji	g	d	-	g	d	-
Olatunji: Ajaja	g	T	P	d	P	T
Dance of the Dogun	G	-	g	d	g	d
standard accompaniment	P	-	g	T	-	d

Universal Grooves (Arthur Hull)

Rocker Rhythm	**1**	.	*	.	**2**	.	*	.	**3**	.	*	.	**4**	.	*	.
--junjun	O	-	O	-	-	-	-	-	O	-	-	-	O	-	-	-
--kenkeni	-	-	-	-	O	-	O	-	-	-	-	-	O	-	-	-
Heartbeat	O	-	O	-	-	-	-	-	O	-	O	-	-	-	-	-
double heartbeat	O	O	-	-	O	O	-	-	O	O	-	-	O	O	-	-
rolling to the one	x	-	-	-	-	-	-	-	-	-	-	-	x	x	x	x

4/4 (Olatunji)

	1	.	*	.	**2**	.	*	.	**3**	.	*	.	**4**	.	*	.
junjun bell	-	-	x	x	-	-	x	x	-	-	x	x	-	-	x	x
junjun	O	-	-	-	M	-	-	-	O	-	-	-	M	-	-	-
djembe (play X4): a.	G	-	P	-	G	-	P	-	G	-	P	-	g	d	-	-
b.	G	-	P	T	-	P	T	-	G	-	P	-	g	d	-	-
c.	g	d	-	-	g	d	-	-	g	d	-	-	g	d	-	-

12/8 (Olatunji)

	1	.	.	2	.	.	3	.	.	4	.	.
bell	x	-	x	-	x	x	-	x	-	x	-	x
junjun	O	-	-	M	-	-	O	-	-	M	-	-
djembe (X4): a.	G	-	g	d	-	-	-	-	-	-	-	-
b.	G	-	g	d	g	d	G	-	-	-	-	-
c.	G	-	g	d	g	d	G	-	g	d	-	-
d.	G	-	g	d	g	d	G	-	P	-	-	-
e.	G	-	g	d	g	d	G	-	P	T	-	-
f.	G	-	g	d	g	d	G	T	g	T	g	-

12/8 Dance Warmups

	1	.	.	2	.	.	3	.	.	4	.	.	
Olatunji: Zungo	G	-	g	d	g	d	G	-	P	T	-	-	
Xochimochi	G	-	g	D	-	d	G	-	g	d	g	d	
--variations...	G	-	d	g	-	D	G	-	g	d	g	D	>]
	G	-	d	g	-	D	G	d	g	d	g	D	]
	G	-	g	T	g	d	G	-	g	T	-	d	>]
	P	-	g	d	g	d	G	-	G	D	P	d	

Rhythm Foundations

Use these exercises for solo practice or to share with others.

1. **Rhythmic breathing**
   Vary the counts, tempo, and balance between inbreath and outbreath.
2. **Rhythmic movement**
   Use your favorite form of yoga, timing each move. Try also creative movement, again with a rhythmic structure.
3. **Rhythmic awareness**
   --Repeat and contrast the different drum tones (bass, rim, slap).
   --Rhythmic alternation of right and left hands; switch hands for same patterns.
   --Rhythmic breathing while playing
   --Heighten awareness of the melodic shape of a rhythm
   --Fine tune awareness of timing and feel, using basic single-part rhythms
   --Fine tune awareness of simple polyrhythms (with partner, drum loop, or metronome)

Sample Tempos, in bpm (here, pulses per minute)

sultry swing = 78
Rolling Stones = 78-84
standard 4/4 = 96
swing beat: 96-108
rocking shaker = 102
roots funk (Incognito) = 104
driving beat = 108

Youssou N'Dour swing = 114
lively driving beat = 114-120
driving disco 4 = 120
samba = 120-138
Mamady Keita 6/8: 150
Mamady Keita 4/4: 175-180

Standard Djembe Patterns

In the earlier section, "In Search of the 'Mother Rhythm,'" generic patterns were derived as "lowest common denominators" by simply counting where different kinds of notes were found most often in a 12- or 16-beat bar, among several dozen traditional rhythms. The less simplistic but more lifelike answer to the same search gives us an array of several "most common" djembe parts--all actual and living entities. (These might be considered children of the Great Mother.) While each in turn has their inevitable variations, it is remarkable how widespread and fundamental are these few basic patterns.

4/4

	1	.	*	.	2	.	*	.	3	.	*	.	4	.	*	.
1. *Senegal, Mali, Guinea:* Aconcon, Bolon, Balakulania, Dalah, Diansa, Dennadon, Fankani, Kassa, Lafé, Lamba, Sunu, Timini, Tordo	P	(T)	-	T (d)	P	-	g	d	P	(T)	-	T (d)	P	-	g	d
2. *Senegal, Mali, Guinea:* Aconcon, Diansa, Fankani, Frekoba, Kassa	P	-	(g)	T (d)	P	-	G	-	P	-	(g)	d	P	-	G	-
3. *Senegal, Guinea, Ivory Coast, Ghana, Benin, Nigeria, Congo:* Akiwowo, Bwanga, Ekonga, Gota, Kebendo, Kpanlogo, Kuku, Kurubi, Lamba, Mombassa, Moribayassa, Shiko, Timini	G	-	P (g	T d)	G	-	g (P)	(d)	G	-	P (g	T d)	G	-	g	(d)
4. *Guinea, Congo:* Balakulania, Boushay, Dalah, Kassa, Kuku, Lafé, Yembela	G	-	g	d	-	-	P	(T)	G	-	g	d	-	-	P	(T)
5. *Senegal, Mali, Guinea, Ivory Coast, Benin:* Aconcon, Dennadon, Diansa, Frekoba, Gota, Kuku, Kurubi, Timini, Tordo, Wollosidon	P	T	-	d (D)	g	(d)	P	-	P	(T)	-	d (D)	g	(d)	P	-
6. *Senegal, Mali, Guinea, Ghana:* Diansa, Gahu, Kakilambe, Kebendo, Makuru	g (G)	d (D)	-	d	G	-	P	-	G	-	d	-	G	-	d	-

Notes:

- This distillation is an attempt to arrive at some predominant feels. The differences here between slaps and rim tones, on beats that are not primary downbeats, are minor. On the other hand, note the greater emphasis on bass notes in patterns 3 and 4, which roughly corresponds to a geographical shift south among the countries represented here.
- Note the difference in feel between the closely related first pattern (4 downbeats, in bold), second pattern (6 downbeats, including the bass notes), and third pattern (8 downbeats, 4 down/low alternating with 4 up/high). The "g d" in the first pattern is more of a doubled pickup note, than a downbeat, because of the much greater stress on the downbeats marked with slaps (**P**).
- The fourth pattern, by dropping the downbeat on the "2," gains the "offbeat" feel of the Afro-Latin clave (also a typical junjun pattern).
- The fifth pattern restores the downbeat on the "2," but offers a distinct flavor with the added emphasis on the second and tenth notes (**T**). The doubled slap beats simultaneously produce both a four-feel and a three-feel in the resulting interval to the next stressed downbeat (the "2" or the "4").
- Traditional rhythms typically combine, as polyrhythms, two or more of these different feels (Aconcon, Diansa, Kassa, and Kuku are all good examples). Many parts also feature combinations of these feels within a single bar--for example, those distilled into the hybrid pattern of pattern 6. Variations on the foundation patterns can be found throughout the Latin and Middle Eastern sections.

12/8

	1	**.**	**.**	**2**	**.**	**.**	**3**	**.**	**.**	**4**	**.**	**.**
1. *Mali, Guinea:* Djaa, Djabara, Dununba, Kakilambe, Linjen, Mandjani, Maraka, Sedeba, Soli, Sorsornet	**P**	–	(g)	**T**	(g)	(d) (D)	**P**	–	(g)	**T**	(g)	(d) (D)
1a. *Guinea, Ghana:* Abioueka, Fume Fume, Jewe, Linjen, Soli	**G**	–	(G)	**D** (T)	g	d	**G**	–	(G)	**D** (T)	g	d
2. *Guinea, Congo:* Abioueka, Sedeba, Etumba Nambuaka	**P** (G)	–	**T** (D)	–	g	**d**	–	**T**	–	**T**	(g)	(d)
3. *Guinea, Ghana:* Fume Fume, Linjen, Mandjani, Sorsornet	**G** (P)	–	**D** (T)	–	**g**	d	**G** (P)	–	**D** (T)	–	**g**	d
4. *Ghana, Congo:* Adowa, Baye, Bintin, Fume Fume, Kakilambe	**G** (g)	–	g	(d)	**P**	–	**G** (g)	T	(g)	d	**P**	–
5. *Guinea, Ghana, Congo:* Fume Fume, N'kisi, Soli, Tiriba	**G**	–	–	d (G)	**g**	–	**G**	–	–	d	**g**	–
6. *Guinea:* Mandjani, Nantaloma, Soli, Sorsornet	**P**	–	–	d (T)	g	d	**P**	–	–	d	g	d

Notes:
- Pattern 1 is best represented in the large body of rhythms known as Dununba. The emphasis in this insistent dance is on the four primary downbeats. This pattern also serves as a strong accompaniment to many 12/8 rhythms.
- Pattern 1a differs from Pattern 1 mainly in the shift from slap to bass notes on the primary downbeats (corresponding again to a southward shift in geography).
- Pattern 2 is polyrhythmic in itself, as it blends a binary and ternary feel.
- Pattern 3 establishes a strong binary feel of six downbeats moving across the ternary pulse.
- Pattern 4 keeps the binary feel but, of the six downbeats, reduces the emphasis on the second and fifth, resulting in an overall feel of: X x X X x X. Pattern 5 makes this feel even more pronounced by dropping the second and fifth downbeats altogether (X - x X - x).
- Pattern 6, while similar to pattern 5, brings the pulse back to a simpler 6/8 feel, by emphasizing only the primary downbeats 1 and 3.
- For good examples of polyrhythms combining these various kinds of patterns, see Fume Fume, Mandjani, or Sorsornet.

Percussion: Bells and Claves

4/4

Patterns for Clave or Bell

	1	.	*	.	2	.	*	.	3	.	*	.	4	.	*	.
basic	X	-	-	X	-	-	X	-	X	-	-	X	-	-	X	-
Son	X	-	-	X	-	-	X	-	-	-	X	-	X	-	-	-
Bossa Nova	X	-	-	X	-	-	X	-	-	-	X	-	-	X	-	-
Gahu	X	-	-	X	-	-	X	-	-	-	X	-	-	-	X	-
Nigerian	X	-	-	X	-	-	X	X	-	-	X	-	X	-	-	-
Afro-Cuban	X	-	-	X	-	-	-	X	-	-	-	X	-	-	-	-
Haitian 1	X	-	-	X	-	-	X	-	X	-	-	-	-	-	-	-
Haitian 2	X	X	-	X	X	-	X	-	X	-	X	-	X	-	X	-
Ghana	X	-	X	-	X	-	X	-	X	-	-	X	-	X	-	-
Brazilian	X	-	X	-	-	X	-	X	-	-	-	X	-	X	⌐	-
Reverse Samba	X	-	X̲	-	-	X	-	X	-	X̲	-	-	X	-	X	-
Reverse Son	-	-	X	-	X	-	-	-	X	-	-	X	-	-	X	-
Samba	-	X̲	-	-	X	-	X	-	X̲	-	X̲	-	-	X	-	X
cascara	X	-	X	X	-	X	-	X	X	-	X	-	X	X	-	X
Samba reggae	X	-	-	-	X	-	-	-	X	-	-	X	-	X	-	-

Rumba Claves (Cuba)

	1	.	*	.	2	.	*	.	3	.	*	.	4	.	*	.
Rumba	X	-	-	X	-	-	-	X	-	-	X	-	X	-	-	-
Rumba 2	X	-	-	X	X	-	-	X	X	-	X	-	X	-	-	-
Rumba 3	X	-	-	X	X	-	X	-	-	-	X	-	X	-	-	-
Bo Diddley*	X	-	-	X	X	-	X	-	-	X	X	-	X	-	-	-
Elvis variation*	X	-	X	X	-	X	X	-	-	X	X	-	X	-	-	-
Reverse Rumba	-	-	X	-	X	-	-	-	X	-	-	X	-	-	-	X

*adapted from Sandy Loewenthal in Martin, *Making Music*)

Bells

	1	.	*	.	2	.	*	.	3	.	*	.	4	.	*	.
samba variations...	H	-	H	-	L	L	-	H	-	H	-	L	L	-	L	-
	H	-	H	-	L	L	-	H	-	H	-	L	-	L	L	-
	H	-	H	-	L	L	-	H	-	H	-	H	L	-	L	-
	L	-	L	-	H	H	-	L	-	L	-	H	-	H	H	-
	L	-	H	-	H	-	L	L	-	H	-	H	H	-	L	-
	H	-	H	-	L	-	L	-	H	H	-	L	-	L	L	-
	L	-	L	-	L	-	H	-	-	L	-	-	L	-	H	-
	L	-	H	-	-	L	-	L	L	-	L	-	L	-	H	-
	H	-	L	L	-	H	-	H	-	-	-	L	L	-	H	-
	H	-	L	L	L	H	-	H	-	-	-	L	L	-	H	-
Samba Reggae	L	-	H	-	L	-	H	-	L	H	-	H	L	-	H	-
Korichiwa	L	-	-	H	-	-	H	-	-	-	H	-	-	-	H	-
Conga Habenera	o	-	o	-	X	X	-	o	-	o	-	X	-	X	-	o
Cascara 1	L	-	H	H	-	H	-	H	H	-	H	-	H	H	-	L
Cascara 2	H	-	L	H	-	H	-	L	H	-	H	-	H	H	-	L
basic agogo	H	H	-	L	-	L	L	-	H	-	H	-	L	-	L	-
Afoxe	H	H	-	H	-	H	L	-	H	-	H	-	H	-	L	-
Ijexa 1	H	-	H	-	L	-	L	-	H	H	-	L	-	L	L	-
Ijexa 2	-	-	H	H	H	-	L	L	-	H	-	L	-	L	L	-
Mambo	L	-	H	H	L	-	H	H	L	-	H	-	L	-	H	H
Comparsa	H	-	H	-	L	L	-	-	H	H	-	-	L	-	H	L

12/8 Patterns for Clave or Bell

	1	.	.	2	.	.	3	.	.	4	.	.
short bell	(L)	-	X	-	X	X	-	X	-	X	-	X
--variation (Cuba)	-	X	X	-	X	X	-	X	-	X	-	X
long bell	X	-	X	-	X	-	X	X	-	X	-	X
--variation (Haiti)	X	-	X	X	X	-	X	X	-	X	-	X
Soli bell	X	-	X	-	X	-	X	-	X	X	-	X
6/8 Son	X	-	X	-	X	-	-	X	-	X	-	-
6/8 Rumba	X	-	X	-	-	X	-	X	-	X	-	-
6/8 rev. Son	-	X	-	X	-	-	X	-	X	-	X	-
6/8 rev. Rumba	-	X	-	X	-	-	X	-	X	-	-	X
rev. long bell	X	X	-	X	-	X	X	-	X	-	X	-
rev. Soli bell	X	-	X	X	-	X	X	-	X	-	X	-
*salsa clave**	X	X	X	-	X	X	-	X	-	X	-	X
--variations...	-	X	X	-	X	X	-	X	-	X	-	X
(from Mauleón)*	-	X	X	-	X	-	X	X	-	X	-	X

9/8 clave

	1	.	.	2	.	.	3	.	.
	X	-	X	-	-	X	-	X	-

Junjun Exercises

(adapted from Michael Wall, Djembe and Mande Music website)
http://tcd.freehosting.net/djembemande/patterns.htm

4/4

	1	.	*	.	2	.	*	.	3	.	*	.	4	.	*	.
steady pulse	x	-	x	-	x	-	x	-	x	-	x	-	x	-	x	-
	O	-	-	-	M	-	-	-	O	-	-	-	M	-	-	-
	M	-	-	-	O	-	-	-	M	-	-	-	O	-	-	-
Uffunu	O	-	-	O	-	-	O	-	O	-	-	O	-	-	O	-
	O	-	-	O	-	-	O	-	O	-	-	O	-	-	M	-
Diansa (fast)	O	-	-	M	-	-	O	-	O	-	-	M	-	-	O	-
	M	-	-	O	-	-	M	-	M	-	-	O	-	-	M	-
	O	-	O	O	-	O	O	-	O	-	O	O	-	O	O	-
	M	-	O	O	-	O	O	-	M	-	O	O	-	O	O	-
	O	-	O	O	-	O	-	O	O	-	O	-	O	O	-	O
	O	-	O	O	-	M	-	O	O	-	M	-	O	O	-	O
	O	O	-	O	-	O	O	-	O	O	-	O	-	O	O	-
	O	O	-	M	-	O	O	-	O	O	-	M	-	O	O	-

	1	.	*	.	2	.	*	.	3	.	*	.	4	.	*	.
reggae feel	-	-	x	x	-	-	x	x	-	-	x	x	-	-	x	x
	O	-	-	-	-	-	-	-	O	-	O	-	-	-	-	-
Yembela	O	-	O	O	-	-	-	-	O	-	O	O	-	-	-	-
highlife	O	-	-	-	M	-	-	-	O	-	-	M	-	-	-	-

	1	.	*	.	2	.	*	.	3	.	*	.	4	.	*	.
downbeat	x	x	-	-	x	x	-	-	x	x	-	-	x	x	-	-
Fanga	O	-	-	-	-	-	-	-	O	-	O	-	-	-	-	-
Fanga variation	O	-	-	-	M	-	-	-	O	-	O	-	M	-	-	-

	1	.	*	.	2	.	*	.	3	.	*	.	4	.	*	.
clave feel	x	-	-	x	-	-	x	-	x	-	-	x	-	-	x	-
	O	-	-	-	M	-	-	-	O	-	-	-	M	-	-	-
	M	-	-	-	O	-	-	-	M	-	-	-	O	-	-	-

	1	.	*	.	2	.	*	.	3	.	*	.	4	.	*	.
Kassa feel	x	x	-	x	-	x	x	-	x	x	-	x	-	x	x	-
	O	-	-	-	M	-	-	-	O	-	-	-	M	-	-	-
	M	-	-	-	O	-	-	-	M	-	-	-	O	-	-	-

	1	.	*	.	2	.	*	.	3	.	*	.	4	.	*	.
cascara	x	-	x	x	-	x	-	x	x	-	x	-	x	x	-	x
	O	-	-	-	M	-	-	-	O	-	-	-	M	-	-	-
	M	-	-	-	O	-	-	-	M	-	-	-	O	-	-	-

	1	.	*	.	2	.	*	.	3	.	*	.	4	.	*	.
highlife ride	x	-	x	x	-	x	x	-	x	-	x	x	-	x	x	-
	O	-	-	-	M	-	-	-	O	-	-	-	M	-	-	-
	M	-	-	-	O	-	-	-	M	-	-	-	O	-	-	-
	-	-	O	-	-	-	O	-	-	-	O	-	-	-	O	-
Sunu (kenkeni)	O	-	-	M	-	-	O	-	O	-	-	M	-	-	O	-
	M	-	-	O	-	-	O	-	M	-	-	O	-	-	O	-
	O	-	-	M	-	-	M	-	O	-	-	M	-	-	M	-
	M	-	O	-	-	O	-	-	M	-	O	-	-	O	-	-
	O	-	M	-	-	M	-	-	O	-	M	-	-	M	-	-
	M	-	-	O	-	O	-	-	M	-	-	O	-	O	-	-
	O	-	-	M	-	M	-	-	O	-	-	M	-	M	-	-
	M	-	O	-	-	-	O	-	M	-	O	-	-	-	O	-
	O	-	M	-	-	-	M	-	O	-	M	-	-	-	M	-

12/8 Junjun Exercises

	1	.	.	2	.	.	3	.	.	4	.	.
short bell	x	-	x	-	x	x	-	x	-	x	-	x
pulse (Ibo)	O	-	-	O	-	-	O	-	-	O	-	-
Mandjani	O	-	-	O	-	-	O	-	-	-	-	O
Bembe	O	-	-	O	-	-	O	-	O	O	-	-
Bintin (songba with stick)	-	O	O	-	O	O	-	O	O	-	O	O

	1	.	.	2	.	.	3	.	.	4	.	.
long bell	x	-	x	-	x	-	x	x	-	x	-	x
pulse	O	-	-	O	-	-	O	-	-	O	-	-
Camberto (low drum)	M	-	-	O	-	-	O	-	-	O	-	-
Daome, Zepaule, Yanvalou	-	O	O	-	O	O	-	O	O	-	O	O
Djaa	O	-	O	O	-	-	-	-	(O	O)	-	O

	1	.	.	2	.	.	3	.	.	4	.	.
Soli bell	x	-	x	-	x	-	x	-	x	x	-	x
pulse	O	-	-	O	-	-	O	-	-	O	-	-
Soli (songba)	O	-	-	-	M	-	M	-	-	O	-	-
Djabara (songba)	O	-	M	-	M	-	M	-	O	O	-	O

	1	.	.	2	.	.	3	.	.	4	.	.
pulse	x	-	-	x	-	-	x	-	-	x	-	-
like short bell (Mahi)	O	-	O	-	O	O	-	O	-	O	-	O
like long bell	O	-	O	-	O	-	O	O	-	O	-	O
like Soli bell	O	-	O	-	O	-	O	-	O	O	-	O

	1	.	.	2	.	.	3	.	.	4	.	.
pulse 2	x	-	x	x	-	x	x	-	x	x	-	x
Sorsornet (kenkeni)	-	-	O	-	-	O	-	-	O	-	-	O

	1	.	.	2	.	.	3	.	.	4	.	.
pulse 3	x	x	-	x	x	-	x	x	-	x	x	-
Tiriba--junjun	O	-	-	-	O	-	O	-	-	-	-	-
--songba	M	-	-	O	-	-	M	-	-	O	-	-
--kenkeni	O	O	-	M	-	-	O	O	-	M	-	-

Breaks

4/4

	1	.	*	.	2	.	*	.	3	.	*	.	4	.	*	.
universal break	X	-	X	X	-	X	-	X	X	-	X	-	X	-	-	-
--variations...	X	-	X	X	-	X	-	X	X	-	X	X	X	-	-	-
	Pt	-	g	d	-	g	-	g	d	-	g	-	g	(d)	-	-
	g	-	g	d	-	g	-	g	d	-	g	d	g			
	g	d	g	d	-	d	-	d	g	-	g	-	P	-	-	-
	g	d	-	d	g	-	g	d	-	d	g	-	g	-	-	-
end break	g	-	g	D	-	D	-	d	G	-	P	-	P	-	-	-

12/8

	1	.	.	2	.	.	3	.	.	4	.	.	
break 1	g	(d)	(g)	d	-	d	g	-	g	d	-	-	>
	F	-	-	-	(g)	d	g	d	g	d	-	-	
break 2	Pt	-	d	P	-	d	P	-	d	P	-	-	
break 3	PT	P	d	P	d	-	P	d	-	P	-	-	
break 4	x	-	x	x	-	x	-	x	x	-	x	x	
break 5	g	d	g	-	P	T	P	-	g	d	g	-	

Pointers to Remember When Drumming

1) Remember to breathe.

2) Stay relaxed.

3) Always listen for, feel, and play with the central pulse of the rhythm and the group.

4) Play softer, not louder; and notice how the texture of the music improves.

5) Beware the too-many-djembes syndrome. Pick up a shaker or bell.

6) Watch the dancers and share the common energy with them.

7) If nobody's dancing, your music is probably missing something. Go deeper.

5. Rhythm Culture: Where We Go

While many challenges stand ahead for realization of a global community with equality and harmony among all, the global drumming community has unquestionably become a major positive force in the world, and exists in great and growing numbers everywhere from small towns to big cities. It extends across all cultural, racial, ethnic, political, financial, and geographical boundary lines. The power of this community to effect positive changes is now strong and will continue to grow stronger.

The power and effectiveness of the global drumming community to make a positive influence and effect change will to a large degree depend upon our ability to communicate, respect, organize and co-operate within our community.

--Paulo Mattioli

Tension, Intention, and Attention

Drumming is the releasing of tension. Where does the tension come from? It hardly matters: it could be stress from our jobs, the contained energy of urban life, psychological and physiological issues...or simply the dynamic tension of life, always seeking expression and new creation. Releasing this tension is inherently healing, bringing our mind/body to a state of equilibrium. The release also makes room for our intention to manifest.

As drummers, what is our intention? It helps to be clear. In a narrow sense, it hardly matters what the content of our intention is. Do we want to support dancers in their creative expression? Show off our manual dexterity? Align ourselves with the cosmic pulse? Motivate troops marching into battle? Whatever our intention, being clear about it will undoubtedly help it to become manifest in the world, through our drumming.

Looked at another way, it *does* matter what our intention is. If our aim is egoistic or material in nature, we may succeed as drummers, but the result will be inherently shallow and unsatisfying. If our intention is rather to harmonize with other people and with the natural world, I believe the results will be more deeply rewarding for all concerned.

You are what you drum. You drum what you are.

Drumming demands our full attention. There's no better one-pointed meditation. At least, none more challenging. Because always the fullest moment is rapidly passing. Do we let it pass us by, while we think of other things, or do we jump on and ride, for all we're worth?

Quest for Excellence

The following exercises were developed by Lars Chose. They can be adapted to any area of personal or professional development. Lars is a Performance Enhancement Coach and can be reached at lars@netidea.com

1. **Intention**
Finish the following statement: My intention/purpose/aim is to...

2. **Relaxation**
Slowly breathe out, repeating the word "relax" 6 times; at the end of the exhale, hold the breath out while saying "hold" 4 times; then as you inhale, say "release" 5 times. While breathing, relaxing, and releasing in this way, visualize yourself performing at your best in your activity.

3. **Affirmation**
Replace negative self-talk with positive messages of affirmation.
Mentally rehearse activity, including imagery of being at your optimum energy level. Eliminate negative thoughts through visualized imagery (e.g., write down, then burn or erase off a blackboard).

4. **Vision**
Complete the following statements:
--My long-range goal is...
--For this to happen, I need to...
--The rewards are...

5. **Assessment** of your present level of performance:
Analysis of elements   Measurement method   Present level

6. **Goal Setting**
Set realistic goals for yourself, something measurable. List on a card:
Start Date   Present level   Goal   Strategy   Target date

7. **Visualize** replacement of present levels by goal-improvements from Exercise 6.

8. **Imaging**
Use each sensory mode (visual, auditory, kinesthetic, smell, taste).
Visualize yourself in a performance scenario: in the past, in the future; focusing on
        specific skills, and in the whole context.
Repeat practice: daily, 10 min; before, during, after performance; before/after sleep.
Awareness: zoom focus in, out; go from broad to narrow; include sound, sensations,
        emotions, thoughts. Multi-track: do many activities at the same time.

9. **Arousal leveling**
Imagine your most recent performance event. Feel the energy arise.
Raise your level of energy arousal, increasing brightness with repetitions.
Evaluate your levels of relaxation, confidence, energy, attention, awareness, control.
Compare your worst time, best time of performance, especially re. energy arousal.
Regulate level of energy arousal through core breathing (2-5" below navel).
Use words or images to enhance desired level of energy.

New Directions

As Fodeba Keita pointed out when first bringing African village dances to the European stage, much is lost when departing from the group energy of the circle. "In our African villages, the same dance may last a whole night without tiring anyone. The dances are...executed in the middle of a ring of spectators who also take part almost as much as the dancers and musicians" (Charry, p. 212). This non-passive audience becomes active through its own dancing, singing, and clapping.

Compare such a configuration with the conventional western stage, where the players and audience are separated, face-to-face, into "us" and "them," the impossibly talented performers and their goggle-eyed groupies. While it seems impossible to avoid such layouts in many pre-existing venues, there is always another model to turn to, just over the horizon.

Whenever possible, try to facilitate a circular arrangement of players, audience, and dancers. If nothing else, the energy directed into and out of the circle will be more powerful than the linear, one-way energy emanating from a conventional stage. I suggest a semicircular arrangement of musicians, with the inner circle loosely completed by the area used by choreographed or trained dancers, or those dancers from the audience who voluntarily gravitate toward the center. The rest of the audience forms an outer ring. The boundary between the outer and inner circles is variable, so that the audience may be encouraged to join the dancing in the center, and to clap and sing with the rhythm and chants, when appropriate to the overall intention of the event.

> The Creator wants us to drum. He wants us to corrupt the world with drum, dance and chants. After all, we have already corrupted the world with power and greed....which hasn't gotten us anywhere - now's the time to corrupt the world with drum, dance and chants.
> --Babatunde Olatunji

6. Resources

Books

Brown, Thomas A. *Afro-Latin Rhythm Dictionary: A Complete Dictionary for all Musicians.* Van Nuys, CA: Alfred Publishing, 1984.
Essential reference for conga and percussion ensemble parts, in standard music notation.

Charry, Eric. *Mande Music: Traditional and Modern Music of the Maninka and Mandinka of Western Africa.* Chicago: University of Chicago Press, 2000.
Definitive, encyclopedic, scholarly (yet personal) study of West African music-- its origins, its instruments, its language and technique.

Chernoff, John Miller. *African Rhythm and African Sensibility.*
A Westerner looks deeply into African musical culture.

Davis, Wade. "The Art of Shamanic Healing." Shadows in the Sun: Travels to Landscapes of Spirit and Desire. Edmonton: Lone Pine, 1992.
Powerful encounters with natural peoples and places around the globe, including a chapter on Voudoun rites.

Flatischler, Reinhard. *The Forgotten Power of Rhythm.* Mendocino: LifeRhythm, 1992.
Investigation, shared through exercises, of our essential rhythmic nature in breath, heartbeat, walking, percussion.

Hart, Mickey, with Jay Stevens. *Drumming at the Edge of Magic: A Journey into the Spirit of Percussion.* San Francisco: HarperSanFrancisco, 1990.
Excellent introduction to world music by eclectic Grateful Dead drummer.

Hull, Arthur. *Drum Circle Spirit: Facilitating Human Potential Through Rhythm.* Tempe, AZ: White Cliffs Media, 1998.
A handbook of drum circle etiquette, sensitivity and technique, mostly for facilitators or those who would take on this role, whether in part or full-bore. The most useful section for me listed some core "universal grooves" to depend on in any situation. The first night I tried one, a 6/8 bell pattern over a campfire drone, it set the tone into a higher trance of group spirit. This stuff really works!

Martin, George, ed. *Making Music: The Guide to Writing, Performing and Recording.* New York: Quill, 1983.
A potpourri of tips and lore from the popular music world, assembled by the Beatles' producer.

Mauleón, Rebeca. *Salsa Guidebook for Piano & Ensemble.* Petaluma, CA: Sher Music, 1993.
Authoritative and accessible reference on Afro-Latin music and its rhythmic elements.

Matthews, Bill. Drum Talk: *33 Handdrum Dialogues for Two Players, From Traditional African and Afro-Caribbean Ensemble Rhythms.* Seattle, Luna Percussion (n.d.).

Core rhythms in box notation, plus tips on technique and drum tuning.

Moreira, Airto. Airto: *The Spirit of Percussion*. Wayne, N.J.: 21st Century Music Productions, 1985.
Airto is as fine a communicator on a basic human level, as he is a master percussionist for all occasions. Key advice and grooves from Brazil.

Moses, Bob. *Drum Wisdom*. Cedar Grove, NJ: Modern Drummer Publications, 1984.
Tons of licks for kit drummers, adaptable to hand drums. Explores many 4/4 grooves with a variety of feel, plus topics such as independence, organic drumming, movement and dance, and singing.

Olatunji, Babatunde. *Drums of Passion Songbook*. Transcribed and Edited by Doug Lebow. New York: Olatunji Music, 1993.
22 classics from the master who brought African drumming into popular awareness in North America. Includes Akiwowo, Fanga, Frekoba, Jin-go-lo-ba, The Beat of My Drum.

Plainfield, Kim. *Advanced Concepts: A Comprehensive Method for Developing Technique, Contemporary Styles and Rhythmical Concepts*. Miami: Manhattan Music Publications, 1992.
Kit drum master lays out patterns and exercises for the funk-minded drummer.

Redmond, Layne. *When the Drummers Were Women: A Spiritual History of Rhythm*. New York: Three Rivers Press, 1997.
"In the mother goddess cultures of ancient Europe, the rhythm clans come alive in Layne's fascinating and insightful book." --Mickey Hart

Reed, Ted. *Latin Rhythms for Drums and Timbales*. Clearwater, FL: Ted Reed, 1960.
Another classic guide, adding numerous rhythms and variations to the repertoire of the Afro-Latin ensemble.

Werner, Kenny. *Effortless Mastery: Liberating the Master Musician Within*.
Werner is an accomplished jazz musician but speaks as the friend and mentor of the musical beginner or performer alike. Take it easy, he says. Relax. Get in touch with what this magic called music is really about. Listen. Get out of the way, enough to hear what the music wants to say, where it wants to go. If you can do this--feeling your musical "I" to be as large as time itself--then you can say in the larger sense, "I am a master."

Wilson, Sule Greg. *The Drummer's Path: Moving the Spirit with Ritual and Traditional Drumming*. Rochester, VT: Destiny, 1992.
African-American drummer shares his wisdom and learning regarding all aspects of the art and life of the hand-drummer.

Audio CDs

African/Latin Drumming, traditional and modern

- Abdul Kabirr and Soto Koto Band, Gumbay Dance! -- hot high life Afro-Brasil -- compilation covering everything from carnaval to trance
- Alpha Yaya Diallo, The Message -- Juno award winner features highlife guitar master
- Babatunde Olatunji, Drums of Passion: The Beat -- C. Santana sits in
- Bakongo: Drumming Music for Dancers -- It's party time, straight from the roots
- Bomba, lo que bomba te dá -- world-class salsa from top Edmonton band
- Cascabulho, Hunger Gives You a Headache-- great non-stop dance energy from Brazil
- Cheikh Lo, ne la thiass -- Cuban-influenced singer-guitarist in soul-lyrical groove
- Cheikh Lo, Bombay Gueej -- a more energetic mix from protege of Youssou N'Dour
- David Thiaw, African Skies -- upbeat bright and high-life sound
- Edwina Lee Tyler, Drum Drama -- virtuoso African woman on djembe
- Fatala, Gongoma Times -- all star band plays hot, features Alpha Yaya Diallo electric
- Gabrielle Roth and the Mirrors, Initiation -- Five universal rhythm-moods
- Kanda Bongo Man, Amour Fou (Crazy Love) -- highlife classic by Congolese band
- King Sunny Ade, E Dide/Get Up -- cool groovin' by the master of highlife
- Mamadou Ly, Mandinka drum master -- with ultratight trio
- Mamady Keita, Hamanah -- a dozen variations on Dununba
- Mamady Keita, Nankama -- everything by this master is great
- Mamady Keita, Wassolon -- the djembefola par excellence
- Nii Tettey Tetteh -- gentle, original mastery of traditional music from Ghana
- Salif Keita, Folon -- soulful vocals fill out master's mellow grooves
- The Best Best of Fela Kuti -- A hot mix of "The Black President's" powerful hits
- The Best of Tito Puente -- classics by the Cuban salsa king: "El Rey del Timbal"
- Thione Diop -- Know Your Culture -- hottest young Senegalese djembe star
- Youssou N'Dour, The Lion -- early, full-mood classic from the Senegalese star

Funk, Fusion and Jazz

- African Travels -- dance hall compilation layering tribal beats with electric funk
- Arabian Travels -- middle-east grooves with funky bass mixes for dance
- Brent Lewis/Peter Wood, Thunder Down Under -- natural/aboriginal-style rhythm textures
- Celso Machado -- hot lounge jazz guitar in Amazonian jungle
- Dr. John, Creole Moon -- The wizard of the bayou is at it again with world-funk gumbo
- Eric Dolphy, Out to Lunch -- rhythm slow and unique, in the moment
- Herbie Hancock, Dis is Da Drum -- 90's jazz/drum/funk
- Herbie Hancock, Head Hunters -- jazz fusion classic
- Incognito, 100 Degrees and Rising -- British soul funk dance
- Jack DeJohnette, Parallel Realities -- eclectic compositions from the great jazz drummer

- James Brown, 20 All-time Greatest Hits -- still great
- James Brown, Live at the Apollo 1995 -- keep it funky, JB
- Joe Zawinul, My People -- ex-Weather Report-man with world groove
- Latin Travels -- another six degrees classic roots-funk-fusion for dance
- Leon Parker, Awakening -- clean, movable jazz with great roots foundation
- Michael Franti & Spearhead, Stay Human -- get-down funk with conscious rap
- Pharoah Sanders, Message from Home -- 90's release, African roots
- Red Hot and Cool, Stolen Moments -- acid jazz and rap, compilation, vets and new kids
- Santana, Sacred Fire -- Live in South America
- The Brand New Heavies -- vocal and funk grooves

Videos

Stomp Out Loud
Smash Off-Broadway percussion show takes to the streets with brooms, basketballs, bungie cords, sewer pipes, kitchen knives, playing cards...anything that will make a rhythmic texture. In one joyful hour this group will make you aware of the rhythm pervasive in every act of living.

Tap Dogs
Possibly even more inspiring than Stomp Out Loud! These Aussie foot-stompers cross all the boundaries while pounding out tight percussive polyrhythms on every variety of surface. Backed at times by frenzied kit drummers, these unstoppable dancers will have you climbing the walls with them: in time.

Selected Websites

(if these links expire, search for title phrases)

African Beat - great comprehensive resource list for African music: CDs, Videos, Books.
http://www.rhythmtraders.com/html/africa.html

Alternative Culture Magazine's Rhythm Section - the author's own site with additional drumming topics, rhythms, lessons, sound files, exercises, resource links, and online ordering for this book.
http://www.alternativeculture.com/music/rhythm.htm

Djembe and Mande Music - top quality list of resources, references and reviews re. West African drumming.
http://tcd.freehosting.net/djembemande/

Djembe-L Mailing List FAQ and Drumming Resources - the most comprehensive website for hand drummers, drum makers, drum teachers, dancers...
http://www.drums.org/djembefaq/index.htm

Drum Track Zone - drum tracks, loops, and samples.
http://www.synthzone.com/drums.htm

Percussion Africaine - by Jean Vaucher of Montreal - one of the best sites on the Net for information on African drum culture and rhythms.

http://www.iro.umontreal.ca/%7Evaucher/Djembe.html

Rhythm Catalog from Larry Morris - authoritative source reference for many West African and Latin rhythms found here.
http://www.drums.org/djembefaq/rhycat.htm

Synth Zone - links and resources for drum programs, midi, hand drumming and more.
http://www.synthzone.com/

World Music Reviews - includes reviews of African, World and Latin music.
http://www.technobeat.com/

Rhythm References Online

(if these links expire, search for title phrases)

Cultural Context for Djembe Rhythms:
http://home.acceleration.net/clark/PaperVu/context.htm

Djembe and Mande Music: http://tcd.freehosting.net/djembemande/

Djembe Country Index: http://rz-home.de/%7Ewtower/djembe/rhythmen/

Drums and Percussion Page Groove Archive: http://www.cse.ogi.edu/Drum/groove/

Djembe-L email discussion list: http://www.drums.org/djembefaq/faqv1.htm

Folilia Rhythm Catalog: http://arthur.ebel.free.fr/nezpales/Partitions/catalog.html

Jan Verhaert's Rhythm Notation Catalog:
http://www.iro.umontreal.ca/~vaucher/Music/JVRhythmes.html

Jas's (Jeff Senn's) Dumbek Rhythm Page:
http://www.maya.com/local/senn/rhythm.html

Jean Vaucher's Rhythmes d'Afrique de l'Ouest:
http://www.iro.umontreal.ca/%7Evaucher/Music/Rhythmes.html

Karim's Annotated Rhythm Catalog: http://alpheus.hep.sci.osaka-u.ac.jp/~karim/africa/percu/rhythm_djembe.html

Larry Morris's Rhythm Catalog: http://www.drums.org/djembefaq/rhycat.htm

Rhythm Planet Catalog: http://members.tripod.com/rhythm_planet/

Rhythmaddicts: http://www.rhythmaddicts.com/

West African Percussion Notation and Soundfiles: http://home.wanadoo.nl/paul.nas/

Rhythm Index

Navigation: press Ctrl-G and enter the desired page number.

Roots Jam 2 CD Audio

Instructions

1. Insert CD into any CD audio player or computer CD drive.
2. Use the controls of your player (or the computer directory for your CD drive) to select and play each track you want. <u>Underlined patterns below are 1-4 minutes long for play-along practice</u>.
3. For best results (especially in hearing bass beats), use headphones or good quality speakers.

Index of recorded rhythm tracks:

Track No.	Rhythm	Page
1.	G, D (bass beats)	7
2.	g, d (rim beats)	7
3.	P, T (slap beats)	7
4.	G - D - g d g d	8
5.	D - d g - g d g D - D - d g d g	9
6.	<u>6/8 (3 parts)</u>	10
7.	<u>Ethiopian walking rhythm</u>	12
8.	<u>handing exercise, version 1</u>	12
9.	<u>handing exercise, version 2</u>	12
10.	<u>short bell</u>	13
11.	straight reel	14
12.	swung reel	14
13.	<u>Dununba djembe</u>	14
14.	2/4 pattern: x - - x x - - x	15
15.	<u>long bell</u>	15
16.	<u>jazz bell</u>	15
17.	<u>Son clave in 4/4</u>	15
18.	<u>Son clave in 6/8</u>	16
19.	<u>6/8 pulse</u>	18
20.	<u>3/4 pulse</u>	18
21.	<u>Zepaule: junjun and bell</u>	19
22.	<u>Fanga (ensemble)</u>	26
23.	<u>Kakilambe 4/4 (ensemble)</u>	29
24.	<u>Lamba (ensemble)</u>	32
25.	<u>Mandjani (ensemble)</u>	52
26.	<u>Sorsornet (ensemble)</u>	56
27.	<u>Tiriba (ensemble)</u>	56
28.	<u>Bembe (ensemble)</u>	58

Roots Jam 2
African and Afro-Latin Drum Rhythms

About the author:

Nowick Gray has been a writer, teacher, and workshop leader for over twenty-five years, and a drummer since 1990. His popular book *Roots Jam: Collected Rhythms for Hand Drum and Percussion*, and instructional webpages have helped beginning, intermediate, and performing drummers understand and play traditional African-based rhythms since 1996.

Nowick has studied with a number of world drumming masters including Mamady Keita, Babatunde Olatunji, Alpha Yaya Diallo, Thione Diop, and Nii Tettey Tetteh. He has facilitated a variety of drumming events ranging from weekly jams and rhythm study, to annual 24-hour drum circles and all-night trance dances. Nowick drums for ongoing trance and African dance classes and has performed with Moving Company and Moving Mosaic, based in Nelson, B.C.

Visit the author's websites for additional drumming topics, rhythms, lessons, sound files, exercises, resource links, and online ordering for this book: www.alternativeculture.com - www.djemberhythms.com

ROOTS JAM 4

World Beats

Rhythms
Wild!

NOWICK
GRAY

- Dive deep into African drumming styles from around the world.
- Find simple notation for djembe, dunun, conga, tabla and batucada parts from Guinea, Mali, Cuba, Brazil, Belize, India.
- Groove on tribal beats for hip hop and DJ mixes, samba bands, kirtan, dance classes, or drum circles.
- Explore archetypal music patterns, polyrhythm, improvisation, and drum culture.

DjembeRhythms.com

Roots Jam 3

Arrangements for

West African Drum and Dance

by

Nowick Gray

Cougar WebWorks
© 2007 by Nowick Gray

email: now@djemberhythms.com
Web: http://djemberhythms.com

Cover Art: Natasha Bird (http://poipixies.com)

Recording: Percussion Studio software (http://www.henrykellner.com/PercussionStudio/)

A note about the recordings:

Purists will no doubt take exception to the recording of the audio material via software rather than with live drumming. Actually the Percussion Studio software that I use is based upon live drum samples; it's just that here they are arranged note by note. The advantage for the student is exact precision of tonality and timing, which is a challenge to achieve live in recording. The advantage from a production standpoint is that the result is much more economical and efficient. In any case, the recorded audio tracks are meant more for guidance and inspiration than to stand alone as performance pieces; the real performance is up to you, the reader / listener / player.

You can purchase the full set of 16 traditional and 27 original arrangements as .mp3 audio files from my website at:
http://djemberhythms.com/books/order-roots-jam-drum-rhythm-books/ You can also order other *Roots Jam* books and audio files there. See page 61 of this book for a full index of the audio files.

Library and Archives Canada Cataloguing in Publication

Gray, William N., 1950-
     Roots jam 3 : arrangements for West African
drum and dance / by Nowick Gray.

Also available in electronic format.
Also available with a variety of accompanying materials: a compact disc
     containing arrangements for 16 traditional dance rhythms, and/or a

  compact disc containing 27 original compositions, or a CD-rom
  containing similar material in mp3 format.

Includes bibliographical references.
ISBN 978-0-9682033-6-1

     1. Percussion instruments--Studies and exercises. 2. Drum--Studies and exercises. 3. Musical meter and rhythm--Africa, West--Studies and exercises. 4. Percussion music--Teaching pieces. 5. Percussion ensembles--Teaching pieces. I. Title.

MT655.3.G785 2007a   786.8'1224'076   C2007-904963-X

Roots Jam 3: Arrangements for West African Drum & Dance

Table of Contents

2

African drum music is a perfect example and training ground for that core concept that The Mayan Oracle *calls "complex stability." When the part you're playing, however simple or complex it is in itself, is solid and stable, it can help hold the whole complex polyrhythm steady in time, alive and coherent and . . . yes, even spacious. As Mamady Keita says, to play the djembe well implies "mastery of time." When the timing is precisely stable, then even a high-tempo piece can be perceived in its completeness, as if time stands still – and then a wonderful sense of space, and consequently also freedom, opens up within the music.*

Why Roots Jam 3?

This volume, third in the Roots Jam series, continues my effort to record my own learning of West African drumming and to share it with others. Along with this learning of traditional rhythms and arrangements has come an interest in composing and arranging original pieces. The boundaries between "traditional" and "original" in this book are not totally distinct. There are a few original phrases in the collection of traditional rhythms, and the arrangements themselves are products of my own selection process; meanwhile many of the individual patterns in the "Original Compositions" come from traditional or other recorded sources, and are combined here in new arrangements.

Since the publication of *Roots Jam 2* in 2002, I have moved from playing with a dance troupe in Nelson BC to the larger city of Victoria. Here I had the good fortune to connect right away with Byron and Lynn Weaver of Moondance Dynamic Arts, who were putting on West African dance classes, at a time when another drummer had also just arrived to help out with drum instruction and arrangements.

Jordan Zinovitch had been drumming for just four years, but with an intense learning curve under master teachers in New York (Bembe Bangoura, Ousmane Sylla) and Guinea (Gbanworo Keita). After weekly classes and several performances with Jordan for nine months, I traveled with him to Portland, Oregon in 2003 for a weekend workshop with Famoudou Konate. That inspiring contact led to further study for both of us the following winter with Famoudou in Guinea, West Africa, as part of a larger group of 18 students, in the village of Sangbarala and the city of Conakry, where we drummed for five hours a day for the better part of a month.

Learning that material was a challenge which is ongoing. Again I have been fortunate to have the opportunity to put the learning into practice by playing for dance classes in Victoria, both with Lynn's Moondance company and with Ilana Moon's Dancing Moon Multicultural Arts Company. In the latter group I took on the additional responsibility of musical arrangement in coordination with Ilana's choreography, and of instructing the other drummers of the ensemble in their parts. It has been my pleasure as well to share this knowledge with beginning drummers in a classroom setting, in locations ranging from Saltspring Island and Victoria to Koh Phangan, Thailand and Hobart, Tasmania.

In addition to the learning and inspiration from my primary teachers, Jordan and Famoudou, I have also had the opportunity since *Roots Jam 2* to learn from Mamady Keita's live workshops and written material, from Jordan Hanson's drum classes in Victoria, and from the teachers of the Tambacounda drum camp in Mendocino, California: Moussa Traore, Abdoul Doumbia, Abdoulaye Diakite, and others. To my previous sources of written notation I have added the excellent books by Famoudou and Ibro Konate, Mamady Keita, Abdoul Doumbia, Serge Blanc, and Age Delbanco (see Resource list at the end of this volume).

My usual disclaimer is in order here: that I cannot guarantee that my own transcriptions are accurate from my live and recorded learning experiences, or even from other written sources (which themselves are not always reliable or consistent). Rather than attempt to be the authoritative recorder of certain teachers' rhythms and arrangements, I aim to draw from the wide range of available material, to present here my own arrangements and choices of parts, while trying to remain faithful to the traditional forms as much as possible.

On one hand, the rhythms of the Malinke drum culture are almost infinite in their variation; on the other hand, out of those variations emerge certain constant and universal phrases and motifs. Not only are there the standard accompaniment parts for 4/4 and 12/8 timings; the solo phrases, too, often cross over between rhythms; and finally you come to the place where even these "different" time signatures blur one into the other. With all of the foregoing in mind, I have done my best to distill those variations that have come to me and to present them in what I hope is a pleasing arrangement – yet another variation in the tradition.

The primary inspiration for this book has been to collect and make accessible a cohesive and comprehensive body of material for use with dance classes or troupes. That application has its own set of rewards and limitations, geared as it is toward stage performance and highly choreographed dance and rhythm arrangements. I hope also that this rich musical tradition can inspire and feed more open-ended and participatory venues, in the mode of village-style dance, where the aim is powerful and joyful community celebration, and drummers and dancers can play together more freely.

A final note of thanks to those few teachers I have mentioned here, especially Jordan Z. and Famoudou; to Lynn and Ilana for allowing me the opportunity to play for their dance classes and performances; and to all those others (acknowledged in *Roots Jam 1 & 2*), who have shared their knowledge and inspiration with me along the way.

Real music is not for wealth, or honour, nor even the joys of the mind. It is a path of salvation and realization.

– Rumi

4

Rhythm Notation Guide

Instrument terms:

Djembe – Standard West African bell-shaped hand drum. In an ensemble, it helps to have djembes of different pitches playing together: djembe 3 lowest, djembe 2 mid-range, djembe 1 highest for lead parts, breaks and solos.

Dunun – Double-headed drum played with sticks. Various combinations are possible. Basic configurations include side-mounting on a stand or chair, or strapped to another dunun. This way it is common to play an attached bell on top, with the weaker hand. Another common setup is to play dununs in combination in the upright position, on a floor or mounted on a stand. In this setup usually sticks are used in both hands and the bell is left out.

Dununba – The largest of the family of dununs.

Sangban – Medium-sized dunun

Kenkeni – Smallest dunun

Basic notation for djembe:

The primary notation in this book, as in *Roots Jam* (1996) and *Roots Jam 2* (2002) is based on the traditional Yoruba "oral notation" terminology as taught by Babatunde Olatunji. It mimics the standard range of sounds produced by the West African djembe.

G: Gun ("Goon") = bass beat with strong hand in center of drum head
D: Dun ("Doon") = bass beat with other hand

g: go = rim tone with strong hand: middle joint of fingers; fingers closed
d: do ("doe") = rim tone with other hand

P: Pa = slap with strong hand: sharp glancing stroke with fingertips
T: Ta = slap with other hand

P or **T** = slap muffled by other hand placed first on head to dampen it

 - : = unplayed note, marking a place to feel the underlying pulse or timing

(G) = parentheses indicate optional note

Gt, Dp, Pt, gf = flams. (Gt=GT, Dp=DP, Pt=PT, gf=gd) Play two notes almost as one single beat, in the order written.

gd or **PT** = two notes played at double time, at the beginning of a roll. Similar to a flam; but here there are distinctly two notes played quickly one after the other, whereas the flam notes are closer to being struck simultaneously.

Map of Notes on Drum Head:

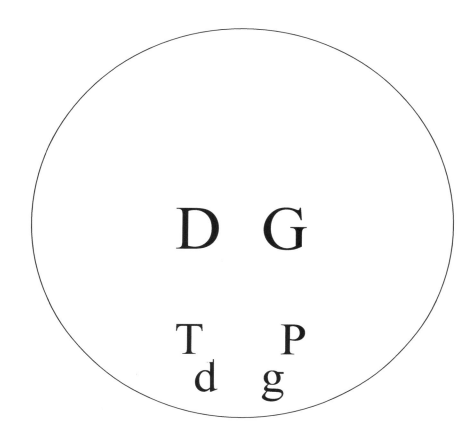

Dunun notation

x = dunun bell, usually played with weaker hand

O = open (stick) beat on any dunun; usually implies bell note struck at same time

o = note on kenkeni or higher-pitched dunun; usually includes bell

M or **m** = muted note on dunun, with stick pressed to drum head; usually with bell

(O) = parentheses indicate optional note

Arrangement notation and terms

4/4	1	.	*	.	2	.	*	.	3	.	*	.	4	.	*	.

Each of these lines of grid boxes represents a single **measure** or **bar** of musical time, generally the length of a recognizable and repeatable pattern or **phrase**.

12/8 (2 X 6/8)	1	.	.	2	.	.	3	.	.	4	.	.

☐ = a single box in the grid for one **beat**: either a **rest** (-) or a struck **note** (sometimes two)

4/4 = from standard musical notation, 4 quarter notes (= 8 eighth notes or 16 sixteenth notes) to a measure. Notes are spaced in **binary** form, evenly numbered between downbeats.

6/8 or **12/8** = denotes time in **triplet** groupings (each with 3 "eighth" notes), usually four triplets to a measure (12/8)

1, 2, 3, 4 = **pulse** of basic **downbeats**

* = in 4/4, marks secondary downbeats (these could also be considered **upbeats** – see Lesson 1, below)

. = intermediate beats: **offbeats**. The most commonly used offbeat is the **pickup**, coming just before and giving momentum to the downbeat.

handing = normally alternates, with **R** L **R** L emphasis in the binary 4/4 patterns; or **R** L R **L** R L emphasis in the triplet-based 12/8 patterns (reverse if lefthanded)

> = between measures, continue on to play next measure or multiple measures; or within a measure, denotes place to start playing a phrase off the break (often around the **4**). Two-bar phrases are also implied by a blank heading after the first bar.

|: , :| = beginning, end of a repeating multiple-bar phrase

X3 = repeat bar or phrase a given number of times before moving on

[G - | or **[D |** = pickup notes sometimes used to start a phrase before the "one" (or first note) of a measure

alt. or **var. =** alternate part; or variation played in sequence with main part

echauffement = French for "heating up" – phrase that's usually repeated for three or more measures, sometimes with an increase in tempo, signaling an upcoming break to a new dance section or ending.

Features

Drumming Workshop

Here is a workshop progression that you can use for self-learning or for teaching others. The rhythms build step by step so that basic accompaniment patterns can be learned quickly, with proper handing and timing. The other objective of these lessons is to illustrate the different variations of feel: from downbeats to upbeats to offbeats to polyrhythms (4 across 3 or 3 across 4).

Lesson 1: Stretching Time and Space

Here's a little exercise to demonstrate the flexibility of time and space in West African music.

a) x x x x > b) x - x x - x > c) x - - x x - - x

We start with a) four straight notes, evenly spaced . . . or rather, struck without a sense of much space between them: toc toc toc toc.

In b) we stretch them a little, inserting a small bit of space/time between each pair. The result is "swing," in which we play those four notes of straight 4/4 time more like four notes out of six in 6/8 time. The extra two unplayed "beats" are rests.

In c) we simply stretch a little further, inserting extra space - in fact an extra rest - between each of the original pairs of struck notes. We're back to the binary format of 4/4, but still with the swung feel of space between the notes. We've gone through "swing" and arrived at "samba."

x		x		x		x	
x		-	x	x		-	x
x	-	-	x	x	-	-	x

Lesson 2: Downbeats and Upbeats

	1	**.**	*****	**.**	**2**	**.**	*****	**.**	**3**	**.**	*****	**.**	**4**	**.**	*****	**.**
1. basic downbeat	O															
2. basic downbeats	O								O							
3. double time	O				O				O				O			
4. upbeat/reggae 1	O				o				O				o			
5. upbeat/reggae 2					o								o			
6. upbeat/reggae 3					x	x							x	x		
7. double time	O		x	x	O		x	x	O		x	x	O		x	x

Lesson Notes:

Line 1. In this example we start with one downbeat in the full measure, on the **1**.
Line 2. Here the downbeat is doubled, to come at the **1** and the **3**. Alternatively, we could refer to the 3 as an upbeat, giving more weight or stress to the **1**'s downbeat.
Line 3. Doubling the downbeats again. Here the pattern is consistent with the basic timing of the 4/4 measure, with primary downbeats at **1**, **2**, **3**, and **4**, and primary upbeats in between (*****).
 Line 4. Here we notate clearly with smaller o's (higher-pitched beats) that the 2 and 4 are upbeats rather than downbeats. This is the basic feel of reggae.
Line 5. Here the downbeat is left out altogether, unplayed; or as in much reggae music, the downbeat bass is so low as to be felt rather than heard, while the upbeat is the sharp "chuck" of the rhythm guitar or "tak" of percussion.
Line 6. More of the distinctive reggae feel of the upbeat rhythm guitar. This can also be swung or stretched to a more laid-back feel: [x - x] instead of the straight [x x].
Line 7. Doubling the time and reinserting the downbeats gives us a steady downbeat-upbeat pulse. The doubled upbeats [x x] provide momentum directly into each following downbeat.

Lesson 3: Offbeats

Here we depart from the marching grid, the binary pulse of downbeats and upbeats, by moving the emphasis to an offbeat. All the offbeats are marked in the top timeline as (.). Normally in a djembe rhythm these notes are all played by the weaker hand (D, d, or T), filling in space or keeping time between the strong-hand downbeats (G, g, P). They could also be considered upbeats if we think of the whole measure as having eight downbeats (1 * 2 * 3 * 4 *). The eight offbeats or smaller upbeats lie in between. Placing notes and stresses there gives a rhythm projection, momentum, rounded space and a funky feel – especially when space is created around them by leaving the downbeats unplayed.

	1	.	*****	.	**2**	.	*****	.	**3**	.	*****	.	**4**	.	*****	.	
1. clave	x	-	-	x	-	-	x	-	x	-	-	x	-	-	x	-	
2. dunun	O	-	x	O	-	x	O	-	O	-	x	O	-	x	O	-	
3. djembe	g	d	P	d	g	T	g	d	P	d	g	T	g	d	P	-	
3a. djembe	P		g	T		d	P		g	T		d	P				
4. djembe a)		.		.		.		.		.		.		.	g	d	>
b) |:		P		g		P		d		T	P		g	d		D	>
c)	P	T			-		D	P		T			-		g	d	:|
5. djembe														...	P	T	>
	g	d	P	T		P	T	g	d	P	T			P	T		
6. djembe	P	T	P	T	-		G		-		D		-				
7. djembe	gd	g	d	P	T		P		gd	g	d	P	T		P		
	g	d	g	d	P	T		P		gd	g	d	P	T		P	

Line 1. The feel shifts to triplets (grayed in). The underlying binary structure of 4/4 is reestablished going into the basic downbeats at 3 and 1.

Line 2. Same basic offbeat clave feel applied to a dunun pattern, with bell notes added for flavor, emphasis, and reinforcement of the timing.

Line 3. In this djembe solo pattern, the triplets continue through the whole phrase until the very end, when there is just time enough for a final binary space to start again. **Line 3a** uses a different chain of triplets and ends on the 4.

Line 4. Here's a classic solo phrase from Famoudou Konate demonstrating the use of offbeats. a) Begin off the break with the [g d] at the end of the measure. b) Here I use the handing he teaches, but notice how each beat in the initial strong-hand sequence of the measure [- P - g - P] falls on the offbeats. In fact, of the nine notes in this measure, seven come on the offbeat. c) From the end of the phrase, return to the beginning of measure (b) and repeat. This device of using the [g d] to set up a series of offbeats with a space on the downbeat (1 in this case) can be applied to other downbeats as well. For example, try these as exercises for solo practice (CD track 19):

	1	.	*	.	**2**	.	*	.	**3**	.	*	.	**4**	.	*	.
	g	T		T	T		T		g	d	P		P	d	g	
	g	d	P	T		d		T		d		T	P		g	d
	G		g	d	g	d		T		d		T	P		g	d
	G		g	T	P		g	T		d		T	P		P	T
	gd	g	T	P			P	T	P	T		d		T	G	

Line 5. Another way to provide interest and complexity to a 4/4 rhythm is to offset a phrase so the downbeat comes in the middle of it, played with tones instead of slaps. The phrase [P T g d P T] is played and heard as a group of continuous notes; but usually it is arranged to "turn the corner" of the measure, so that the first tone [g] falls on the 1.

Line 6. Yet another way to get off the downbeat train is with triplets, played on top of the underlying 4/4 structure. Here we play three notes [P T P] in the time normally taken up by four; these are even further "off" the grid than the "offbeat" spaces reserved in the 4/4 measure, so that we have to notate them in threes, and hear them "outside of" rather than "in between" the notes of the other drum parts. Lines 5 and 6 may be played together, for instance, in Sinte.

Line 7. Triplets can also be played "inside" the beat, with three notes [gd g] played in the space normally taken by two. This is accomplished not with a triplet, per se, but simply a doubling of the first note – at least for convenience of notation. An alternate way to notate (and play and hear) this roll would be as a triplet [g d g]. But the difference, at high tempo, is so slight as to be imperceptible, so the point is rather moot. It's the same kind of subjective flexibility that comes into play with "swing," where the length of space between two notes can stretch between [x.x] and [x–x]. It's simply a matter of feel, and taste.

Finally, the lead soloist can weave in and out of all of these variations fluidly. Downbeat, upbeat, offbeat, outside or inside the beat . . . all of these are possible realms to explore. Always in ear and mind and body are the foundation parts keeping the tempo and pulse and downbeat going; and if these are strong and the soloist sensitive, there is no limit to the intricacy and beauty of his or her elaborations.

Lesson 4: Downbeats and Offbeats in 6/8 Time

Here we can see the same range of possibilities as in 4/4, for playing around the downbeat pulse.

	1	.	.	2	.	.	3	.	.	4	.	.	
1. downbeat	O			x			O			x			
2. djembe	G	(d	g)	D	g	d	G	(d	g)	D	g	d	
3. djembe	P		g	T			P		g	T			
3a. alt. handing	P		d	P			P		d	P			
3b. with pickup	P		g	T		D	P		g	T		D	
3c. alt. pickup	P		d	P		D	P		d	P		D	
3d. accomp.	P		g	T	g	d	P		g	T	g	d	
4. upbeat	x			o			x			o			
5. pulse, pickup	x		x	x		x	x		x	x		x	
6. binary feel	x		x		x		x		x	x		x	
7. djembe	g	d	G	D			g	d	G	D			
8. offbeat dun.		x	x		x	x		x	x		x	x	
9. offbeat ken.			x		x	x			x		x	x	
10. djembe			P		g	T			P		g	T	
11. solo phrase	dg	d	P	**T**		d	**g**		P		g	d	>
		T		**d**		T		d	g		P		

Downbeats and Upbeats

Line 1. Here the basic downbeat is established, one bass beat for every six notes, with the bell marking the pulse in between.

Line 2. The classic "mother rhythm" maintains the pulse with bass notes, filling in offbeats with tones. Note that with triplets, the bass downbeats require alternating hands. Playing this rhythm without some of the tones (d g) is a part for Tiriba.

Line 3. The classic, almost universal 6/8 accompaniment djembe rhythm. 3a shows an alternate handing. 3b and 3c give the option of a bass pickup note. 3d shows a variation or additional part. With more notes filled in, you can see why the standard handing is preferred, as the regular alternation of hands is required.

Line 4. Sometimes the pulse will mark the upbeat more than the downbeat, for contrast. This is the kenkeni part for Guinea Fare.

Line 5. Here's the standard dunun bell pulse for 6/8 rhythms. The momentum and timing is enhanced and reinforced with the use of the pickup.

Binary Feel

Line 6. A common variation on the dunun bells establishes a binary feel in the first half of the bar [x - x - x -] before grounding back in the triplet pulse in the second half.

Line 7. Some rhythms, like Sorsornet, lean even more heavily on a binary feel, carrying it through the whole measure. We might even think of such rhythms as 3/4 instead of 6/8 (see below) – except for the more identifiable 6/8 parts accompanying such patterns in the ensemble.

	1	.	*	.	2	.	*	.	3	.	*	.
	g	d	G		D		g	d	G		D	

Offbeats

Line 8. The vast family of Doundounba rhythms relies almost universally on this offbeat dununba bell part and on the similar offbeat kenkeni part.

Line 9. The kenkeni alternates between playing single and double offbeat notes.

Line 10. The offbeat djembe part, also played in Doundounba, matches the kenkeni rhythm. Note that this is the same pattern as the main accompaniment djembe pattern in Line 3, which sets the pulse in Doundounba and most other 6/8 rhythms; except that here it is offset away from the downbeat.

Line 11. In this solo phrase (from Soli) notice how the played notes weave in and out of the pulse (grayed boxes). Anchor the phrase and monitor that the timing is tight where the played notes align with the pulse (notes in bold).

With all three of these offbeat rhythms, it is next to impossible to practice them without having a strong accompanying downbeat played alongside. Otherwise we inevitably allow a sense of downbeat to gravitate onto one of our played notes. This is only natural, since we are conditioned to play these exact same patterns with the pulse on the played notes, as in lines 3 and 5 above. Practice s-l-o-w-l-y and diligently, with a patient partner or steady metronome supplying the downbeat in the empty space (gray squares) in the pattern where it belongs. As well it helps to really feel in the body and breath the presence of that missing downbeat. For instance we can voice the dununba bell pattern as "**Nn** ti ti **Nn** ti ti **Nn** ti ti **Nn** ti ti . . ."; and the djembe pattern as "**Uhn** uhn Pa **Uhn** go Ta **Uhn** uhn Pa **uhn** go Ta . . ."

Lesson 5: Handing and Timing for Basic 4/4 Djembe Parts

Following a simple progression we can learn the two most commonly played accompaniment djembe parts, with proper handing and timing.

	1	.	*	.	2	.	*	.	3	.	*	.	4	.	*	.
	G		g	d	G		g	d	G		g	d	G		g	d
	G		g	d	G		P		G		g	d	G		P	
	G		g	d	-		P		G		g	d	-		P	
alt. handing	D		g	d	-		P		D		g	d	-		P	

These patterns start with a straightforward downbeat and upbeat feel, and move us to a clave feel (grayed squares). The rhythm we have arrived at is best known as Kuku.

12

		1	.	*****	.	**2**	.	*****	.	**3**	.	*****	.	**4**	.	*****	.
		G		P	T	G		P	T	G		P	T	G		P	T
		G		P	T	G		g	d	G		P	T	G		g	d
		P		P	T	P		g	d	P		P	T	P		g	d
		P			T	P		g	d	P			T	P		g	d

These patterns start as the previous group did, with the bass pulse on the downbeats, but substitute slaps for tones on the upbeats. With a series of further substitutions (practice each line by itself until the handing is effortless!), we arrive at the final line, which is practically a universal accompaniment djembe part in 4/4 rhythms from West Africa. Trying to master this rhythm by itself is deceptively challenging for beginners; so I recommend using this progression to get there in gradual steps, reinforcing the right/left handing along the way.

Koreduga – A Time Puzzler

We might well call this eccentric rhythm that of the trickster. The timing is in the oddball signature 9/8, which to our struggling ears we can break into more bite-sized chunks. The basic rhythm is:

o - o - o - O o -
g - d - T - d P -

This group of notes combines familiar phrases from 4/4 and 12/8 rhythms and melds them together. One way we can hear it is like this, 4 + 5:

g - d - | T - d P -

While counting in 5 is generally unheard of, we can recognize the standard triplet phrase, [T - d P - -], so really what's happening is the final rest gets dropped; or rather, the final double rest [- -] gets shortened to a single rest. Come to think of it, this isn't so uncommon after all. Remember the clave pattern [x - - **x - - x -**]?
That's 3 + 5, where once again the 5 comes from a shortened triplet.

Getting back to Koreduga, our 4 + 5 then is really more of a 4 + 3 + 2. It begins with the binary feel, switches to a triplet feel and then quickly back to the binary.

Another way to hear it is 6 + 3, with the initial 6 having a binary feel:
o - o - o - | O o -

This phrase is reminiscent of the Mendiani sangban in 12/8:

O - O - O - | x M - ...

where the phrase extends by doubling the triplet (thereby increasing the 9 to 12 total notes).

O - O - O - x M - x M - = 6 + 3 + 3

That Mendiani sangban phrase actually begins just after the **4**:

	1	.	.	**2**	.	.	**3**	.	.	**4**	.	.
sangban	O		O		x	M		x	M	>	O	

In this layout, the 6 + 3 + 3 counting is broken up and becomes 4 + 3 + 3 + 2, as we begin our counting from the **1**. But there's something compelling and familiar about that grouping of 6 notes with a binary feel at the beginning of the phrase we hear, so let's recapture it by shifting our timing grid instead.

	4	.	.	**1**	.	.	**2**	.	.	**3**	.	.
Mendiani S	O	>	O		O		x	M		x	M	
	1	.	.	**2**	.	.	**3**	.	.	**4**	.	.
Mendiani D	O		x		x		x	x		O	O	

The first thing we notice is that the phrasing of the Mendiani dununba is identical, at least in where the beats are placed – except that its phrase starts just after the **1** instead of just after the **4**. Played together, these two patterns basically make a "round" (think "Row row row your ... / Row, row, row ...").

Once we can think of phrases as recognizable melodies, freed from their normal starting places (>) in the traditional arrangements (or our propensity to want to lock them into such grids), the correspondences abound.

	.	>	**1**	.	.	**2**	.	.	**3**	.	.	**4**
Mendiani sangban	O		O		O		x	M		x	M	
	.	.	**2**	.	.	**3**	.	.	**4**	.	>	**1**
Mendiani dununba	O		x		x		O	O		O	O	
	.	**2**	.	.	**3**	.	>	**4**	.	.	**1**	.
Soli sangban	x		M		M		x	O		x	O	
Soli dununba	O		x		x		O	x		O	x	
	.	**2**	.	.	**3**	.	.	**4**	.	>	**1**	.
Konden dununba	O		O		M		x	M		x	O	
Tiriba sangban	O		x		M		x	M		x	O	
Guinea Fare sangban	x		O		O		x	O		x	M	
	1	.	.	**2**	.	.	**3**	.	.	**4**	.	>
Tiriba dununba	O		x		O		O	x		x		x
Guinea Fare dununba	O		x		x		x	x		x		x

Bell and Clave Patterns Summary

The more bell patterns we learn for the West African dununs, the more we realize that the number of combinations is fairly limited. One traditional limitation is that there are seldom more than two notes in a row struck in a given pattern. Another limitation is that there are seldom even two rest notes in a row. This makes sense when we think of the bell as the timekeeper - if not a metronome, then at least marking the passage of time steadily, without any ambiguous or crowded spaces. Thus the most common patterns over the space of a half-bar of 4/4 time are as follows:

1	.	*	.	2	.	*	.
X		X		X		X	
X		X	X		X	X	
X	X		X	X		X	
X	X		X		X	X	
X		X		X	X		X

These same patterns can be repeated or used in various other combinations to complete the bar, for example:

	1	.	*	.	2	.	*	.	3	.	*	.	4	.	*	.
Sofa dununba	X		X	X		X	X		X		X		X		X	

While the above patterns nearly exhaust all the possibilities (given the traditional rules of thumb), there are a few other possibilities allowed, which we might as well have in our toolkit. Also it is useful to include a few other basic rhythms commonly used to establish and maintain the pulse: the clave, samba and juju patterns.

4/4	1	.	*	.	2	.	*	.	3	.	*	.	4	.	*	.
straight pulse	X		X		X		X									
Lamba sang/ken	X		X		X		X	X								
Lolo kenkeni	X		X		X	X		X								
juju pulse	X	X			X	X										
rev. juju pulse			X	X			X	X								
samba pulse	X				X	X		X								
clave	X			X			X									
Sofa dununba	X		X	X		X	X									
cascara	X		X	X		X		X								
Kassa sangban	X	X		X		X		X								
Kassa dununba	X	X		X		X	X									
Sofa sangban	X	X		X	X		X									
Lamba sang/ken	X	X		X	X		X	X								
Lafe dununba		X	X		X	X		X								

While the above rhythms are typical of the West African dunun bells, many also migrated to the New World with African slaves and found their way into the Afro-Latin ensembles as separate bell and clave parts. The rhythms below generally depend on one of the patterns above for the first half of the bar, and continue with variations that feature a greater use of space in the second half of the bar.

4/4	1	.	*	.	2	.	*	.	3	.	*	.	4	.	*	.
--Son											X		X			
--Bossa Nova											X			X		
--Gahu											X				X	
--Samba									X		X		X			X
--reverse Samba										X			X		X	
(--variation)										X	X		X		X	
(--variation)										X		X	X		X	
--Conga Habanero										X		X		X		X
--Ijexa									X			X		X	X	

It's interesting to note that nearly all of the examples with the first beat unplayed are these completion patterns in the second table, which pick up their momentum from the first half of the bar. But there is no reason why we can't add to the possibilities of first-half patterns with such phrasing (the venerable Mendiani dununba rhythm in 6/8, for example, makes use of just such a pattern).

It's also remarkable how few possibilities there are that don't belong (to my knowledge), to any recognizable traditional pattern. Or maybe it's just a matter of time. Just recently I found rhythms containing three previously unnamed patterns in the above chart. There is truth here in the saying, "Nothing new under the sun."

The same mapping exercise can be applied to the 6/8 side of the extended family of West African rhythms. In this case we can confine the map to the six squares of the 6/8 bar, assigning names of notable rhythms that begin with these patterns. Again, some of the patterns will simply repeat, and some will be completed in a 12-beat phrase with another of the patterns here. For the sake of a comprehensive view of the possible patterns in this grid, I have included a few djembe rhythms as well.

6/8	1	.	.	2	.	.
pulse	X			X		
P - g T - -	X		X	X		
pulse with pickup	X		X	X		X
short bell	X		X		X	X
long bell, Son	X		X		X	
rumba, Fula Fare	X		X			X
rev. long bell, Haitian, salsa	X	X		X		X
Sorsornet kenkeni	X	X		X	X	
salsa 2		X	X		X	
Doundounba		X	X		X	X
Doundounba kenkeni, djembe			X		X	X
rev. Son, rev. rumba		X		X		
Soko djembe		X		X	X	
Mendiani dununba		X		X		X

Listen to your music, and do what you know you have to do to feel whole, to feel complete, and to feel you're fulfilling your destiny. You'll never be at peace if you don't get that music out and let it play. Let the world know why you're here, and do it with passion.

– Dr. Wayne Dyer

West African Drum Chakras

Inspired by some of the drumming lore I have heard, I present here another kind of map to use in your creative arrangements, based on the 7 chakras. Looked at in this way, the music of this tradition can be appreciated as a complete body-mind-spirit experience.

(flute)

7 Crown – djembe solos/improvisation
6 Third Eye – djembe melody/ride/lead/solos
5 Throat – djembe harmony/accompaniment 2/ride
4 Heart – bass djembe accompaniment
3 Solar plexus – kenkeni
2 Sex center – sangban
1 Root – dununba

(shekere)

For those unfamiliar with the chakra system, I offer here a brief description of the above.

1. The dununba establishes the foundation, the solid grounding of the earth.
2. The sangban moves the hips and activates the kundalini or rising life energy.
3. The kenkeni enacts the will to gather the rhythmic elements around its tempo.
4. The bass djembe flows from the heart and connects the hearts of all who hear it.
5. The accompaniment djembe expresses the creative harmony of the music.
6. The lead djembe understands the rhythm through all of its elaborate melodies.
7. The djembe solos dance above the body and melody with pure and free spirit.

For more on the chakras and what they generally represent in our lives, see the following resources online:
   http://alternativeculture.com/spirit/chakra.htm - general introduction
   http://alternativeculture.com/spirit/chakras.htm - meditation through the chakras
   http://alternativeculture.com/spirit/balance.htm - comprehensive chakra life-map

Grow Your Own Drum and Dance Group

There is a definite power in drumming for drumming's sake, either with other drums and percussion, or even alone. Nothing compares, however, with drumming for dancers. Drumming and dancing are fused together in the West African tradition. The interplay between the two elements is synergistic. Each feeds the other, until the vortex of energy is more than the sum of the two. We gain more life force from this activity than we use up.

If you don't yet have access to a group of dancers to play for, there are a number of possibilities. One approach is to practice with other drummers and percussionists until you have a set of pieces to perform. Be careful of expectations: dancing will happen spontaneously if the drumming is good enough; conversely, even if an event for dancers is organized but the drumming falls short, few dancers will be inspired to take the floor!

Besides inviting audience participation on the dance floor, you can enlist dancers or poi/fire spinners to join you in performance. The visual dynamic adds a great attraction for street busking or a drumming show; and having a core of enthusiastic dancers can animate others to join the dance energy.

The most reliable way to drum for dancers is to collaborate with a dance class teacher or facilitator. Classes that can make good use of live West African style drumming include not only dance classes of that tradition, but other styles of dance as well, including trance, jazz, modern, Afro-belly, and hip-hop. Even a single djembe can fuel a powerful trance dance class.

While this book can provide you with material to inspire many types of percussion events or dance classes, the ensemble rhythms included here are specifically arranged for traditional West African dance. If you have a dance teacher or choreographer to work with, the basics are in place. What is needed then is to fill out the group with competent and enthusiastic drummers. Even beginners can quickly learn the necessary supporting parts, with the help of this notation or some live instruction, and a little patience and practice.

Besides the work of the dance class drum ensemble, if you become familiar with this material you can use it as a basis to teach others. Virtually any city in the world will have at least a half a dozen people eager to learn this style of drumming. While there may be a long road ahead of some players before they can hold a strong and fast tempo for a dance class, the journey is begun, and satisfaction is enjoyed in the meantime for the inner dance.

Lead Djembe Drumming and Soloing

Traditional Solos and Improvisation

Contrary to popular belief, traditional drum soloing on the djembe is not simply free improvisation. Master djembe players such as Mamady Keita and Famoudou Konate play and teach a style of soloing based on "traditional solos," a series of rhythmic variations each corresponding to a particular dance move. Besides being tailored to the movements of the dance, these solo phrases will reflect the underlying melody of the dununs (particularly the sangban) and the accompaniment djembes. A gifted soloist will also depart from the prearranged solo phrases to improvise with free creativity . . . always with the structure and feel of the traditional rhythms and dance in mind.

In comparing the traditional solos of different teachers, villages, or regions of West Africa, one realizes that the tradition is not fixed, nor is there a commonly agreed upon arrangement of solos (or other parts) for any given rhythm. Dance moves likewise will vary, even among "traditional" teachers from the same area. So there is some freedom for the lead djembe player or arranger to pick and choose from traditional solo parts, as well as to create and play new variations. **The "djembe 1" parts in the arrangements that follow could be considered as the basic starting point for the lead djembe, with the "solos" as additional options.**

To summarize: the grounding for the soloist begins with traditional parts and phrases, and when improvising, (s)he plays around the foundation melody of the supporting instruments (whatever the choice of parts may be for a given rhythm). Deep knowledge of all the parts is definitely recommended as preparation for such a role. Then the key is to listen, and to play around that melody in various ways to reinforce, to embellish, and to accentuate the pulse and the spaces of the music. All of this happens with the ears and hands, while the eyes focus on the dance moves, to play with those. It all comes back to the dance.

Breaks, Intros and Endings

While playing solos to match the sequence of dance moves, the lead djembe player will mark the transitions from one move to another by calling a break (or "call"). Here are the most commonly used breaks (see Fula Fare for more possibilities in 12/8).

4/4	1	.	*	.	2	.	*	.	3	.	*	.	4	.	*	.
	this		is	a		u	-	ni	ver	-	sal		break			
universal break	g		g	d		d		d	g		d		g			
--variation	gf		g	d		d		d	g		d		P			
--variation	gf		g	d		d		d	g		P	T	P			

12/8	1	.	.	2	.	.	3	.	.	4	.	.
	g		g	d		d	g		g	d		
--variation	gf		g	d		g	d		g	d		
	gd	g	d	g	d		g	d		g		

Normally the other players keep playing their regular parts while the lead djembe calls the break for the dancers to change moves. Where these breaks occur in the arrangement is variable. Here are some different approaches:

1. *Counting bars.* Often a choreography will call for a set number of moves between transitions. In that case the lead drummer will either need to count or feel the right number of bars (usually 4 or 8), or watch for a dancer's cue. With an 8-bar move, play the solo measure for 7 bars and the break for the 8th. With a 2-bar solo phrase, this means three repetitions (making 6 bars) then bar 1 for the 7th, then the break.

2. *Signal from dancer.* The dance teacher or other dancer will give a visual or voiced signal for the drummer to call a break. This can be tricky to time correctly. Since dance moves generally alternate between right and left, it's important to start the new solo phrase – and also the break leading into it – on the correct side.

3. *Drummer initiates break.* The drummer has to have a good sense of how long each dance move should be. While this option may seem like the easiest approach, it's even more important here for the drummer to be aware of the alternating sides of the dance moves.

Introductions and endings to rhythms, especially in performance situations, can be made more dynamic with a special break for that purpose. Some traditional intros and endings are included with the rhythm arrangements in this book; many more are possible. Another way to lend dynamic to an arrangement is to play a "long break," a sequence of many measures of changing patterns. Such a display of timing (and memory) of the players of the ensemble can add to the audience appeal of a presentation between dances, or in place of dancers. Ibro Konate's book (see Resource list) is an excellent resource for long breaks.

Here is an example of one of many possible intro breaks for Kuku:

	1	.	*	.	2	.	*	.	3	.	*	.	4	.	*	.	
(Ken Doumbia)															g	d	> |
|:	P	T	P	T	P		g	d	P	T	P	T	P		g	d	
	P		g	d	P		g	d	P		G		D		g	d	x3 |
(O : duns only)	-		-		-		-		-		O		O		O		
3rd time: …															Pt		
|:	g		d		g		Pt		g		d		g		Pt		
	g		d		G		D		G		-		-		Pt		x3
> universal bk.	gf		g	d		d		d	g		d		g				

Arranging Solo Phrases

A complicated arrangement of multiple solo phrases can be challenging to learn, and also to remember in the heat of performance. It may be better to simplify. If you are ambitious and want to string together a long sequence of variations, it will help to make use of some device to aid your memory. Here are some examples:

1. *Number association.* You can associate the number of each solo with the character, structure or feel of that phrasing. For example, is there a 2-bar phrase for solo number 2 or 4? Does solo number 6 have a 6/8 feel to it?

2. *Visual reference.* You can picture the shape of the notation layout on the page, or recall visually the progression of solos.

3. *Structural layout.* Many traditional solo progressions begin with the simpler phrases and work naturally up to the more complex, building variations on the basic rhythmic structure. While it's true that the solos should match the dance moves, there is usually a good match between many of the moves and many of the possible solo phrases, so you do have some freedom in choosing your progression. You can build a sequence that has some internal logic and is easy to remember. For a good example of this approach, see notation for Lafe, Sofa (4/4) and Yankadi (12/8).

Notation for Rolls Practice

The signature of the solo drummer is the roll, made by doubling the first few notes of a phrase. A doubled first tone followed by another tone makes a group of notes that can also be notated, played and heard as a triplet (see gray boxes below in the first two lines). The roll can be extended to 4, 5, 6, 7 or more notes in the same fashion.

To become fluent in these rolls, practice slowly at first, and play in time with your foot or a metronome keeping the pulse. It also helps to learn rolls beginning with both right and left hands, as some rhythms will call for one or the other in order for the handing of the larger phrase to work out most easily. Play CD tracks 17-18 as practice exercises.

4/4		1	.	*	.	2	.	*	.	3	.	*	.	4	.	*	.

3-note roll	gd	g		d	g	T			P	T		G		T		P
--alt. feel	g d g															
--mid-phrase	gd	g	T	P	D		P	T	gd	g	T	P	D			
--in series	gd	g	T	gd	g	T	P	T	P				gd	g	T	P	T
4-note rolls	g	d		d	g		gd	gd	P	T		T	P		PT	PT
5-note roll	gd	gd	g	T	P			T	P		D		P		T	
--alt. feel	gd	g d g														
6-note roll	G				D			PT	PT	PT	P	T				
--alt. feel								PT	P T	P T P	T					
7-note roll	gd	gd	gd	g	T			P	T		D		P		T	
--alt. feel	gd g d	g d g	T													
3-5-7 combination	gd	g	T			gd	gd	g	T		gd	gd	gd	g	T	
tone/slap exercise	gd	gd	gd	g	T		g	d	PT	PT	PT	P	d		P	T

12/8	1	.	.	2	.	.	3	.	.	4	.	.
3-note roll	gd	g	T	P			gd	g	T	P		
4-note roll	gd	gd	P	T			gd	gd	P	T		
5-note roll	gd	gd	g	T			gd	gd	g	T		
6-note roll	gd	gd	gd	P	T		gd	gd	gd	P	T	
7-note roll	gd	gd	gd	g	T		gd	gd	gd	g	T	
roll-to-roll series	gd	g	T	gd	g	T	gd	g	T	gd	g	T
tone/slap exercise	gd	gd	g	T	g	d	PT	PT	P	d	P	T
mid-phrase (Soli	P	T	gd	gd	P	T		D	P	T	gd	gd	>
or Doundounba)	P	T		D	P	T	gd	gd	P	T		

More Soloing Tips

1. **Use primarily slaps** to be heard above the other drums, and tones for variation and emphasis, and for calling the break. Bass notes are less useful for the soloist because they are harder to hear in the ensemble, but they can add subtlety and a funky feel to your phrasing; they are also useful as pickup notes.

2. **Make good use of space.** Remember to play with and around the accompaniment parts, especially the sangban. Play with *offbeat* phrases that weave in and around the downbeat, as in the examples noted earlier. This requires always listening. For much of the time while soloing, "Less is More." In general, leave space after the 4 in any solo phrase leading into the break, as a cue of anticipation; and for additional emphasis, mark the 4 with a slap or flam.

3. **Smile, have fun, and engage** with the dancers, the other drummers, and the audience. You are a front for the band, a visual focus, and a channeler of energy.

West African Dance Rhythm Arrangements

Djole	1	.	*	.	2	.	*	.	3	.	*	.	4	.	*	.	
intro (all)	X		X		-		-		-		-		X		X		>
	-		-		-		-		-		-		-		-		>
	X		X		-		-		-		-		X		X		>
	-		-		-		dg	d	P		dg	d	P	-			
djembe 1	G			d	g				G				g	d	g	d	>|
	g			d	g				G				g				
djembe 2	P		P	T		T	g	d	P		P	T		T	g	d	
djembe 3	G		g	d	G		P	T	G		g	d	G		P	T	
ken/san combo	o		X		O		x		o		x		O		O		
dununba	O		x		M		x		O		O		M		x		
sangban	x		x		O		x		x		x		O		O		
kenkeni		o	o			o	o			o	o			o	o		

solos...	1	.	*	.	2	.	*	.	3	.	*	.	4	.	*	.	
1	G		T	P					G				g	d	g	d	
2	G	D	P	D			g	d			P				g	d	
3	P		P	T		T	g	d	P		P		P	T	g	d	
4			g	d			P	T			g	d			P	T	
5	G			d	g				G				g	d	g	d	>|
	g			d	g				G				g				
6	Pt				g	d			Pt	G			g	d	g		
7	g	d			g	d			P				g	d	g	d	
8	P		P	T		T	g	d	P		P	T		T	g	d	>
	P		P	T		T	g	d	P		P		P	T	g	d	
9	gd	g	d	g	T				gd	g	d	g	T		P		
10	P	T		T		T		D	P	T	P		P			D	

Doundounba Rhythms

This is the term for a whole family of rhythms known as "the dance of the strong men," popular in the Hamanah region of interior Guinea. I saw it performed in Famoudou Konate's home village of Sangbarala for days on end; and there, reportedly for the first time, the dance was done also by "strong women."   Normally the rhythm is characterized by a constant offbeat dununba and kenkeni part, with the accompaniment djembes keeping the pulse, the sangban providing the distinctive melody for the given rhythm out of thirty or more possible variations, and the lead djembe players taking turns running through the set of solo phrases.

The primary break and "onbeat" dunun parts here are adapted from parts that come from a different rhythm altogether – Konden – because they are easier to play, and because the dance teacher I was working with wanted this feel for the piece. But we called it Doundounba because we used those dance moves and djembe solos. For more advanced players and for a more traditional arrangement, use the "offbeat" dunun parts and alternate break indicated here.   The dununba and sangban parts are from the "mother" Doundounba rhythm, Dunungbe, while the kenkeni and djembe accompaniments and solos are generic Doundounba patterns.   Note how djembe 3 matches the kenkeni, and functions as a "round" when offset with djembe 1.

Doundounba	1	.	.	2	.	.	3	.	.	4	.	.	
intro	gd	g	T	P			gd	g	T	P			>
	gd	g	T	P			gd	g	T	P			>
	gd	g	T	P		g		P			PT	P	>
	T	P		gd	g	d	g	T	P				>
Doundounba bk.	P	T	g	T	P	T							
alt. bk. (Konden)	g		g		g		g						
djembe 1	P		g	T		(D)	P		g	T		(D)	
djembe 2	P			T	g	d	P			T	g	d	
djembe 3			P		g	T			P		g	T	
onbeat (Konden)													
sangban	O			O		O	M		x	M		x	
dununba	O		x	x		O	O		x	x		O	
kenkeni	x		o	x		o	x		o	x		o	
offbeat duns:													
kenkeni		x	o		o	o		x	o		o	o	
sangban	M		x	x		x	x		O	O		x	>
	M		x	x		x	x		O	x		x	
dununba		x	x		x	x		O	O		O	O	>
		O	O		x	x		O	O		O	O	

Doundounba	1	.	.	2	.	.	3	.	.	4	.	.	
solos...													
1	P		g	T	g	d	P		g	T	g	d	
2	g	d	P	T	P	T	g	d	P	T	P	T	
3	P	T	g	T	P	T	P	T	g	T	P	T	
4	P	T	g	T	P		P	T	g	T	P	D	
5	P	T	P	T	g	d		T	P	T	g	d	
6	P	T			g	d	P	T	G		g	d	
7	P		P	T	g	d	P	T	P	T	g	d	
solos with rolls...													
8	gd	g	T	P			gd	g	T	P			>
	g			-			-			-			
9	gd	g	T	P			gd	g	T	P			>
	g			-		P		P		P			
10	gd	g	T	P			gd	g	T	P			>
	gd	g	T	P			gd	g	T	P			>
	gd	g	T	P		g		P			Dp		>
	-			-			-			-			
11	gd	g	T	gd	g	T	gd	g	T	gd	g	T	>
	gd	g	T	gd	g	T	gd	g	T	P		D	>
	PT	PT	P	T		T	P		P	T			g
(alt)	PT	PT	PT	PT	PT	PT	PT	PT	P				g
12	P	T	gd	gd	P	T		D	P	T	gd	gd	>
	P	T		D	P	T	gd	gd	P	T		D	>
	PT	PT	P	T		T	P		P	T			g
echauffement	g	T	P	T	P	T	g	T	g	T	g	T	
end	gd	g	T	P			gd	g	T	P			g

Fula Fare	1	.	.	2	.	.	3	.	.	4	.	.
dununba	O		x	O			O		x	O		
--alt.		O	O	M	x			O	O	M	x	
sangban	O		x	M		x	O		O			O
> variation		O		O		O	O			O		O
kenkeni	o		x	o		x	o		x	o		x
djembe 1	P		g	T	G		P	d	g	T	G	
djembe 2		d	g		P			d	g		P	
djembe 3	G		P	D	g	d	G		P	D	g	d
solos...	1	.	.	2	.	.	3	.	.	4	.	.
1	P		g	T	G		P	d	g	T	G		> ⌐
	P	d	g	T	G		P	d	g	T	G	
2	P	D	P	T	P		P	D	P	T	P	
3	P		P	d	G		P		P	d	G	
4	P	D	gd	g	D		P	D	gd	g	D	
5	T		P	T	gd	g	T		P	T	gd	g
exit	P	d	g	d	P	D	P	d	g	T	P	
call & variations	g		g			(d)	g		g		g	
a	gd	g	d	g	d			g	d		g	d
b	gd	P	T	P			g	d	g	d		
c	gf		g	d			d		d	g		g
d	g	T	P	d	P	T	g	T	P	T		> ⌐
	g		g			d		d		D		

Solos
As with many of the rhythm arrangements, here you can be flexible in choosing additional solos from the djembe accompaniments and variations. You can even create solos using phrases from the call variations, as long as the primary call remains distinctive.

Call Variations
a. Note the handing to emphasize the downbeat pulse with the strong hand. This variation adds a final [d] after one of the standard 12/8 calls (p. 19).
b. Play with the emphasis on the pulse beats (the 1, 2, and 3).
c. Note the similarity to the 4/4 universal break, with this 12/8 version lacking only the last beat.
d. The first measure could be repeated several times as an echauffement (of which this phrasing is typical in 12/8), before ending with the standard call (here with bass for the final note).

Guinea Fare	1	.	.	2	.	.	3	.	.	4	.	.	>
call	g	d	g		P	T	P			g	d	g	>
	d		g	d			g						
--alt.	P	T	P		g	d	g			P	T	P	>
	T		g	d	g		g	d		g			
sangban	M		x	O			O		x	O		x	
kenkeni	x			o			x			o			
dununba A O	O		x	x			x	x		x		x	>
B	x		x	x			x	x		x		O	
A B A B A > C:	x		O	x		O	x		O	x		O	
for solos use...													
djembe 1 D	P		D	g		T	P		d	g			>
	P			g		T	P		d	g		D	
--alt. 1	P	D		d	g		P		g	d		T	>
	P		g	d	P		P		g	d		D	
djembe 2	P			**d**	g		P			**d**	g		
--alt.	P			d	g		P		g	d	P		
djembe 3	P		D		d	g					D		>
	P				d	g						D	
--alt.	P				g	d					G		>
	D	G			g	d					D		
djembe 4	G		P	T		d	g			P	T		

Djembe 2 Timing
Note that the timing of this pattern is different from the usual accompaniment part [P - g **T** - -] or [P - g **d** - -]. Here the pulse comes on the first of the tone pair instead of the second - a tricky difference to get correctly at first.

Kassa	1	.	*	.	2	.	*	.	3	.	*	.	4	.	*	.	
djembe 1	g	(d)	P	T			P	T	g	d	P	T	G		P	T	
djembe 2	P			T	P		g	d	P		G	T	P		g	d	
djembe 3			g	d			P				g	d			P		
sangban	x		x	O		x	M		x		x	O		x	M		
kenkeni	o	o		m		x	m		o	o		m		x	m		
--alt	o		x		o		x		o		x		o		x		
--alt	o		x		x		o		o		x		x		o		
dununba	O		O	O		x	x		x		O		O		O		
upright: D-S-K	D		D	D			S		K		D		D		D		
solos...	1	.	*	.	2	.	*	.	3	.	*	.	4	.	*	.	
1	gf		g	d		T	g	d	P		P		P			T	
2	g	d	G	T		D	P		g	d	G	T		D	P		
3	g	d	G	T		D	P		g	d	G	d	G		P		
4	G		G	T		T		D	G		G		g	d		D	
5	P			T	g	d	P	T	P			T	g	d	P	T	
6	g	d	P			T		T	g	d	P			T	g	T	
7	gd	g	T	gd	g	T	gd	g	T		-		-		-		
8	g		g	d		g	d		g	d		g	d			d	>
	g	d		D	g	d		D	P	T		D	P	T		D	
9	P̲		P̲				P̲				g	d	G				>
	P̲		P̲				P̲		g	d	g	d	G				
10	G	d	g	D	g	d	G	d	g	D	g	d	G		G		>
	G						P̲		P	T	P		G				
11	G	T	gd	g	T	P		T	gd	g	T	P		T	gd	g	>
	d	P	d	g	T	g	d	P		-		-		-		-	
12	Pt		g	d		Pt			g	d		Pt		g	d		>
	Pt		g	d		Pt			g	d							
echauffement	P	T	P	T	P	T	g	d	P	T	P	T	P	T	g	d	

The following arrangement of Kassa adapts the traditional drum parts to a different set of instruments, in this case a mobile samba-style band I play for, Masala. The order of parts here can serve as a sample guide to bringing different instruments into the mix, in single or multiple layers.

KassaMasala	1	.	*	.	2	.	*	.	3	.	*	.	4	.	*	.	
repinique call:	XX		x	x		XX		x	x		XX		x	x			>|
	XX		x	x		XX		x	x		-		-		-		
snare (rpt...)	XX		x	x		X	x	x	X		X		X			X	
cowbell join			L	L			H				L	L			H		
snare break X2	XX	x	X		XX	x	X		XX	x	X		-	-	-		
tambourim	X			X	X		x	x	X		x	X	X		x	x	
repinque	x		X	X			X	X	x		X	X	x		X	X	
agogo 1	L		L	H		H		L	L		L			H	H		
lo surdo	O		O	O		x	x		x		O		O		O		
--alt.						(	M		M		)						
mid surdo	(M)		x	O		x	M		(M)		x	O		x	M		
hi surdo/shakers	o		x		x		o		o		x		x		o		
kenkeni	O	O		M		x	M		O	O		M		x	M		
clave	x				x				x		x		x				>|
	x				x				x		x		x				
agogo 2	H		L	H		L	H		H		L	H		L	H		
snare	x	x	X			X		X	x	x	X			X	x	X	
doumbek	P		P	T		T	g	d	P		P	T		T	g	d	
1	**.**	*****	**.**	**2**	**.**	*****	**.**	**3**	**.**	*****	**.**	**4**	**.**	*****	**.**	
doumbek bk 1	P			T	g	d	P	T	P			T	g	d	P	T	
doumbek bk 2	g	d	G	T		G	T		g	d	G	T	G		P		
repinque solo	x		x	x		x	x		x	x		x	x			x	>|
	x	x		x	x	x		x	X	X		x	X	X		x	
repinque solo	x	X	X	x	X	X	x	X	X	x	X	X	x		x		>|
	x			XX			X	X	X		x						
snare solo	x	X	xx	x	X	X		X	xx	x	X	X		X	xx	x	>|
	x	X	x	x	X	x	x	X									

Kuku	1	.	*	.	2	.	*	.	3	.	*	.	4	.	*	.	
djembe 1	G		g	d				P	G		g	d			P		
djembe 2	G		T		d	g			G				G				
djembe 3	G				G				P		T		g	d			
kenkeni 1	o	o			o	o			o	o			o	o			
sangban 1	O		x	M		x	O		O		x		x		O		
sang 1 variations	M		x	O		x	M		M		x		x		M		x4
> var. 1	M		O	O		x	M		M		O	O	x		M		
> var. 2	M		x	O		x	O		x	O		x	O		M		
> var. 3	O		O	O	O			O	O		O		O		M		
dununba 1	x		x	O		x	x		(M)		x		O		O		>
	O		x	O		x	x		(M)		x		x		x		
--alt. duns:																	
kenkeni 2	x		o		x		o		x		o		x		o		
sangban 2	M		x		O		x		M		x		O		x		
dununba 2	x		x	O		x	M		x		x	O		x	M		
--alt. duns:																	
kenkeni 3	o		x		o		x		o		x		o		x		
sangban 3	x		O	O		x	M		x		O	O		x	M		
dununba 3	O		O		O		x		M		x		M		x		

Dunun Parts

As with other rhythms arranged here, there are several options to choose from among the dunun parts. I have arranged the possibilities here in three groups, where each group of 3 parts works well within itself.

Group 1 is the preferred choice. A kenkeni can be mounted on the sangban to play the [M] notes as high [o] notes (with or without a second kenkeni playing its own part alongside). The variations of sangban/kenkeni here are especially fun to play, though challenging at first. Note that variation 3 matches the universal break.

Groups 2 and 3 consist of parts that are relatively easier to play for less experienced drummers.

Solos

All of these choices (on the following page) are probably too many to try to squeeze into one arrangement – though it can be done! Ultimately the choice comes down to what you like and what goes well with the moves of the dance.

Kuku solos	1	.	*	.	2	.	*	.	3	.	*	.	4	.	*	.	
1	g		g	d				Pt	P		P	T			P		>
	G		g	d				P	G		g	d			gf		
2	G		T			d	g		G				G				>
	G		T			d	g		P		T			g	d	
3	g	d			T	g	d	P	g	d			T	g	d	P	
4	G				G				P		T			g	d		x3
	P		T			g	d		P		T			g	d		x1
5	G		g	d	G		P		g	d	g	d	G		P		x3
	gf		g	d	G	T	P		gf		g	d	G	T	P		x1
6	P	T	P	T	g	d	P		P	T	P	T	g	d	P		
7	G		T	P	T				G				D				>
	G		T	P	T			D	g		g			g	d		
8	g		G	T̲		T̲		D	g		G		T̲			(D)	
9	T		g	d				P	T		g	d			T		
10	D		-		-			P	D		-		-		P		>
	D		-		-			P	D		g		d		P		
11	g	d			D	g	d	G	g	d			D	g	d	G	
12	G	D	g	d	G	D	P		G	D	g	d	G	D	P		
13	g	d	P	d	g	T	g	d	P	d	g	T	g	d	P		>
	G				D				G				D				
echauffement	g	T	P	d	P	T	g	T	g	T	P	d	P	T	g	T	
end break	g	d	g	T	P	T	P	T	P	T	P	T	P	T			x3
	g	d	g	T	P	T	P	T	P	T	P	T	P	T	P	T	>
	P	T	P	T	P	T	P	T	P	T	P	T	P				>
end on final 1	P		g	d		T	P		G				G		G	G	

Lafe	1	.	*	.	2	.	*	.	3	.	*	.	4	.	*	.	
break	gd		g	d		d		d	G		D		G	D		d	>
	G		D		G	D		d	G		D		G	D			>
	P	T	g	d	P	T		d	G		D		G	D			
djembe 1	G		g	d			P		G	d	g	d	P		G		
djembe 2	P			T	P		g	d	P			T	P		g	d	
djembe 3			P	T			P	T			P	T			P	T	
kenkeni	x		x	x		o	o		x		x	x		o	o		
--var. 1	x		o	o		x	(m)		x		o	o		x	(m)		
--var. 2			o	o		o	o				o	o		o	o		
sangban a	x		x	M		M		x	O		O		O	O		x	>
b (var. 1)	x		O	O		O		x	O		O		O	O		x	
b (var. 2)		O		O		O		x	O		O		O	O		x	
--echauffement	O		x	O		O		x	O		O		O	O		x	
dununba	O		x	x		x		O	O		O		O	O		O	
--var. w/ kenk.		o	o		x	x		O	x		O		x	O		x	
--var. 2 w/ kenk.		o	o		x	x		O	O		O		O		o	O	
--echauffement		O		O		O		O	O		O		O		O	O	

Lafe Solos (next page)
Many of the 4/4 rhythms can share solo parts just as they share common accompaniment parts. The same can be said for the rhythms in 12/8. In addition, certain rhythms are even more closely aligned in the cultural tradition of West Africa, to the point that even the names of some rhythms are interchangeable. Djole and Makuru are one example (4/4), the Dounounba family is another (12/8).

Lafe has a fairly generic 4/4 feel: note the common djembe and kenkeni patterns, and the way that the sangban and dununba parts use the phrasing of the 4/4 universal break. Thus the solo phrases that follow are a good point of reference for other 4/4 rhythms in need of solos, or for improvising in 4/4. Also they can serve as useful exercises in distinguishing tones and slaps, playing rolls in various combinations, and refining the timing of offbeat sequences.

Lafe solos	1	.	*	.	2	.	*	.	3	.	*	.	4	.	*	.	
1	g	d		T	P		P	T	g	d		T	P		P	T	
2	g	d		T	G		P		G			T	G		P		>
	g	d		T	G		P		G		g	d	P	T	P		
3	gd	g	T	P		g		P		g	d		T	P			>
	G			D					PT	PT	PT	P	T				
4	gd	g	T	P		g			P	T		g		P	T	g	>
	P	T		g		P		T	gd	g	T	P	T		P		>
	G			D					G				D				
5	gd	g	T	P		gd	g	T	P				gd	g	T	P	>
	T				G				D				Pt	Pt			
6	gd	g	T	gd	g	T	P	T	P				gd	g	T	P	>
	T				gd	g	T	P	T				gd	g	T	P	>
	T				G				D				G				
7	g	d	P	T			P	T			P	T	G				
8	gd	g	d	g	T				gd	g	d	g	T		g		>
	P				d				P				d				
9	gd	g	T	P	D		P	T	gd	g	T	P	D				
10	gd	g	T	P	T		T	P	T		P	T	gd	g	T	g	>
	d		P	T	P		P	T	P		P	T	gd	g	T	g	>
	d				-				-		Pt		Pt				
11　　D	gd	g		D	PT	P		D	gd	g		D	PT	P		D	
	gd	g							PT	P	T	P					

Makuru	1	.	*	.	2	.	*	.	3	.	*	.	4	.	*	.	
intro	gf		g	d		d		d	g		d		g				>
	G		T		G		T		G		T		G				>
	g		-		-		g	d	g		P	T	P				
djembe 1	G		P		g	d			G		T				g	d	
djembe 2	d		P					d	g		T		P			g	
djembe 3	G	d	(g)	d	G		T		G		d		G		T	
kenkeni	x		o	o		x	x		x		o	o		x	x	
--faster	o		x		o		x		o		x		o		x	
upright duns	O			O	O		o		O		O		O		o	
sangban (alt.)	(M)		x		x			O	(M)		x		x			O	
dununba (alt.)	O	(O)		O	O		x		O		O		O		x	
solos...	1	.	*	.	2	.	*	.	3	.	*	.	4	.	*	.	
1	g		d	g	d				G		T			G			
2	g	d	P	D	g	d			g	d	P	D	g	d			
3	P		D	P	D		P		D			d		g	d		>
	P			d		g	d		P			d		g	d		
4	P			d	g			P			P		T			D	>
	P			d	g			P								D	
5	P		P	d		d	P		P		P	T			P		>
	P		P	d		d	P										
6	g	T	P	d	P	T	g	T	P								

Arrangement

Makuru is often played as a companion piece to Yankadi (see p. 45), in the arrangement: Yankadi > Makuru > Yankadi. Transition breaks are as follows:

Makuru bks.	1	.	*	.	2	.	*	.	3	.	*	.	4	.	*	.	
bk. after Yan I	P		g	d		T			d	g	P		T				>
O = duns	O		O					g	d	g	P	T	P				>
(all play: O = G)	O		O		O			O		O		O				>
	G			d		T	g	d	g	P		T				
> Makuru > ...																	
echauffement	g	d	g	d	g	d	g	d	P	T	P	T	P	T	P	T	x3
> then	P		g	d		T			d	g	P		T				
> Yan II intro bk	see Yankadi notation																
> Yan II cont. >																	
after Yan II > O	O		O		O			O	O		O			O		>
(all play: O = G)	O		O		O			O								

Mendiani	1	.	.	2	.	.	3	.	.	4	.	.	
sangban	O		O	x	M		x	M		O			x4
--var.	O		O	x	M		x	M		x	O		x2
kenkeni	o		x	x		o	o		x	x		o	
dununba		O		x		x	x	x		O	O		x4
--var.		O		O		O		O	x		O	O	x1
--alt.	O		x	x		O	O		x	O		x	
--alt.	O		O		O		O		x	M		O	
dun/sang comb.	O	O		x		o		x	o		O		
--alt. (upright)	O		o	o		O		O	o		O		
call	gd		g	d		g	d		g	d			
djembe 2	P		g	T		(D)	P		g	T		(D)	
djembe 3	P			T	g	d	P			T	g	d	
djembe 1	P				P			D	P		g	d	
--alt.	P		g	T	P		G	D	P	T	g	d	
solos...	1	.	.	2	.	.	3	.	.	4	.	.	
1	g	T	g	d	P	T	P	T					
2	g	T	P	T	g	d	P	T	P	T			
3	P	T	G	T	P		P	T	P	T		D	
4	g	d	P	T	P	D	g	d	P	T	P		
5	P	d	P	d	g	T	P		P	T	G	T	
6	P	T			g	T	P	T	G		g	T	
7	g	T	g	T	g	T	g	T	g	d	P		>
	P	T									PT	PT	>
	P	T		g		P		d	g	T	P		>
	P	T		-			-			-			

Timing

Notice how the distinctive djembe 1 part cuts across the 12/8 time, with its binary 3/4 feel marked by the slaps. In this emphasis its timing is reinforced by the binary feel of the sangban. For an even funkier feel, you can swing the djembe 1 part as you might with a 4/4 part - slightly stretching, for example, the [g d] at the end. The alternate djembe 1 part has the same timing and feel but simply adds extra notes to the core rhythm.

Sinte	1	.	*	.	2	.	*	.	3	.	*	.	4	.	*	.
djembe 1	g	d		T	G		T		G			T	G		T	
djembe 2	g	d	P	T			P	T	g	d	P	T			P	T
djembe 3	P			T	g	d	g	d	P			T	g	d	g	d
kenkeni	x		x		o		o		x		x		o		o	
sangban	O	O		O	x		x		O		O		x		x	
dununba	O		x		M		x		O		O		O		x	
--alt	M		x	M		x			O	O		O		O		x
solos...	1	.	*	.	2	.	*	.	3	.	*	.	4	.	*	.
1	P			T	g	d	g	d	P			T	g	d	g	d
2	g	d	P	T		(D)	P	T	g	d	P	T	(G)		P	T
3		P	T	P	T				G				G			
4	g	d		T	G	T			G			T	G	T		
5	G	T		D	P			T	G	T			g	d		
6	P		P	T		T	g	d	P		P	T		T	g	d
												(-	P	d)		
break:																
bk/signal	P	T		P	T		gf		g	d		g	d			D	>
lead djembe:	P		P		P			D	P		P		P			D	>
	P	T		D	P	T		D	P	T		D	P	T		
duns accomp:	O		O		O			-	O		O		O			-	>
	o	o			o	o			o	o			o	o		

Short Break, Longer Break
The break sequence above consists of a primary break of one measure, or an extended break of three measures. An arrangement can be built using either the short form or longer form, as an intro, ending, or to mark transitions and break moves in the dance. A pickup note is often used before the start of the break: [D], [G -] or [P -].

Djembe Solos
Solo 2 adds different flavors via the optional bass notes, representing variations of the djembe 2 accompaniment. Solo 3 uses a slow triplet at the beginning of the phrase. Solo 4 is a variation of the djembe 1 part.

Sofa	1	.	*	.	2	.	*	.	3	.	*	.	4	.	*	.	
djembe 1	P			T	P		g	d	P			T	P		g	d	
djembe 2	g	d	P	T			P	T	g	d	P	T			P	T	
djembe 3	g	d		G					D				g	d			
--2-bar var.	g	d		G					D				g	d	P		>
	g	d		G					D				g	d			
dununba	x		x	x		x	O		O		O		O		O		
--alt.	x		x	x		x		O	O		O		O		O		
sangban	O	O		x	M		x		O		O		M		x		
kenkeni	o		x		o		x		o		x		o		x		
--alt	x		x		o	o		x	x		x		o	o		x	
--alt.	x		x	o		x	m		m		x		x		x		
solos...	1	.	*	.	2	.	*	.	3	.	*	.	4	.	*	.	
1a	P			T	P		g	d	P			T	P		g	d	
1b	P			T	P		g	d	P	T	g	d	P		g	d	
2a	P			T	P		G		P		g	d	P		G		
2b	P		g	d	P		G		P	T	g	d	P		G		
2c	P			D	P	T	G		P	T	g	d	P	T	G		
3	P	T		D	P	T		D	P	T	G	D	P	T		D	
4a	g	d	P	T			P	T	g	d	P	T			P	T	
4b	g	d	P	T			P		g	d		T	G		P		
5	G		g	d			P				g	d			P		>
			g	d			P				g	d			P		
6	Pt		P	T			Pt		P	T			g	d		d	>
	g				G				G				G				
7	gd	g	T	P	T			P		gd	g	T	P	T		P	

Djembe Parts and Solos

Note how the solos draw from the basic accompaniment djembe parts and expand on them with variations. The assignments are not fixed. For example, solo 2a or 4b could well be maintained throughout as a basic accompaniment. The solo variations can be built in sequence, or chosen to match more the character of the dance moves. Any solos can be repeated if appropriate to the dance.

End Breaks
The end breaks that follow could by adapted for use as intro breaks, or as breaks in the middle of an arrangement to add dynamics.

Sofa: end bks	1	.	*	.	2	.	*	.	3	.	*	.	4	.	*	.	
Break I																	
echauffement	g	d	g	T	P	T	P	T	g	d	g	T	P	T	P	T	X3
> then univ. bk:	gf		g	d		d			d	g		d		g		D		>
--djembe(s):	P			T	P			D	P			T	P			D		>
	P		P	T	P			T	P			d	g				
--dunun(s): O	x			x	x			O	x			x	x			O		>
	x		x	x				x	x			O	O				
Break II																	
echauffement	g	d	g	T	P	T	P	T	g	d	g	T	P	T	P	T	X3
> then univ. bk:	gf		g	d		d			d	g		d		g				>
--sangban/duns:	O	O		x	M		O		O		O		O		O	O		>
	O	O		O	O	O			O		O		O		O	O		>
	O	O		O	O	O			O		O		O		O			
--djembes:	-		-		-			P		T		P		T		P	T	>
	P	T		T	P	T		T	P		T		P		P	T		>
	P	T		T	P	T		T	P		T		P		T			
Break III																	
echauffement	g	d	g	d	P	T	P	T	g	d	g	d	P	T	P	T	x4
D	P		P			P	T		D	P		P		P	T		D	>
	P	T	G	d	P	T	P		g		g		g	d				>
	g		g		g	d			-				-					

We cannot expect you to be with us all the time, but perhaps you
could be good enough to keep in touch now and again.

- Sir Thomas Beecham to a musician during a rehearsal

Soko	1	.	.	2	.	.	3	.	.	4	.	.	
intro break	PT	P	T	g	d		P	T		G	D		>
duns play GDs	PT	P	T	g	d		G	D		G	D		>
	PT	P	T	g	d		P	T		G	D		>
	G		G		G		G		Pt				>
call	gd	g	d	g	d		g	d		g			
djembe 1	P		P	T	g	d	P	(T)	P	T	g	d	
--alt.	P		g	d			P		g	d			
djembe 2		T		d	P			T		d	P		
djembe 3	g		d				G			D			
kenkeni	x		x	x		x	x		x	x		x	
				o	o			>	o	o			
sangban	O		x		x		O	O		O	O		>|
O on 1 can be M	O		x		x		x	x	>	O	O		
dununba	O		x	x		O	O		O	O		O	>|
	O		x		x		x	>	O	O		O	
alt. dun parts:													
kenkeni	o	x		o	x		o	x		o	x		
sangban	M	x		x	x		O	O		O	O		>|
	M	x		x	x		x	x		O	O		
dununba	O		x		O	O		O			O		>|
	O		x	x		x	x		O	O		O	
solos...	1	.	.	2	.	.	3	.	.	4	.	.	
1	G	d	g	-	P		G	T		G	T		
2	P	T	P	-	g	d	P	T	P	(D)	g	d	
3	G	T	P	-	P	T	-	T		d	g		
4	-		P	-	g	d	-	T	P	-	g	d	
5	-	T	P	-	g	d	P	T		D	g	d	>
	P			-	g	d	P	d	g	T	g	d	x3
6	-			-	g	d	P	T		D	g	d	>
	P			-	g	d	P			Pt			
end break: D	P			T		D	P	T		T		d	>|
duns: d g = O O	g												

Dununba and Sangban - Come into the rhythm from the call, on 4 (> , bar 2). These interlocking parts are great fun to play; they produce a dramatic rolling sound as the bass notes bounce off each other. To learn them, it helps to really feel the dununba pattern leaning *into* the pulse [O **O**], and the sangban pattern leaning *on top of* the pulse [**O** O]; the combined effect at the pulse is thus [O **O** O].

Kenkeni - A rare case of drum notes offset from bell notes; tricky to learn at first.

Solos - With these offbeat parts, it really helps to feel the unplayed pulse notes [-].

Soli	1	.	.	2	.	.	3	.	.	4	.	.
call	gf		g	d		g	d		g	d		
djembe 1	g	d	P		G	T	g	d	P	D		T
djembe 2	P		g	T			P		g	T		
djembe 3	g		G			d	g		G	D		d
kenkeni	x		x		o	o	x		x		o	o
--var.	o		o		x		o		o		x	
sangban (a)	O		x		M		M	>	x	O		x
--var. (b)	O		x		M		M		x		x	O >
(c)		x	O		x	O		x	O	O		x
a-b-c-a a-b-c-a												
dununba (a)	x		O		x		x		O	x		O >
(b)	x		O		x	x	x	>	O	x		O >
--var. (c)	O		O		O	O		O		O		O
echauffement	g	T	P	d	P	T	g	T	P	d	P	T >
	g	d	g	T	P	T	g	d	g	T	P	T >
	P	d	g	T	P	T	P	T	P	T	P	T >
	g	T	P	d	P	T	g	T	P	d	P	T >
	g	T	P	d	P	T	g	T	P	d	P	T >
	g	T	P	d	P	T	g	T	P	T		>
	gd	g	T	gd	g	T	P	T	P	T		
exit d	g	T	g	d	P	d	g	T		PT	P	T >
	P	T		PT	P	T	P	T		PT	P	T >
	P	T		PT	P	T	P	T				d >
	g	T	g	d	P	d	g	T		PT	P	T >
	P	d	g	-			-			-		

Dununba and Sangban - Come into the rhythm from the call, on 4 (> , bar 2).

Solo Phrases and Variations
These can be arranged to taste and for the choreography. Solo 5 makes use of a variation on the seventh bar, leading into the break. The basic 2-bar phrase is repeated 3 times, totalling 6 bars, then the variation on bar 7, plus the break, produces the required 8-bar total. Multi-bar phrases can be used with some flexibility for long dance moves; just end with the measure required by your count before the break, leaving space after the 4 for anticipation. For example, playing solo 9 for a 12-bar move, you could include the optional (T) for the first three repetitions (making 9 bars), but drop it on the fourth time through, ending on bar 11, and continuing into the break for bar 12.

Soli solos	1	.	.	2	.	.	3	.	.	4	.	.

1	P		g	T	g	d	P		g	T	g	d	
2	g	d	P			T		P	D		T		>
	g	d	P		G	T	g	d	P	D		T	
3	P	T	P			d	P	T	P	D		d	
4	g		g	d		T	P		g	d		T	>
	P		G			T	P		G			T	
5	g	T	P	d	P	T	g	T	P	d	P	T	>
	P		G			T	P		G				
--bar 1 last time	gd	g	T	gd	g	T	gd	g	T	P		T	
6	G	-	G	D	g	d	G	-	G	D	g	d	
7	gd	g	T	P		g	d	P		PT	P	T	>
	P	d		PT	P	T	P	d		PT	P	T	>
	P	d		G			D			G			
8 Gt	g	d	P	T		Gt	g	d	P	T		Gt	>
	g	d	P	T		Gt	g	d	P	T			>
	gd	g	T	P		g	d	P		P			>
	gf			-		P̲		P̲		P̲		Gt	
9	g		P		P	d	g		P	D			
	gd	g	T	P	(T)		gd	g	T	P	(T)		
	g				P̲		P̲		P̲				
10	P	T	gd	gd	P	T		D	P	T	gd	gd	>
	P	T		D	P	T	gd	gd	P	T			
11	G	d	g	D	P		G	d	g	D	P		>
	P	d	g	T	P		P	d	g	T	P		>
	gd	g	T	P	T		gd	g	T	P	T		>
	gd	g	T	P	T			D	P	T			>
	PT	P	T	P	g		PT	P	T	P	g		>
	TP	T	P	T	P		-			-			
12	dg	d	P	T		d	g		P		g	d	>
		T		d		T		d	g		P		>
				PT	P	T	P	d	g				

Arrangements

Here are two sample arrangements for Sorsornet. In both, all the drums join in the **long breaks** (including the end break), which are signaled by the call from the lead djembe. Only the lead djembe plays the **short break** to signal a change in dance moves, while the other drummers continue to play through with their regular parts.

Binary vs. Triplet Feel

Sorsornet has a distinctive binary feel set by the dununba and sangban parts and the bass djembe (3) accompaniment, the breaks, and other parts. It could almost be considered a 3/4 or 6/4 rhythm for this reason, except for the standard 12/8 parts that cut across this binary grain (kenkeni, djembe I:2, and many of the solos). Note the additional interest created by the matching offbeat kenkeni and solo I:3 parts.

Sorsornet	1	.	.	2	.	.	3	.	.	4	.	.	
call (short bk.)	g	d	g	d	g	-	g	d	g	d	g	-	
call (intro, long)	g	d	g	d	g	d	g	d	g	d	g	-	
long break:	O	O	O		O	O	O		O	O	O		>
(djembes match)	O	O	O		o		o		o		o		
djembe 3	g	d	G		D		g	d	G		D		
djembe 1	P	T	P		G			D		g			
djembe 2	P		g	T			P		g	T			
dununba	O	O	O		M		x		O		M		
sangban	x		x	O	O		x	x		O			
kenkeni	x	o		x	o		x	o		x	o		
Arrangement I:	L - 1 - L - 1 - L (L = long break; 1 = solo 1)												
1	G	d	P	D	g	d	G	d	P	D	g	d	
2		d	g	d		D	G		g		g		
3	d	P		d	P		d	P		d	P		
4	g			d	g	d	g			d	g	d	
5	PT	P	T	P	T		G	T	g	d	P		>
	gd	g	d	g	d		G		P		P		
L - 1 - L - 1 - L													
6	P		g	T			P		g	T		D	
7	P			T	g	d	P			T	g	d	>
	g			d	g	d	g			d	g	d	
8	G	T	g	d	P		G	T	g	d	P		
9	P			T	g	d	P			T	g	d	>
	g			d	g	d	g			d	g	d	
10	d	P		d	P		d	P		d	P		
L - 1 - L - 1 - L*													
*end bk: call >	G	D	G		G	D	G		G	D	G		>
(duns: long bk.)	G	D	G		gd	g	d	g	d	g	d		>
	P	T	P										

Sorsornet	1	.	.	2	.	.	3	.	.	4	.	.	
Arrangement II													
djembe 1 or 2	P	T	P		G		D		g				X3
>	P	T	P		P	T	P		P	T	P		
djembe 1 or 2	P	T	P	T	g	d	P	T	P	T	g	d	
solos...													
1	P	T	P	T	g	d	P	T	P	T	g	d	
long break													
2	G	T	g	d	P		G	T	g	d	P		
long break													
3	g	d	g	d	g	d	g	d	P	T			>
	P		g		P				g	d			
long break													
4	gd	g	T	P	T		gd	g	T	P	T		>
	g	d	g										
short break													
5	PT	P	T	P	T		PT	P	T	P	T		>
	g	d	g										
long break													
6	-			-			-			-	g	T	>
	-	T	P	-	g	T	-	T	P	-	g		>
	P	T	P										
long break													
7	g	d	P	d	g	T	g	d	P	d	g		>
	P	T	P										
short break													
8 (rpt. 5.)													
long break													
9 (rpt. 2.)													
long break													
10 (rpt. 1.)													
end bk.													

Tiriba	1	.	.	2	.	.	3	.	.	4	.	.	
intro:	gd	g	d	g	d	g	T			P			x3
	P			P			P						>
break	gd	g	d	g	d			g	d		g		
djembe 1	D	P	d		P		D	P		D	P		
djembe 2	G			d	P		G			d	P		
djembe 3	G			D	g	d	G			D	g	d	
sangban	O		O			x	M		x	M		x	
dununba	O		x		O		O	x		x		x	
kenkeni	x		x	o	x		x	x		o		x	
--alt.	x		o		o		x		o		o		
solos...	1	.	.	2	.	.	3	.	.	4	.	.	
stage entrance	D	P	d		P		D	P		D	P		
1	D		T	G	d	g	D	P		G	d	g	
2	P		g	T		D	P		g	T		D	
3	G	d	g	D	P		g		g	D		T	
4	P		g	T		D	P		g	T		D	
5	D		T	G	d	g	D	P		G	d	g	
6	P		d	g	d		P	D		G		D	
7	gf		P	T			P	T	gf		P	T	>
	G		P	T	gf		P	T			P	T	>
	gf		P	T	G		P	T	gf		P/	T	>
			P	T	gf		P	T	G		P	T	
8	g	d	P	T	P	T	P	T			d	d	>
	g		P		P		G	T	P	D	g	d	>
	g			gd	g	T	gd	g	T		D		:|
...add before bk:	g	d	g	d			T	P		g	d		

Tiriba solos	1	.	.	2	.	.	3	.	.	4	.	.	
...continued...													
9	D		T	G	d	g	D	P		G	d	g	
10	P		P	d		d	P		P		P	T	>
		D	P		P		P	d		d	P		>
	gd	P		dg	T		P		P	d		d	>
	P		P		P	T		D	P		P		>
	P	d		d	P		gd	P		dg	T		>
	P		P	d		d	P		P		P	T	>
		D	P		P		P	d		d	P		
11 exit	gf		P	T			P	T			P	T	>
			P	T	gf		P	T			P	T	>
			P	T	gf		P	T	gf		P	T	:|
...add before bk:	gf		P	T	gf		P	T	gf		P		
(dununba...)	O		x		O		O	x		x		x	
(djembe 1...)	D	P	d		P		D	P		D	P		
end break:	D		-	P		D	D		-	P		-	>
	D		-	P		D	D		-	P		-	>
	P		T	P		T	P		T	P		-	>
all play:	P		T	-		T	P		-	P		-	

Offbeat Solos

Tiriba is a tricky and interesting rhythm, with the basic feel of djembe 1, for instance, pulling off the pulse with the slaps after the 3 and 4. In addition, some of the solos (7, 10, and 11) have a 3/4 structure and feel. Solos 1 and 6 can swing either way.

Counting Phrases and Ending Solos

In solo 7, the whole phrase is 4 bars long, so a break bar after that would yield an undesirable odd number, throwing the dancers off balance. The solution is to end the phrase with the [P/] in the third bar, then play a break for the fourth bar. Repeats can follow the same rule, yielding a total of 4, 8, 12 or 16 bars for this solo pattern including a final break. Solos 8 and 11 are 3-bar phrases, so either they can lead directly into a standard break for the fourth bar; or if repeated to a 6-bar total, they can lead to the extra transition pattern for bar 7 before the break in bar 8.

End Break

Tiriba has a distinctive end break which switches to a 4/4 feel. It is possible for the duns and accompaniment djembes to play through the first three bars of the end break while continuing their parts in 12/8, while the lead djembe cuts across the timing in 4/4 (see the juxtaposition above). It's an interesting challenge! For a simpler dynamic, have the duns or the other djembes join the lead djembe.

Yankadi bks	1	.	.	2	.	.	3	.	.	4	.	.	
regular break	g		g	T		T	g			P	d		d >
(also intro)	P			d	g	d	g			g	d		
solo, end part I	P		P	d		d	P		P				>
	P		P	dg	dg	d	g	d		P	T		
--var. bar 2	P		P	dg	d	g	d	g		T	P		
solo, end part II	P		P	d		d	P	T	P				>
	P	T	P	d	g	d	P			P			
end break (I, II)	g		g	T		T	g			P	d		d >
	P		P	d		T	g			g	T		

Yankadi/Makuru Arrangement

Yankadi is often played as a companion piece to Makuru, in the arrangement: Yankadi (I) > Makuru > Yankadi (II). The **regular break** is used during both parts of Yankadi to signal dance move changes (other parts continue playing through). The **end break** follows each part. After Part II the final break is in 4/4 (see Makuru, p. 33, for this and the other Makuru breaks.)

The solo variations above can be used as distinctive signals to anticipate the coming end break; this is appropriate especially if the lead djembe plays the related djembe 1 part below throughout the dance, instead of a sequence of many solo variations.

Yankadi	1	.	.	2	.	.	3	.	.	4	.	.	
djembe 1	P		P	d		d	P		P				X3
	P		P	d		d	P		P	D		D	X1
djembe 2	P			g	d								>
	gf			gf			P		T				
djembe 3	G			P		D	G			d	g		D
upright duns I	O		O	o		o				O			>
	O			o			o			o	o	O	
upright duns II	O		O			O	o		o				>
	O		O				o			O	o		
kenkeni with I	x		x	x		x	o		o	x		x	>
	x		x	x		x	o		x	o			
kenkeni with II	x		x	o		o	x		x	x		x	>
	x		x	o		x	o		x	x		x	
alt. dun parts:													
kenkeni	o		x	x		x	o		x	x		x	
sangban	M		x	O		x	M		x	x		x	
dununba	O		x	x		O	O		x	x		O	

Dunun Parts

For variety, the upright dununba/sangban combination can change parts from I to II in the arrangement with Makuru. These work well with the associated kenkeni part if there is another player or if a bell part is desired. An alternate setup for dununs is the more standard set of three matching duns with attached bells.

Solo Sequence

The sequence of solos here is arranged to show how phrases can be linked to each other when they are structurally similar. Such an arrangement has the musical advantage of embellishing a given theme with some consistency; and it has the additional advantage of aiding the memory of a long sequence. Of course, if dance moves are involved then the choice of parts may need to be adjusted to match.

Yankadi	1	.	.	2	.	.	3	.	.	4	.	.	
solos...													
1a	G			P		D	G		d	g		D	
1b	g		g			T	G		d	g			>
	G			P			G		d	g			
2a	g		P		P	d	g		T	P		d	>
	g			-			-			-		d	
2b	P		P		P			D	P		P		>
	P			-			-			-		d	>
	g	d	g		d		-			-			>
	-			-			-			-			
3a	P		g	P		g	P				g		>
	P		g	P		g	P					d	
3b	g		P	g		P	g				P		>
	g		P	T	P	T	P	T	P	T		d	
4a	g	d	g		P	T	P		g	d	g		>
	P	T	P		g	d	g		P	T		d	
4b	g	d	g		P	T	P			g		g	>
	d		PT	P	T	P	T	P	T	P		d	
5a	g	d	P	T	g	d	P	T	g	d	P	T	>
	g	d	P	T	g	d	P	T	g	d		d	
5b	PT	P	T	gd	g	d	PT	P	T	gd	g	d	>
	PT	P	T	gd	g	d	PT	P	T	P		d	

Original Compositions

The titles largely reflect my travels in Asia and the Pacific while composing and compiling this collection.

Arambol Moon	1	.	*	.	2	.	*	.	3	.	*	.	4	.	*	.	
dunun set hi	o	o	o	O		o										-	>
dunun set lo									O	o		O	o	o	O		
djembe 2	P		T		P		g	d	P		T		P		g	d	
djembe 3	P		d		-		T		-		d		P		-		
djembe 1	g	d		D	g		G			g		d	P		G	D	
solos...																	
1	G	D	g	D			T		D		T		D		P		
2	g		P		dg	d	g	T	P		g	T	d		P	T	
3	g		T		g	d			PT	P	T	P	D		D		
4	P	T	dg	dg	P	T		D	P	T	dg	dg	P	T		D	>
	P	T		D	P	T		D	P	T		D	g			D	
5	G		g	d		P	D		G		gd		g	d	P		

Ban Bang Bao	1	.	*	.	2	.	*	.	3	.	*	.	4	.	*	.	
dununba	O		x		x			O	O		x		O		O		
sangban	O		O		M		x		O	x			O		x	O	
kenkeni	x		x		o	o			x	x			o	o	x	x	
agogo	H		H		L		L		H	H			L		L	L	
djembe 2	G		P	d	g		g	d	G	D	d		d	g			
djembe 3	P	T		D			G	D	P	T	D		g	d	G	D	
solos...																	
1	G			D	P		g	d	G			d	P	d	g	d	>
	G		D		P		g	d		d	g		T	d	-	d	
2	P		P	d	G		G	T	g	d	P	d	g	T	g	d	
3	P	d	g		g	T	G	D	P	d	g		g	T	G	D	>
	P	d	g		P	d	g	d	P	T	G	D	D		T		
4	G			D	P	d		d	P		d		P	d	g	d	>
	G	d	P	T			T		T	G	d	g	T				
5	G		G	T		d	g	D		d	P	d	g	d		d	
6	g		P	d		T	g		P	d	T		g		PT	P	>
	T		gd	g	d		P		g	D		D	P	T	P		
7		P	g		P		d		T	P		g	d			D	>
	P	T							D	P	T			g		d	
end: var. bar 2	P	T		D	(g	d)	G	D	P	T	D		g	d	G	D	

Banana Boat Bop	1	.	.	2	.	.	3	.	.	4	.	.
dununba	O		x	x		x	O		x	O		x
sangban	O		x		M		M		x	O		x
--variation	O		O		O	O		O		O		O
bell	x		x	x	x		x		x	x	x	
kenkeni	o		x		m		x		m		o	
djembe 1	G		g	(d)	(P)		G		P	T	g	(d)
djembe 2		D		P		P		g	d		D	G
djembe 3	g	d						g	d	G		D
solo 1	G		g		g	d		d	P	D		T
solo 2	g	T	P		g	d	G	T	P	D		d

Black Rock Dive	1	.	*	.	2	.	*	.	3	.	*	.	4	.	*	.
kenkeni	o		o		x		m		o		o		x		m	
toms				O	O		o					O	O		o	
sangban bells	x	x			x	x			x	x			x	x		
sangban drum	O	O							O		O					
shaker	X				X				X				X			
stick/clave	x		x			x		x			x		x		x	
agogo	L		H		L		H				L		H		H	
djembe 2	g	d		g	D		P		g	d			P		D	P
djembe 1a	g	d	P	T		T		T	g	d	P	T		P	d	g d
djembe 1b	P	T		D	P	T	G	D	P	T		D	P	T	G	D
djembe 1c	G		D		P	d	g	d	G	D			T		d	g d	>
	G		G	D	P	d	g	d	G	D		d	P		g	d

Bollywood Reggae	1	.	*	.	2	.	*	.	3	.	*	.	4	.	*	.
tumba	O		x		O		x		O		x		O		x	
sangban	O		x		x		O		O		x		x		O	
dununba	O				x				O				x			
surdo	O								x							
sticks			x	x							x	x				
bell	x		x	x		x			x	x		x	x	x		L
djembe 1	g	d	g	d	P			d	P		D		g	d	G		>
	d	g	d	g	d	g		T	P		d	P		D		P
djembe 2	G			d			g		D		g		g	d	P	d
djembe 3	G			d	G			d	G					d	G		d

Bombay Xmas	1	.	.	2	.	.	3	.	.	4	.	.
tambourine	X		-		X		-		-		X	
sangban	O		x	x		O	x		x	x		O
kenkeni	o		o	x		o	o		o	x		o
dununba	O		x		O		x		x		O	
djembe 1	g		-		g	T	P		T	G		D
djembe 2	G		g	d	g	d	G		g	d	g	d
djembe 3	P		-			-	g	d	G	D		

Elephant Garden	1	.	*	.	2	.	*	.	3	.	*	.	4	.	*	.	
kenkeni bell	x		x		x	x		x	x		x		x		x	x	
kenkeni drum					o	o				o	o				o	o	
sangban	O	O				x	x		O		x		x		O		
dununba	x	O			x	O		M	M				x		O		
djembe 1	P	T		T	P		g	d	P		G		P	D	g	d	
djembe 2	P	T	G		P	T		D	P	T	G		P	T		D	
djembe 3	G			D			G		P		T		g	T	g		
solo 1	G		g	d	G	(D)	G	D		d		d	G		G	D	
solo 2	g			D	P			g		g	d		D	P		G	>
	g			D	g		G	d		d		D	P		G		
solo 3	G		D		g	d	G			D		g	d	G	D	g	
solo 4	G		G		g	d	G		G		g	d	P		g	d	>
	P		D			-		D	P		-		G		-		
solo 5	G		g	d	g		g	d	G		g	T		T	G		>
	G		g	d	g		g	d	G	T		T	g		g	d	
solo 6	P	T	G		P		g	d	G		P	d			g		
solo 7	G		P	T	g		P	T	G	d	P		g	d		d	
break	g	d	G	d	g	D	g	d	G	d	g	D	g	d	gd	gd	

Funkin Fiji	1	.	*	.	2	.	*	.	3	.	*	.	4	.	*	.	
djembe 1	g			D	P		g		g	d		D	P		G		>
	g			D	d	G	d		d			D	P		G		
djembe 2	P	d	g		g	T	G	D	P	d	g		g	T	G	D	
djembe 3: solo 1	g		T		-		g		-		g		D	G			
solo 2	G		g				G		g		G		g	d	g	d	
solo 3	G		T			P		G		g	d	G	d	P			
solo 4	G			d		d		d	G			d	g		P		
drum set	X	x	x	x	X	x	x	x	X		X		x	x			>
	x	x	X		x	x	X		x	X		x	X				
percussion	x		x	x	X̲		x	x	x		x		X̲		x		>
	x		x	x	X̲		x	x	x		X̲		X̲		X̲		
toms	-		O		-		o	o	-		O		-		o	o	
bass	X		X	X	-		X		-		X		-		-		
cymbal	x				x				x				x			x	
snare		x				x							x				>
		x				x			x		x		x			x	
bell	X				X				X				X				
clave			x	x			x	x			x	x			x	x	

Gadzookie	1	.	*	.	2	.	*	.	3	.	*	.	4	.	*	.
bell 1	x		x		x		x		x			x		x		
bell 2	-		x		-		x		-		x		-		x	
stick	x		x		x		x		x		x		x		x	
sangban			O		O						O		O			
dun/kenkeni	O	O			O	O			o	o			o	o		
djembe 1	P			P			P		g		g	d		(g	d)	
djembe 2	g		d		P				g	d	G		g	d	g	
djembe 3		d	g		G				d	G		d				

Goa Gone	1	.	.	2	.	.	3	.	.	4	.	.	
bell	x		x		x	x	x		x		x		
clave			x		x		x			x			
stick		x	x				x	x					
sticks	x		x	<u>x</u>	x	x	<u>x</u>	x	x	<u>x</u>	x	x	
shaker	x			x			x			x			
quinto	-		-		gf		-		gf	-			>
	-		-		g		d		g	d			
conga	g	d	P	T		T	P		P	T		T	>
	P	T	P	d		D	P	T	P			D	
djembe 1	G		g	d	G		G		P	T	G		
djembe 2	P			d		D	G		g	D	G		>
	P			d	G	D				D	g		
dununba bell	x	x		x		x	x		x	x		x	
dununba drum	O	O						O					
kenkeni bell			x	x	x	(x)			x	x	x	(x)	
kenkeni drum				o		o				o			
sangban	O		O		O	O		O		M		O	>
		O		O		O		O		O			>
			O					O				O	>
	O	O	O			O	O	O		O	O	O	>
	O	O		O	O	O		O	O	O		O	
tumba	O	O	O			O	O	O					>
	O		O		O				O	O		O	
surdo	O		O		O		O				O		>
	O		O	O		O	O				O		

Halloween Funk	1	.	*	.	2	.	*	.	3	.	*	.	4	.	*	.
djembe 1/toms	g	d	g		P		G	D			g	d	G	D		
djembe 2/conga	g		P			T		T	g		P		T		P	
djembe 3/tumba	G				g			D	d		D	P				d
sangban/tumba	O		x	x		O	O		x		x		x	x		O
dununba/surdo	O		x		O		x		O	x		O	x		O	
kenkeni/agogo	o		x	m		x	m		o		x		o		x	

Hepe	1	.	*	.	2	.	*	.	3	.	*	.	4	.	*	.	
snare	x		x		x		x	x		x		x		x	x		
sangban		x	O	O		x		x	x		O		O		x		>
	x	x	O	O		x		x	x		O		O		x	xx	
dununba	O			O			M							O		M	
drum kit	x	x	x	o	x			o	x	x	x	o	x	x	o	o	
djembe 1	G		D			g	d	g	d	G	D			d		d	g	d	>
	G	D	P	d	g			g	d	G	D			d		d	g	d	
djembe 2	G		D			P	d		d	P			d	P		d	g	d	>
	G	d	P	T			T			T	G	d	g	T			
djembe 3	G			T			P		-			g		T		P	

Home at Last	1	.	*	.	2	.	*	.	3	.	*	.	4	.	*	.	
shaker	x			x			x				x		x				
agogo			H		H								H		L		
djembe 2	g	D		d	G					d	g		P		P		
djembe 3	G	D		d	g	d	g	D	G		g	d		d	g		
conga (LH)	D			d					D		d		T				
tumba (RH)			g				P		G		P			g			
sangban	x		M		x			x		x		x		x		O	
dununba	O	O		O		O	O		-		O		O		O	O	
>	O	O		O	O		x	x	x		M		M		x		

Hot Pants	1	.	*	.	2	.	*	.	3	.	*	.	4	.	*	.	
guitar/guiro	x	x		x		x	x			x		x	x	x	x		
djembe 1	G		D		P	T		d	g		P	T		d	g		
djembe 2	g	d	P										g	d		T	>
													g	d		T	
djembe 3	g	d		g	d		G		g	d		g	d		G		
agogo H			x		x				x		x				x		
agogo L			x				x				x				x		
clave			x		x				x		x			x			
kenkeni	O	O		x	x		O	O		x	x		x		x		
dununba/bass											O		O				
tamb/shekere	X	x	x	x	X	x	x	x	X	x	x	x	X	x	x	x	
sangban	O			o					O	O		o					>
	O			o		O	O		O			o					>
	O			o			O		O	O		o					>
	O	o		o		o			O	O		o					

Island Hut	1	.	*	.	2	.	*	.	3	.	*	.	4	.	*	.
kenkeni	x		o		o	o		x	x		o		o	o		x
bell	-		x		x		x	x	-		x		x		x	x
sangban	O		O	x		x	M		O		O	O		x	M	
dununba	O		x	O		x	O	M	x			x		O	O	
djembe	P	T					g	d	P	T	G				g	d
djembe	P			T	P		g	d	P			T	P		g	d
djembe	P	T		d	P	T	G		P			g	d	P		D

Manifestation4	1	.	*	.	2	.	*	.	3	.	*	.	4	.	*	.	
Intro and break	x		x	x		x		x	x		x		x	x			
[all:]	o		O	O		o		O	O		o		O	O			>
	o					o		O	O	*							
* > sangban										>	O	O		O			
* > all others										>	o		O				
	g	(d)	P	T			P	T	g	(d)	P	T		>	P	T	>
	g	(d)	P	T	G		P	T	g	(d)	P	T			P	T	
		d	G	D		T		d		T		d		T	G		
	P		g	d		d		T	P			T	g	d		D	
kenkeni	x		x		o		x		x		x		o	o		x	
sangban	O		x		M		x		O	x		O	x		M		
dununba	O		x	M		x		O		O		x	M	x		O	
dun/sang	O	X		o	o		O		O		x	O		o	o		
3-dun combo	O		x		o		O		O		x	O		o	o		

Manifestation6	1	.	.	2	.	.	3	.	.	4	.	.	
djembe 1	P		g	T		d	P		g	T			
djembe 2		d	g	T	P		P	T		T	G	(D)	
solo 1		d	g	T	P		g	d	P	T	G		
solo 2		d	g	P		G		P		T	G		
djembe 3	G					D	G		g	d		D	
kenkeni	o		o	x		o	x		x	x		o	
sangban	O		x	M		O	x		M		x		
dununba	x		O		O		x		O		O		>
	x		O		O		-		-		-		
dun/sang	o		O		o		o		O		O		>
	o		O		o		o	x		o		x	
3 duns combo	o		M		M		o		O		O		
	o		M		M		o	x		o		o	

Mayne Man	1	.	.	2	.	.	3	.	.	4	.	.
sangban	O		x		M		x	M		x	O	
dununba		O	x		O	O		O	O		O	x
kenkeni	x		O	O		x	x		O	O		x
djembe 1	g	D	g	D	g		G	d		D	g	D
djembe 2	P		P	T	G		P		P	T	G	d
djembe 3	g			T		d	g	T		D		d
solos…												
1	gd	g	d	P	D		G	d		T		d
2	P	D		P	D		g	d	G			d
3	PT	P	T	P	d		g	d	g	d	P	
4	g	d		g	d		gd	g	T	P		d
5	g		P		g		g	d		T		d
6	g	D		gd	g	T	P	T		D		

Mojo Mendiani	1	.	.	2	.	.	3	.	.	4	.	.
dununba		O		x		x		x	x		O	O
sangban	O		O		x	M		x	M		O	
kenkeni	o	o		o		x	o		m		x	
djembe 2	P		P		g	d	G		P	D	g	d
djembe 3	P	D	(G)			T	P		G	d	g	
djembe 1 solos:												
1	G	D	P			T		g	d	g	d	P
2	G			d	P		g	d	g	d	P		>
	P		G		T		P	d	G		T	
3	G			D		g	d		g	d		g	d	>
	g	d		g	d		g		G		D	
4	G			d		D	G		d		d		D
5	g			g	d	g	d		d		P	
6	g	d	g	D		D			D	g		g	d

Mosquito Farm Blues	1	.	.	2	.	.	3	.	.	4	.	.	
djembe 1	P	T	P	T		T	P	D	G			T	
djembe 2	P		g	d		d	g	D		D	P		
djembe 3	g		g		g	d		d	g		g	d	
kenkeni	x		x	o	o	o		x		x		x	
dununba	O		x		O		M	x		O		x	
sangban	O		M	x		x	x		x	x		O	>
	O		x	x		x	x		x	x		O	
solos…													
1	G		g	D	g	d	G		G		P		>
	G		g	D	g	d	g		g	d	g	d	
2	G		g	T	P	d	G		d	T	P	d	>
	G		G	T	P	d	G		G		G	D	
3	G			D	g	d	G				g	d	>
	g			d	g	d	P		P		P		>
			T	P	D		d		d		D		>
			d		D			g		g	D		>
	G		g	d		D	G		D		P		
4	g		g	d	g	d	g		g	T			>
	g		g	d	g	d		d		T			
5	g		g	T		T		T				d	
	g		g	T		T			P	T	g	d	

Moss Rock	1	.	.	2	.	.	3	.	.	4	.	.	
bell	X	-	x	-	x	x	-	x	-	x	-	x	
dununba	-	-	-	O	-	-	O	-	-	O	-	-	
sangban	O	-	M	-	M	-	O	-	M	-	M	-	
break	Pt	-	G	-	g	d	-	-	-	-	-		
djembe 3	G	D	G	D	G	-	P	T	P	T	P	-	
djembe 2	G	-	g	-	g	-	G	D	-	d	-	D	>
	G	-	g	-	g	-	G	d	g	D	g	d	
djembe 1	Gt	-	g	d	G	-	Pt	-	G	d	g	-	
conga	G	d	P	d	g	d	G	d	P	d	g	d	

New Wave Rave	1	.	*	.	2	.	*	.	3	.	*	.	4	.	*	.	
kenkeni	O			o			O		O			o					>
	o			o	o		O		o			o	o		O		
sangban	O		x	O		x	O		O		x		x		O		X3
	O		x	O		x	O		x	O		x	O		o		
dununba				O			O	O							O	O	
agogo/triangle			L	L			L	L			L	L			L	L	>
			L	L			L	L			H	H					
sticks			x	x		x	x				x			x			
clave	x			x			x				x		x				
maracas	X		X		X		X		X		X		X		X		
djembe 1	G		g	D		d	P			g		G		g	d	P	>
	G		g	D		d	P			T	P			g	d	P	
djembe 2	g	d		D	g	d		D	P		P		P		G		
djembe 3	gd	d	g	d	P		G	D	g	d	G		G			D	>
	P			T			G	T	P			D	g	d			>
	G			D			G	d	g	D		D			g		>
	g			d			g		g				G				

Rising Sun	1	.	.	2	.	.	3	.	.	4	.	.	
djembe 1	G			T		d	g	D		T		D	
djembe 2	P		P		P	d	g		g	d		d	
djembe 3		d	g	d	P		G		g	T	g	d	
kenkeni	O		x	M	x		M			x	x		
sangban	M		x	O		x	M	x			x		
dununba	O		x	x		O	O		x		x	O	
solo 1	G			T		d	G	T		T		d	>
	G			T	g	d	G	T		D		D	

Samba Masala

Samba on the Rocks	1	.	*	.	2	.	*	.	3	.	*	.	4	.	*	.
sangban	M		x		O		x		O		x	M		M	x	
kenkeni	x		x	x	o	o		x	x		x	x	o	o		x
dununba	O		x	M		x	M		x		O		x	O		x
djembe 1	g	d	g	d			T	G	P					g	D	P
djembe 3	G	d	P			d	P			d	g	d			d	G
djembe 2	P			T	g	d	g		g	T		d			d	g
Samba Funk	**1**	.	*	.	**2**	.	*	.	**3**	.	*	.	**4**	.	*	.
djembe 3	g	d	g	D	G		g		g	D		d				
djembe 2	G		g	d	G	D		D		d	g	d	G		g	d
djembe 1	g		g			T		D		d			G		G	
bell		H		L	H			L		H	L	H	L			
sangban	O	x		x	M		x	O		x		x	O		O	
bell/hi-hat	x		x	x		x	x		x		x	x		x	x	
snare/kenkeni		o			o			o	O							
dununba	O			O					O		O	O				
	O			O		O			O		O	O		O		
Nowick's Samba	**1**	.	*	.	**2**	.	*	.	**3**	.	*	.	**4**	.	*	.
djembe 1	P	d	g	d	G		G	T		d		d	G		G	T
djembe 2			P		P		P	T			P		P		P	T
djembe 3	G	D		T		d	g	d	G		D		P	d	g	d
solo 1	G		D		P		g	T		d		d	g		g	d
solo 2	G		D		P		g	D		D		d	g	d	g	d
solo 3	G		D		P	d	g	T		d	g	d	P		g	d
dununba	x			x			x		x		O	O	x	x		
bell		L	L	L	L				H	H		H	H			
sangban/kenkeni		o	o	O		o			o	O		o		o		
	o	O		o			o	O		o		o	o	O		o

> (marker next to dununba rows in Samba Funk)

> (marker next to sangban/kenkeni rows in Nowick's Samba)

Samba Phi Phi

Samba Phi Phi	1	.	*	.	2	.	*	.	3	.	*	.	4	.	*	.	
snare	x	x	x	x	x			x	x	x	x	x	x			x	
cowbell			x				x		x			x			x	x	
woodblock	x		x		x	x		x	x		x	x		x		x	>
	x		x		x	x		x	x	x		x		x		x	
splash cymbal			X														
djembe		d	g		P	T	gd	g		d	g		P	T	gd	g	
tumba	O		O		O		-		O		-		O		-		>
	O		O		O		O		O			O		O			
kenkeni	x	x			o	o			x	x			o	o			
conga	g	d	-		-		g	d	-		-		g		-		
sangban	M		-		M		-		M		O		-		-		
dununba	O		-		-		O		O	O	-		-		-		>
	O		M	M							M		O	O		O	

Snake Island

Snake Island	1	.	.	2	.	.	3	.	.	4	.	.	
tambourine	X			X			X			X			
dununba	O		O		O		x	O		M		x	
sangban	M	x		O	x		O	x		x	M		
kenkeni	o		x		m		o	o		x		o	
djembe 3	P		d	P		D	P		d	P		G	
djembe 2	g		g	d		D	G		g			d	>
	g		g	d		D	G		g	d		d	
djembe 1	P		T		g	d		D		g		D	
quinto	g		d		P		T		d				>
	P		d		g		T		P		d		>
	g		T		P		d		g		T		

Trouble

Trouble	1	.	.	2	.	.	3	.	.	4	.	.
congas	G		G						(g	D	g	d)
G:lo D:hi			g	D	g	d			g	D	g	d
dununba	O		O	x		x	O		x	M		x
	O		x	M		x	O		x	M		
djembe	G		G		g	d	P		g	d	P	
	P		P		G		G		g	T		
kenkeni	o		x		o	o		x		M		o
sangban	x		O		x	x		x	O		x	
conga/djembe	P		G	d	g		P		G	d	g	

Resources

The best place I know of to buy **top-quality drums** (outside of West Africa) is Drumskull Drums - http://www.drumskulldrums.com

The best place I know of to buy **instructional videos, books and CDs** of West African music is African Rhythm Traders - http://www.africanrhythmtraders.com

Books/CDs

Blanc, Serge. *African Percussion: The Djembe.* Trans. Ruth Barnes. 1997.

Delbanco, Age. *The Book of West African Rhythms.* Santa Cruz, CA: Seven Hawk Publishing, 2002.

Doumbia, Abdoul, and Matthew Wirzbicki. *Anke Dje Anke Be: Djembe and Dounou Music from Mali, West Africa.* Vol. 1. 3idesign, 2005.

Franke, Sylvia, and Ibro Konate. *Djembe: Percussion from West Africa.* 2004.

Keita, Mamady. *A Life for the Djembe: Traditional Rhythms of the Malinke.* Trans. Angelika Hansen, Beth Dyer. Arun-Verlag, 1999.

Konate, Famoudou, and Thomas Ott. *Rhythms and Songs from Guinea.* 1997; English trans. 2000, Bettina Kande and Mary Staehelin. Oldershausen, Germany: Lugert Verlag.

Links to West African Drum and Dance Resources

http://DjembeRhythms.com

60

Thanks for reading! If you enjoyed this book, please leave a review (even a brief comment or two helps a lot!) on its page at your favorite online retailer.

Explore the world of rhythms with the other books in the *Roots Jam* series:

- Dive deep into African drumming styles from around the world.
- Find simple notation for djembe, dunun, conga, tabla and batucada parts from Guinea, Mali, Cuba, Brazil, Belize, India.
- Groove on tribal beats for hip hop and DJ mixes, samba bands, kirtan, dance classes, or drum circles.
- Explore archetypal music patterns, polyrhythm, improvisation, and drum culture.

DjembeRhythms.com

Nowick Gray is a drumming performer and teacher with thirty years of experience playing West African rhythms. His popular *Roots Jam* rhythm books, YouTube videos, audio compositions and instructional web pages have helped beginning, intermediate and performing drummers understand and play traditional African-based rhythms since 1996. Nowick has studied with a number of African drumming masters including Famoudou Konate, Mamady Keita, and Babatunde Olatunji; toured with Western African and Brazilian drum and dance ensembles; organized all-night jams and trance dances; played music for yoga and breathwork classes; recorded with electric jam bands; and played tablas for Indian kirtan.

See more books by Nowick Gray at his website, NowickGray.com, or at his Amazon Author Page. Sign up for the "Wild Writings" mailing list for updates, offers and free downloads. Go to: http://djemberhythms.com/sign-up-to-newsletter/

For more information and ordering drum rhythm books and audio, visit http://djemberhythms.com

Audio CD Tracks

Traditional Rhythms

Sequence of parts, tracks 1-16:

Dununba
Sangban
Kenkeni
Dununba and Sangban
Dununba, Sangban, Kenkeni
Djembe 2
Djembe 3
Djembe 2 and 3
Djembe 1, break
Djembe solo 1, break
Djembe solo 2, break
Djembe solo 3, break
Ensemble (w/ Djembe 1 > solos 1-3)

Original Compositions

**To download audio mp3s
go to DjembeRhythms.com**

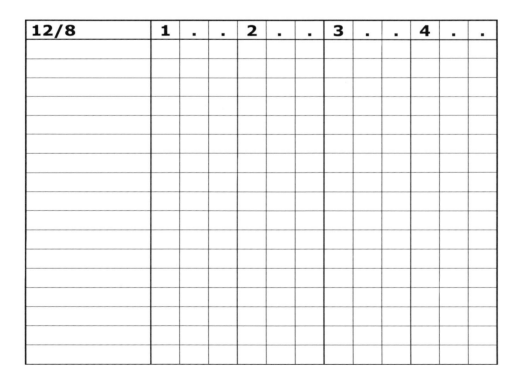

Printed in Great Britain
by Amazon

60364688R00136